For Lizzie Rummel
and Ken Jones
with great respect
and affection

SKI TRAILS
in the Canadian Rockies

CHIC SCOTT

Rocky
Mountain Books

Front cover: Skiing at Mount Assiniboine, photo Vance Hanna
Back cover: Chic Scott on the Rogers Pass to Bugaboos
          Ski Traverse, photo Ron Robinson
Title Page: Mount Saint Nicholas on the Wapta Icefield, photo Gillean Daffern

© Chic Scott 1992

Published by Rocky Mountain Books
#4 Spruce Centre,
Calgary, Alberta T3C 3B3

The publisher wishes to acknowledge the assistance of the Alberta
Foundation for the Arts, and Alberta Culture and Multiculturalism in
the production of this book

Printed and bound in Singapore by
Kyodo Printing Co. (S'pore) Pte. Ltd.
Separations and halftones by
United Graphic Services, Calgary

ISBN 0-921102-13-5

Canadian Cataloguing in Publication Data

Scott, Chic, 1945-
Ski trails in the Canadian Rockies

Includes index.
ISBN 0-921102-13-5
1. Cross-country skiing--Rocky Mountains,
Canadian (B.C. and Alta.)--Guidebooks.* 2.
Trails--Rocky Mountains, Canadian (B.C. and
Alta.)--Guidebooks.* 3. Rocky Mountains,
Canadian (B.C. and Alta.)--Guidebooks.*
I. Title.
GV854.8.C2S36 1992   796.93'2'09711
                         C92-091684-8

CONTENTS

SKIING AREAS

Preface

As far back as 1970, my good friend Lloyd MacKay was urging me to write this book. However I was too busy travelling the globe, climbing and skiing, to get my act together and sit down at the typewriter. By 1974 I had begun to think it was a good idea and I started to organize myself and collect information. I even took the winter off to work on the project. But fate decreed that things should be otherwise and my life swept me along other channels. Someone else wrote the book.

Time and fate however have an uncanny way of bringing things back to you that you thought lost forever. Several years ago, when Tony and Gill asked me to write this book I knew the time was right. I had continued over the years, to ski and explore the trails of the Rockies. I had personally covered most of the ground in this book and had honed my writing and research skills. I jumped at the prospect and now after a year of intense work it is done.

I hope that you find the peace and happiness, gliding along these trails, that I have. Many years ago I realized something was wrong with the society we live in. Somehow out on the trails, with the winter snows around and the mountains gleaming above, I found what was missing. If this book can get more of us out there, safely exploring our Canadian winter wilderness, then my goal will have been achieved.

I wish you happy and safe skiing and a crackling fire and good company at the end of the day.

Chic Scott

Acknowledgments

I would first of all like to thank all those with whom I have shared ski trails over the years. Thank you for your support, good ideas and for help with the trail breaking. I would also like to thank:

Sepp and Barb Renner who shared Assiniboine with me, Blake O'Brian who opened the doors of Skoki to me and Dale Portman and Kathy Calvert who were so hospitable and shared the Jasper trails with me.

Terry Duncan, Neil Jolly, and Perry Davis who helped me collect and sort out information.

Tony and Gillean Daffern, for giving me the chance to fulfill a lifetimes dream and write this book.

Donnie Gardner who gave me an old pair of cut down hickory skis 30 years ago, and got me out cross-country skiing. My life hasn't been the same since.

Skiing in the Canadian Rockies

Skiing in the Canadian Rockies is a wonderful and varied experience. You can enjoy a safe and easy trackset trail, or explore the high and wild back country. You can camp in the solitude of a remote valley or stay in the luxury and comfort of one of our historic lodges.

Skiing in these mountains offers you the opportunity to escape from the noise and rush of our culture. In the winter you need venture only a few hundred metres from the road to enter a world of silence and poetry. In the winter all is clean, new and fresh. The beauty of the snow creations, the wind and the clouds can put new life in your soul. The fresh air and hard exercise can put roses in your cheeks.

The Canadian Rockies has been the home of ski adventure since the late 1920's. Long before the development of ski resorts and mechanical lifts, skiers from around the world journeyed to the Rockies to experience the winter wilderness. Much of that history is still around you. Thankfully, the areas covered in this book are protected as National or Provincial Parks, and little has changed over the years. You can still experience the same adventure and beauty that the pioneers enjoyed.

However there are serious hazards for ski tourers in the Canadian Rockies. You must be well prepared and use good judgement to venture safely in these mountains. The penalty for mistakes can be harsh indeed. Judgement comes with experience and it is advised that you begin slowly with modest trips, then gradually work your way into the more demanding ski tours.

The area covered by this book is very large and there are endless possibilities for ski adventures. We have collected only the most popular and obvious trails. You could spend a lifetime exploring the remote back country and you would rarely encounter a soul.

Good ski touring skills and techniques are required to go very far in these mountains. In addition the Canadian Rockies have some distinctive characteristics which one should become familiar with.

Snow Conditions

The snow which falls in the Rockies is usually dry. During some years the snowfall can be minimal for long periods of time. Because temperatures are often very low, the snow does not consolidate or settle fast. Also as a result of long spells of cold weather combined with a shallow snow pack, a loose and unstable type of snow called depth hoar often develops. Early in the season trail breaking can be extremely frustrating, and it is not uncommon to find yourself breaking trail for long distances, sinking almost a metre into unconsolidated snow. The best months to undertake serious ski touring is from mid February on, when the snowpack is deeper and more consolidated.

You should give serious consideration to the condition of the snow pack before you head out on long distances ski tours. A telephone call to the appropriate agency (see numbers at the back of the book) will give you all the information you need to make a decision.

Avalanches

The snowpack in the Canadian Rockies is often unstable and unpredictable. Snow stability is difficult to evaluate, even for knowledgeable and experienced tourers. Avalanche accidents are a regular occurrence every year and usually occur during periods when professional forecasters are predicting high or extreme hazard. Consequently you are advised to check the avalanche hazard forecast by phoning the appropriate numbers on the final page of this book.

You are also advised to take an avalanche awareness course where you will learn how to travel safely in avalanche terrain and how to recognize signs of snowpack instability.

Ski tourers should all wear an avalanche transceiver, carry a snow shovel, and use probe poles, when skiing in avalanche terrain. Your transceiver should be switched on at the beginning of the tour and worn until you are safely back to the car. Batteries should be fresh and your group should do a check of transceiver operation at the start of the day. Everyone should know how to conduct a transceiver search in the event of an avalanche incident. Avalanche transceivers should not be an excuse to push the limits of safe judgement — remember that despite these electronic devices many avalanches still prove fatal.

You should ski with a high degree of awareness. Most of the tours in this book can be done without exposing yourself or your group to the possibility of being avalanched. If you find yourself anywhere which seems to be steep and dangerous you are likely off route. If you are skiing terrain which makes you nervous, look for a more comfortable route. Keen observation, good routefinding and extreme caution are the keys to safe travel in the Canadian Rockies.

Weather

Weather in the Canadian Rockies can be extreme. There can be long periods of intense cold, where the thermometer drops to -30°C or -40°C. Chinook winds can change this in a matter of hours and raise the temperature well above freezing. Carrying the proper protection against the wind and cold is essential and if your tour takes you above timberline you should be particularly well prepared. A night out in the Rockies can be a serious matter so carry survival equipment on longer tours.

The mean temperature in the Rockies is reasonable however, and the area receives a large amount of sunshine. A typical Rockies day is perhaps -15°C and sunny. Spring time ski touring can of course be a real treat - often a sweater or a windbreaker is all that is needed. An effective sun cream and quality sunglasses are required, particularly later in the season when the sun rises higher in the sky.

Remoteness

Many of the tours in this book take you through wilderness areas. There are no man made facilities on many of the trails and often there will be no other skiers in the area. You are on your own and you must deal with any eventuality with your own resources. Self reliance is the byword in the Canadian Rockies. This remoteness is indeed one of the great attractions of these mountains.

Environment

All of these trails are in National or Provincial Parks where the environment is protected. Cutting of trees and branches is prohibited. All garbage must be packed out.

Emergency Procedures

Before venturing far into the back country you should obtain the knowledge and skills to carry out a few basic emergency procedures. You should know how to build an emergency shelter, how to start a fire and how to stay warm and dry. You should also be familiar with avalanche rescue procedures because it is unlikely that outside help will do more than recover bodies. If you venture onto glaciers you should be able to perform a crevasse rescue.

If you are embarking on any of the more serious ski tours, you should consider registering out with the Wardens or Rangers for some added security. In an emergency you can raise the alarm by phoning the appropriate number listed on the final page of this book.

Equipment and Clothing

Here are few tips on the type of equipment and clothing commonly used in the Canadian Rockies.

Skis Metal edged 'telemark' style skis are popular for back country touring. Waxes are still used but when the going gets steep most folks put on their skins. Cable bindings are still advised for these skis. Fish-scale waxless skis are not recommended. For track-set trails most types of nordic skis are adequate, however one should look for quality equipment - it is no fun to have to walk several kilometres, back to the trailhead, with a broken ski or binding.

Ski Poles Poles which adapt to form an avalanche probe are very popular. However it is recommended that some of the group carry regular sectional probes.

Headgear A warm toque or insulated hat is essential. A balaclava which can be pulled down to cover the face and neck is highly recommended.

Handgear Warm mitts, rather than gloves, are the most effective.

Boots A well made, leather touring boot is best for back country use, and should be a little large to accommodate extra socks. Overboots will add some extra warmth. Some people prefer the double boot approach (an inner and outer boot arrangement) to deal with extreme cold. A lighter nordic boot of good quality with enough room for extra socks is acceptable on track-set trails.

Insulating Materials Down is still the insulating material of choice in the Rockies. The climate is dry and the cold often extreme, necessitating a high quality four season bag. Synthetic pile fabrics are popular for clothing and work very well. Synthetic underclothes are now used almost exclusively.

Shell Materials Simple breathable fabrics are still used in the Rockies during the winter for jackets, shells, overpants, down bags and down jackets. Gore-Tex has been found to ice up seriously on the inside in extremely cold weather.

Avalanche Transceivers Although single-frequency (457 kHz) transceivers are now the standard in North America, many people are still using dual frequency models.

Stoves The butane cartridge stoves are not recommended in the winter because the fuel has difficulty vapourising in the extreme cold.

Food, Gear and Other Supplies

The mountain communities of Banff, Canmore, Lake Louise and Jasper have a wide array of grocery stores and other shops to serve you. White gas for stoves is readily available as is gasoline for your vehicles.

Nordic ski equipment and back country gear can be purchased at:
Mountain Magic (Banff) 762-2591
Monod's (Banff) 762-4571
Mountain Equipment Co-op (Calgary) 269-2420
Spoke and Edge (Canmore) 678-2838
Altitude Sports (Canmore) 678-6272
Wilson's Sports (Lake Louise) 522-3636
Totem Men's Wear & Ski Shop (Jasper) 852-3078
Beyond Bikes (Jasper) 852-4945

Guides

Ski guides or instruction can be obtained through:

The Association of Canadian
Mountain Guides,
Box 1537,
Banff, Alberta,
Canada, T0L 0C0

Weather and Avalanche Info

Weather reports can be obtained in Banff by phoning 762-2088 and in Jasper by phoning 852-3185. A Public Avalanche Awareness Bulletin can be obtained from the Canadian Avalanche Association by phoning 1-800-667-1105. For more detailed information you can always contact the local park warden or ranger office or the park information service.

Grading & Other Trail Info

All trails have been designated as either nordic skiing, ski touring or ski mountaineering. In addition a simple grading system of easy, intermediate and advanced has been used. To apply this system to 150 trails, where the conditions are constantly changing, means that there will be a lot of times when you must use your own discretion.

The grading takes into account that nordic skiing requires less knowledge and experience than ski touring, which in turn requires less than ski mountaineering. Consequently an easy ski along a track-set trail would be less challenging than an easy ski tour. An easy ski mountaineering tour will be much more demanding than may be appropriate for a novice skier.

The following definitions apply to the descriptions and grades used in the book:

Nordic Skiing - takes place on well maintained trails which are usually packed and often track-set. The trails are normally near to the town or road and you will most likely encounter other skiers along the way.

Ski Touring - takes you into the backcountry, usually below timberline but sometimes ventures up into the subalpine. Trail breaking is often required and you may go long distances without encountering any man made facilities or other skiers. Route finding and wilderness survival skills are essential as is proper equipment.

Ski Mountaineering - takes you into the alpine zone, high above timberline. Glacier travel is normally involved and a more advanced level of skill development is required. One should have solid skiing abilities and at least one individual in the group should be completely familiar with all the skills required - route finding, avalanche avoidance and emergency procedures, first aid, crevasse rescue and improvised survival techniques.

Each trail has also been given a grading which should be interpreted as follows:

Easy - trails are normally suitable for a novice or inexperienced skier (within the parameters of the above trail designations). Route finding is not difficult and there are few hills. The length of the trip should always be taken into consideration for beginning skiers.

Intermediate - trails are more challenging and will often have steep hills which require more advanced skiing abilities. For ski tours and ski mountaineering a more advanced level of route finding skills will most likely be required.

Advanced - trails may have extensive sections requiring advanced skiing skills and may also present serious route finding challenges. Often these trips will be isolated and remote and you must rely solely on your own resources and ability.

Times - Times given are for an average party under average conditions. Skiing times can vary greatly depending on the strength and ability of the party, the weight of their packs, and if trail breaking is required, the depth of the snow. What might take several days under one set of circumstances could be skied in several hours in another. You must al-

ways integrate all the factors and arrive at your own estimate of the time your trip will require - the times given are only guidelines.

Distances - are given in kilometres and are noted as being one way, return or loop (be sure to note which of these three when you make your plans). The distances given in the text (i.e. continue 0.5 km along creek then turn right and follow the trail for another 2 km) are approximate - I did not ski these trails with a tape measure. They are accurate enough that with a little judgement you will be able to make the right route choice.

Elevations - are given in metres and are determined from the contour lines on the map. They are intended to give you a good idea of how much climbing will be required on a given trail and what will be the maximum elevation reached. Within the text elevations are referred to as vertical gain to differentiate from a horizontal distance (i.e. ski 100 m vertical gain up the hillside....). These elevations are approximate and one should use a little discretion and judgement in interpreting them.

Directions - are almost always given in the direction of travel (i.e. ski along the right bank of the creek; turn left at the trail junction). Often a compass direction will be given in brackets to add clarity (south). In a few instances the true left or true right bank of a glacier or stream are referred to. In these cases the direction is derived from the direction of flow of the glacier or stream, and may be different from the direction of travel of the skier. For example if you are skiing upstream along the right bank of a creek you are actually skiing on the true left bank!

Maps

Map references given are all to the 1:50,000 National Topographical Series. These can be obtained from private sources such as the ACC office in Canmore or from Map Town in Calgary. If you live far away you can obtain them from the federal government in Ottawa.

Canada Map Office
615 Booth Street
Ottawa, Ontario,
Canada, K1A 0E9.

Take care when using of some of the newer maps where the contour interval is 20 m below 2,000 m and 40 m above. These maps are truly hard to read.

Many of the trails marked on the topographical maps are incorrect. It is best to cross-check with other references wherever possible.

Grid References - many specific objects such as huts are given a grid reference to help you accurately locate the object. (i.e. Bow Hut - GR 355203). On the right hand border of each map you will find instructions on how to use the Universal Transverse Mercator Grid System to locate the object on the map.

Grooming & Tracksetting

Do not expect grooming and tracksetting of the standard to be found in Kananaskis Country and other top nordic centres in North America. Trail preparation in the Mountain National Parks is still done by snowmobile with tracksetting attachments.

Disclaimer

Cross country skiing, whether on a groomed and track-set trail or far back in the wilderness is potentially hazardous and dangerous. Cold weather and exposure, falls, river crossings, avalanches and the possibility of losing ones way are only some of the very real dangers that must be accepted and dealt with if one is to venture onto these mountain trails. For many of us the existence of the dangers forms an integral part of the attraction of this activity.

Hopefully, this guidebook will provide information to help make your time in the mountains a safe and enjoyable experience. However it is only a book - another tool to help you along your way. You must still learn all the techniques and skills required to venture safely into the backcountry, and you must still learn to show good judgement in applying all of these techniques. Furthermore due to continually changing weather and conditions, the information presented in this guidebook provides only a limited part of the overall picture. It is up to you to collect all the information necessary to make intelligent and safe decisions. This guide is NOT a substitute for experience and good judgement.

TRIP PLANNING

You should always have at least an informal plan in the back of your mind, even for the most casual day of skiing. The more serious the trip the better planned it should be. If you do one of the multi-day trips virtually nothing should be left to chance. The following are some items that you should consider when planning your tour:

Register Out Let some one know where you are going and when you will be back.

Route Study the map and any other information so as to be completely familiar with the route. Be aware of options and alternatives along the way.

Team Know the people you are skiing with and their skill and experience level. Don't get them in over their heads.

Times Establish a start time and a finish time. Leave plenty of room in your schedule to deal with the unforeseen. Check your time along the way to gauge your progress. You should decide on a turn back time and stick to it.

Equipment Run through an equipment check before departing. Check the rest of your group for proper skis, boots and clothing and for compatible transceivers.

Weather Obtain the latest weather forecast before starting out.

Snow stability Check on avalanche hazard and snow stability with the local avalanche forecast centre before making a final decision on your route.

Equipment Check-List — to refresh your memory

Skis	Ski goggles	Gaiters
Poles	Pocket knife	Spare mitts, socks
Boots	Toilet paper	Spare underwear
Skins	Camera and film	
Wax kit	Lighter or matches	**If you are going overnight:**
Avalanche transceiver	Lip balm	Tent
Shovel	Sun cream	Sleeping bag
Avalanche probe	Notebook and pencil	Insulated sleeping pad
Snow saw	Appropriate pack sack	Insulated booties
Spare ski tip		Stove and fuel
Compass	**Clothing:**	Pots
Altimeter	Underwear	Pot scrubber
Map	Wool or synthetic socks	Cup, bowl and spoon
Repair kit	Pants or knickers	Toilet kit
First aid kit	Overpants	
Emergency toboggan	Jacket	**For glacier travel:**
Snow study kit	Shirt	Full body harness
Headlamp	Pile jacket or sweater	Rope
Emergency bivouac sack	Down jacket	Several prusik slings
Water Bottle	Toque	Several locking carabiners
Thermos	Mitts	Several regular carabiners
Sun glasses	Polypro gloves	Ice axe

Regulations

Most of the routes in this book are in areas where backcountry use is controlled to some degree. The majority of tours lie within the boundaries of one of five national parks in the Rockies: Waterton, Banff, Yoho, Kootenay and Jasper or are located within a British Columbia provincial park: Assiniboine and Robson. Each of these areas have similar backcountry regulations and to save repetition a summary is provided here.

Backcountry Use Permits

In the national parks it is necessary to get a backcountry use permit if you spend *at least one night* in the backcountry. Permits can be obtained at park information centres. If you are just going out for a day trip then a permit is not required.

Registration

A voluntary registration system is provided by the Parks Service for hazardous activities within the national parks. You are strongly advised to use the service if you are skiing in some of the more remote areas.

It is necessary to register in person during regular office hours at either park information centres or at a warden office as registering out is a contractual agreement that requires a signature. All overdue registrations are checked out. There are two important considerations to bear in mind when you register:

- Because all overdues are checked out you must provide a reasonable estimate of your trip time. This may avoid unnecessary use of costly helicopter flights by rescue personnel.

- You **must** notify the Parks Service upon completion of your trip. This is done by either dropping the registration slip off at one of the warden offices or information centres, or by telephoning the offices or centres. If you are late, phone at your **earliest** convenience. Failure to notify the Park Service of your return or cancellation of a trip is grounds for prosecution.

Rescue personnel will exercise some discretion about when to commence a search. This depends on many factors like weather conditions, amount of time overdue, estimate of the individuals ability, number in party etc. For this reason you must be prepared to spend at least one night out before expecting help to arrive.

Vehicle Permits

All vehicles stopping in a national park are required to have a Park Motor Vehicle Permit — a little sticker that says you paid your entrance fee to the park. These can be obtained at park information centres, or at the east entrance to Banff Park (Canmore), the west entrance to Kootenay Park (Radium) and the east and west gates of Jasper Park (on Highway 16). You can buy either a one day, four day or annual permit. If you intend to stay for longer than a few days the best bet is to pay the $30 (1992 price) for the annual permit.

Travel Information

The bottom line is that public transportation in the Rockies is poor, particularly in the winter. It is almost imperative to have a vehicle if you want to reach most of the trailheads.

The Canadian Rockies can be reached by air, train or bus. Consult your travel agent for schedules and fares.

By Air

There are international airports in both Edmonton and Calgary. It is possible to fly directly to these cities from within North America, and from Europe and Asia. The areas described in this book are only a few hours drive along excellent highways from the airports. In other words it is possible to fly from Europe and be skiing in the Canadian wilderness the following day.

By Train

Jasper is now the only community within the boundaries of this guidebook that is served by regular passenger trains. There are a limited number of trains per week.

By Bus

There are regular scheduled buses which run along the Trans-Canada Highway (Highway #1). These buses stop at Golden, Lake Louise, Banff, Canmore and Calgary. There are also regular scheduled buses which travel Highway #16 between Edmonton and Jasper. Phone Greyhound Bus Lines for further information. Check with Brewster Transport (762-6767) for Icefields Parkway buses.

By Car

Cars can be rented from the major international chains (Hertz, Avis, Tilden, etc.) in Calgary, Edmonton, Jasper and Banff. The highways described in this book are all in excellent condition and are well maintained in the winter. Driving in the Canadian Rockies in the winter is reasonable enough for almost any driver. However the cold can make extreme demands on both car and driver. Be sure that your vehicle has antifreeze adequate for -40°C, and that it is equipped with snow tires, a block heater and a strong battery. You should carry jumper cables in the trunk in the event of a dead battery. If the thermometer plunges it is advisable to plug your car in if at all possible. Propane and diesel powered vehicles can be hard to start on cold winter mornings. It is best not to park on the roadside as high speed snowplows regularly maintain the highways.

Telephone numbers

The telephone exchange for Alberta is (403). The telephone exchange for B.C. is (604).

In the emergency section, where no exchange is indicated, it is assumed that you are calling the nearest appropriate number and therefore are within the same exchange.

Throughout the text of the book, numbers are given with no exchange. These are all in Alberta and are all the (403) exchange.

Where To Stay

When you get off the plane in Calgary or Edmonton you are in major cities each with populations in excess of 700,000. There is an endless variety of accommodation from five star hotels to youth hostels. The four major mountain towns are Banff, Canmore, Lake Louise and Jasper. All of these communities have a variety of hotels, bed and breakfast establishments and youth hostels. More information can be had by writing:

Alberta Tourism
Box 2500
Edmonton, Alberta
Canada, T5J 2Z4
ph. 1-800-661-8888

Ministry of Tourism
Parliament Buildings
Victoria, B.C.
Canada, V8V 1X4

Many cross country skiers are on limited budgets and are looking for more modest accommodation.

Alpine Club of Canada

The ACC operates three 'hotels' and many back-country huts. They are all reasonably priced (particularly if you choose to become a club member) and bookings can be made through the main ACC office in Canmore, Box 2040, Canmore, Alberta, T0L 0M0, (phone 403-678-3200). The ACC facilities are as follows:

The Club House - Located on the outskirts of Canmore, this lovely facility has beds for about 60. There is an attractive library and lounge, complete kitchen facilities, sauna and a bar.

The Canmore Group Centre, located within the town of Canmore has beds for about 50 and all modern facilities. It caters specifically to larger groups.

The Lake Louise Alpine Centre - owned and operated in conjunction with the Southern Alberta Hostel Association the centre offers over 100 beds and a fully modern facility. There are restaurants, saunas, libraries, lounges, and a self serve kitchen. Phone 403-522-2200 for reservations and information.

Huts - The ACC operates many back country huts which tend to be rustic and lean towards a philosophy of self reliance. There is normally no custodian present. Many of the huts referred to in this book (the Class A Huts) are locked with a combination lock. Booking can be a simple matter of exchanging your Visa or Mastercard number for the combination lock number! The huts described in this book are:

Class A Huts - equipped with foamies, cooking and eating utensils, Coleman stoves and lanterns and wood heating stove.
  Elizabeth Parker (Lake O'Hara)
  Stanley Mitchell (Little Yoho)
  Wates-Gibson Memorial (Tonquin)
  Sydney Vallance (Fryatt Creek)
  Fay (Prospector's Valley)
  Bow (Wapta Icefields)

Class B Huts - equipped as above but there is no heating stove. They are much less luxurious.
  Balfour
  Peyto (Whyte)
  Scott Duncan

16

Hostels

The Southern Alberta Hostel Association operates a number of hostels throughout the Rockies. These hostels are moderately priced and during the winter are extensively used by back country ski tourers. Reservations and more information can be obtained by writing or phoning:

SAHA
#203, 1414 Kensington Road N.W.
Calgary, Alberta, T2N 3P9 Canada
Phone 403-283-5551

The Banff Hostel is a large modern structure with beds for 154. Phone 403-762-4122 for information and reservations.

The Lake Louise Alpine Centre is operated in conjunction with the Alpine Club of Canada. See previous page.

Castle Junction Hostel

The Icefields Parkway Hostels - there are several hostels which are much more rustic and are almost like backcountry cabins. These are located along the Icefields Parkway at Mosquito Creek, Ramparts Creek and Hilda Creek. They are inexpensive, but comfortable. Phone SAHA in Calgary for bookings.

The Alberta Hostelling Association operates a number of hostels near Jasper. Information on these can be obtained through:

AHA
10926 - 88 Ave.,
Edmonton, Alberta, T6G 0Z1
Phone (403) 433-5513 or
(403) 433-3139 for reservations.

Whislers (7 km from Jasper)

Maligne Canyon (11 km from Jasper)

Athabasca Falls (south of Jasper)

Edith Cavell Hostel (ski access only)

Commercial Lodges

The Canadian Rockies are blessed with a rich skiing history and some old and beautiful backcountry lodges. These are described where appropriate in the text of this guidebook complete with a contact number for information and reservations. These lodges are not cheap and vary from $80 to $150 per night (meals included). They can however provide a truly memorable experience and are highly recommended. The lodges referred to in this book are:

> Skoki Lodge
> Shadow Lake Lodge
> Banff Sundance Lodge
> Assiniboine Lodge
> Lake O'Hara Lodge
> Dixon's Lodge (Tonquin)

Miscellaneous Huts

There are several other huts which are referred to and described in the text of the book. These are the Egypt Lake and Bryant Creek Shelters which are operated by Parks Canada (Banff National Park) and the Naiset Huts which are operated by B.C. Parks (Mount Assiniboine Provincial Park). Reservations are required and can be obtained by phoning 403-762-4256 (for the Bryant Creek and Egypt lake Shelters), and 604-422-3212 (for the Naiset Huts).

Campgrounds

The Canadian Parks Service plows several campgrounds and keeps them open all winter for folks with RV vehicles. Contact the park information service for more up-to-date information.

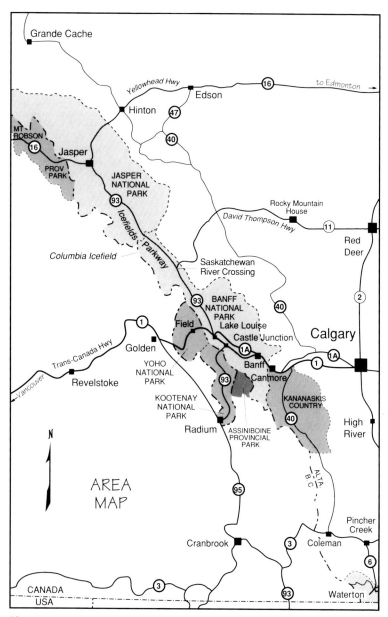

AREA MAP

WATERTON LAKES NATIONAL PARK

Waterton Lakes National Park, the most southerly area covered in this book, is the Canadian section of International Peace Park. Glacier National Park on the U.S. side forms the southern portion. Situated at the extreme south-west corner of Alberta, this small (518 sq km) preserve is popular for its backpacking and hiking trails.

However, Waterton is very much a summer-oriented tourist operation and, with the exception of Kilmorey Lodge, there are no facilities open in winter. Even the grocery store is only open part time.

In good snow periods the skiing, especially in the Akamina Pass area can be excellent. However the area is affected by Chinooks — warm, westerly winds prevalent from December to April — which, when combined with a somewhat lower snowfall than other mountain regions, may result in only marginal skiing.

Access to Waterton Park is via Highway #6 from Pincher Creek, located 48 km north, or by Highway #5 connecting to Cardston, 45 km east. Chief Mountain Highway, which provides access from the United States is closed in winter. Within the Park, the Akamina Highway is the only road open, being plowed to a parking area 2.5 km short of Cameron Lake.

Facilities none in winter.

Accommodation Kilmorey Lodge is the only hotel open in winter.

Information The information centre is closed in winter. Direct any enquiries to the Warden Office (859-2477)located on the right-hand side as you approach the townsite.

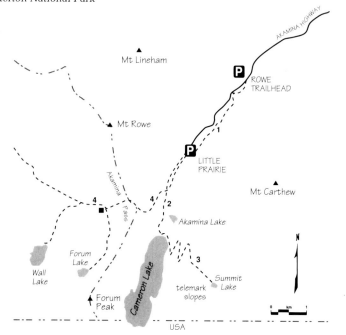

1 DIPPER

Nordic skiing

Grade Intermediate
Distance 6.5 km return
Time 2 hrs
Height gain 50 m
Max elevation 1,680 m
Map Sage Creek 82 G/1

This is a rolling and challenging trail which requires decent snow conditions to be enjoyable. It runs between the Little Prairie parking lot and the Rowe Creek trailhead. You can use two cars and ski the trail only one way if you choose. An interesting trail. Not recommended when icy.

Facilities At the Little Prairie parking lot there are picnic tables, a camp shelter and toilets.

Access Park at Little Prairie parking lot, the trailhead for Cameron Lake Trail.

From the picnic shelter head south (the opposite direction that you would anticipate) into a large meadow. Curve left and cross Cameron Creek on a bridge. Head north alongside Cameron Creek which is often open even in mid-winter. The trail crosses the creek on bridges another three times and ascends and descends numerous short and steep hills. It is very narrow until the final kilometre, where it follows the old bridle road again.

2 CAMERON LAKE

Nordic skiing

Grade Easy
Distance 5 km return
Time 1.5 hrs
Height gain Minimal
Max elevation 1,680 m
Map Sage Creek 82 G/1

The ski trail which follows the unplowed section of the Akamina Highway to the north shore of Cameron Lake is a good trail for beginners but is exposed to the wind resulting frequently in filled-in tracks.

Access Park at the Little Prairie parking lot at the end of the plowed section of the Akamina Highway, 13.5 km west of the town of Waterton.

Facilities Picnic tables, a shelter and toilets at the Little Prairie parking lot.

Options On the return back to the Little Prairie parking lot you can follow a variation on the east side of the road. This is an old road which gives you a nice downhill glide much of the way, if skied in a south-north direction. It begins about half way along the road, opposite the Akamina Pass Trail.

From the parking lot return to the highway, ski around the gate, and continue down the unplowed roadway. Cameron Lake is a scenic spot on a good day to sit and eat your lunch.

Photo Gillean Daffern

Skiing the snow-covered Akamina Highway to Cameron Lake

21

Looking down on Cameron Lake from above Summit Lake. The telemark slopes are off the picture to the left.

Photo Brent Kozachenko

3 SUMMIT LAKE

Ski touring

Grade Intermediate
Distance 13 km return from Little Prairie
Time 4 hrs return from Little Prairie
Height gain 310 m
Max elevation 1,960 m
Map Sage Creek 82 G/1

A scenic trail for telemark skiers who want to make a few turns on the hill west of Summit Lake.

Hazards Not recommended in icy conditions. Telemarking slopes above Summit Lake have the potential to avalanche.

Access Park at the trailhead for Cameron Lake Trail.

Follow the Cameron Lake trail to Cameron Lake and continue along the north shore of the lake to Cameron Creek which is crossed on a bridge. The trail then climbs in 5 long switchbacks up a steepening hillside. The trail itself is not steep but the angle of the slope is. Consequently if there is heavy snow cover you can be traversing under difficult conditions. Half way along the fifth zig the angle eases and from here it is a pleasant ski along a bench and gently down to the lake. You are just below treeline so there are wonderful views across the border to the peaks of Glacier National Park. It is a good place to spend a few hours practising your telemark turns. In good conditions it is a fun descent back to Cameron Lake.

4 AKAMINA PASS TO WALL LAKE & FORUM LAKE   Ski touring

Grade Easy/intermediate
Distance 1.6 km from Akamina Hwy. to Akamina Pass, 4.7 km to Forum Lake, 5.6 km to Wall Lake one way.
Time You can vist both lakes in a 5 hr day
Height gain 220 m to Wall Lake
360 m to Forum Lake
Max elevation 1,800 m at Akamina Pass
1,780 m at Wall Lake
2,000 m at Forum Lake
Map Sage Creek 82 G/1

This is a popular trail with skiers who want something a little more challenging. It has the best snow in the area. When you cross Akamina Pass into British Columbia you are in the Akamina/Kishinena Recreation Area. Snowmobiles are allowed here and for the rest of the tour to Wall Lake you may share the trail with one of these machines.

Facilities There are picnic tables, a camp shelter and toilets at the Little Prairie parking lot. There is an outhouse at Wall Lake.

Hazards Snowmobiles!

Options Forum Lake is perhaps a more exciting destination than Wall Lake, particularly if you are looking for telemark slopes. As well the snowmobiles do not reach here. The trail to Forum Lake branches left about 1 km beyond Akamina Pass. There is a trail sign at this point which may be visible. Follow the trail for a short distance to a ranger cabin which is passed on the left. Just beyond there is another trail junction. Keep left and climb two steep hills to a levelling below the headwall. Here it becomes impossible to follow the trail. Work your way up the headwall (open forest and meadows) following the best line possible, then when it begins to level, continue across to the lake, which will be below you in a deep hollow.

Some people reach Forum Lake from Akamina Pass by skiing south up the boundary cut line then descending through open timber to the lake.

At Forum Lake there are excellent opportunities for telemark skiing. The run back down to the ranger cabin is superb.

Access Park at the Little Prairie parking lot at the end of the plowed section of the Akamina Highway, 13.5 km west of the town of Waterton.

Follow the Cameron Lake Trail for a little more than a kilometre then take the trail to the right to Akamina Pass (trail sign). It is a moderate climb from here to the pass on a wide trail. The trail runs through the trees with little in the way of views. On the left a cut line marks the boundary of the park. The trail now becomes the Akamina Road where there is a possibility of meeting

snowmobiles. Descend gently down the B.C. side, past the Forum Lake Trail, to the next trail branching off to the left which goes to Wall Lake (sign post). The route from here is obvious except at one point where a trail sign points up the ridge to Wall Lake. Do not take this cutoff but continue straight ahead along the obvious trail to the lake. The trail cuts the corner and climbs over the ridge and runs along the creek to the lake. There is an impressive mountain wall behind the lake with many frozen waterfalls hanging on it.

Skiing at Mount Assiniboine

Photo Alf Skrastins

MOUNT ASSINIBOINE PROVINCIAL PARK

Mount Assiniboine Provincial Park is a very popular ski destination. The meadows below Mount Assiniboine offer some of the finest ski touring in the Rockies. There is always plenty of snow, the terrain is open and rolling and the scenery is outstanding.

For information about Mount Assiniboine Provincial Park you should contact the East Kootenay District Office in Wasa, BC, (604) 422-3212. A warden is stationed at Lake Magog Warden Cabin from December 15 to April 15. Once you are in the park, inquiries can be directed to the resident ranger.

Access The park cannot be accessed by motor vehicle. The usual methods of approach to Lake Magog are by helicopter or by ski. The helicopter is quick, comfortable and expensive. Many parties fly in and ski out. For information contact Canmore Helicopters (678-4802) or Canadian Helicopters (678-2207).

There are three ski access routes described in this guidebook. The route from Shark Mountain is the shortest and most popular. The route from Sunshine is somewhat longer and more difficult but still sees some traffic. The route from Banff, over Allenby Pass, although historically the early approach route to Assiniboine, is now rarely skied.

Facilities There are several overnight possibilities of varying degrees of comfort and cost: Assiniboine Lodge, the Naiset Cabins or camping. The lodge is privately managed and is the luxurious place to stay. The Naiset Cabins are similar to the ACC huts and are much less expensive than the Lodge. There is a designated camping area for the truly penurious.

Regulations If you plan on spending a night at the Bryant Creek Shelter you will need a permit from Banff National Park. Helicopter access to the park is restricted to landing at Assiniboine Lodge or the Naiset Cabins, three days of the week only, Wednesdays, Fridays and Sundays. On long weekends, flights are also allowed on Mondays. Flights are limited to the hours between 1100 and 1700.

Naiset Cabins

Map *82 J/13 Mount Assiniboine*
Location Above east end of Lake Magog on bench. GR 973402
Reservations Booking required Dec 1 - May 31. Contact B.C. Provincial Parks
Capacity 28
Facilities Wood stoves, woodpile, axe
Water Magog Creek nearby

Bryant Creek Shelter

Map *82 J/13 Mount Assiniboine*
Location 600 m south-east of the Warden Cabin in the far corner of a meadow on the west side of the trail. GR 043392
Reservations Hut permit required from Canadian Park Service, Banff
Capacity 18
Facilities Wood stoves, woodpile, axe
Water Bryant Creek nearby

Mount Assiniboine Lodge

Mount Assiniboine Lodge is the post card picture of what a ski lodge in the Rockies should be. It is located in the meadows along the shore of Lake Magog, beneath the tower of Mount 'Assiniboine. The beautiful lodge itself was built in 1928 and consists of a central building and several cabins, all constructed of log. It is reached either by a 25 km ski from the Shark Mountain Cross Country Area or a 15 minute helicopter flight from Canmore. The winter season is mid-February to mid-April. Accommodation is about $100 per person with all meals included. Phone (403) 678-2883 for information. GR 972403

In Emergency Contact the Ranger at Lake Magog.

History The meadows below Mount Assiniboine and the mountain itself have been a destination for adventure seekers for almost 100 years. Mount Assiniboine was first climbed in 1901 when British Baronet, Sir James Outram and his Swiss guides Christian Bohren and Christian Häsler reached the summit. Over the years the mountain has become a magnet for climbers from all over the world.

The BC government with totally uncharacteristic foresight created Mount Assiniboine Provincial Park in 1922.

In 1925 A. O. Wheeler built several cabins (Naiset Cabins) which were eventually sold to the Alpine Club of Canada for a minimal amount.

In March of 1928 a young Norwegian ski adventurer, Erling Strom and his aristocratic partner, the Marquis d'Albizzi, skied into Assiniboine over Allenby Pass. After spending a month skiing in the beautiful meadows beneath the striking tower of Mount Assiniboine, Strom was hooked. That summer he returned, and built Assiniboine Lodge which opened for business the following spring. If you visit the lodge today, you can see the names of the early guests carved into the logs high over the main entrance in the dining room.

The early heyday of skiing at Assiniboine was during the thirties and folks came from all over North America to experience the beauty and grandeur of the area. In those days the guests would ski 45 km from Banff, staying at two smaller huts (Ten Mile and Halfway) along the way. Fresh supplies were packed in the same way but staples were brought in the previous autumn and stored in the cellar. During the thirties when you came to Assiniboine you were there for 2, 3 or even 4 weeks. You could relax and adjust to a wilderness pace of living. Today however with the helicopter and the radio telephone, skiers come for two days, with tight schedules. Your stockbroker, your lawyer or your kids can phone you now as easily as phoning across town. 'Civilization' does indeed have mixed blessings.

Strom operated the lodge he had so lovingly built for many years. By the 1940's the winter trade was dying off, although the lodge still operated during the summers. Eventually, the B.C. Government assumed control of Assiniboine Lodge and leased it out to operators.

Swiss born mountain guide Sepp Renner and his wife Barb have operated the lodge, both summer and winter, since 1983. The ski traffic has picked up again and now forms a major portion of the yearly business.

Meanwhile the ACC cabins, which came to be known as the Naiset Cabins fell into disrepair over the years and in 1971 they were sold to the BC Government who completely refurbished them, and who now operate them, charging a minimum fee.

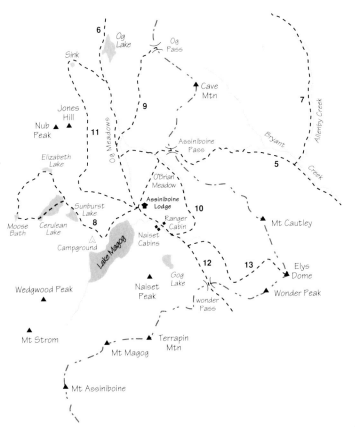

5 SHARK TO ASSINIBOINE VIA BRYANT CREEK   Ski touring

Grade Intermediate/advanced
Distance 25 km one way
Time It is a very full day to ski to Assiniboine and many parties take 2 days. Most parties can ski back out to the Shark parking lot in one day if they get an early start.
Height gain 440 m
Maximum elevation 2,180 m
Maps Mount Assiniboine 82 J/13
Spray Lakes Reservoir 82 J/14

Facilities There are toilets at the Shark trailhead. The Bryant Creek Shelter is located about half way along this tour. The Naiset Cabins and Mount Assiniboine Lodge are located near Magog Lake.

Hazards The slopes of the hillside below Assiniboine Pass offer some avalanche potential.

Access The trail to Mount Assiniboine starts from a large parking lot at the Shark Mountain Cross Country Ski Trails. Drive through the town of Canmore and follow the Smith-Dorrien Trail up the hillside to Whiteman Pass. After 38 km, turn right at Engadine Lodge. Drive past the entrance to the lodge and continue down the road for 5 km to the parking lot.

Most parties who ski to Mount Assiniboine use this route. It is often well packed. Normally skiers will fly into Assiniboine, then ski back out to their cars along this trail. The only real difficulty is the descent from Assiniboine Pass. Many skiers also use this trail for a day outing from Mount Shark.

From the Shark parking lot, follow the Watridge Lake Trail. It is a wide track-set trail with many signs marking the way. After about 2.5 km it climbs for a short distance. This is about as far as the trail will be track-set. It then descends steeply for about 100 vertical-m, crosses the flats then crosses the Spray River on a bridge. On the other side the trail climbs briefly then meanders through the forest for about 0.5 km until it crosses Bryant Creek on another bridge.

From Bryant Creek, climb for a short distance up the hillside to join the Bryant Creek Trail. Turn left along the trail. Soon there is another trail junction and here you stay right (the left fork goes down to a warden cabin). For the next 10 km the trail stays on the right side of the valley. As far as the Bryant Creek meadow it runs along through the forest and is very easy and clear to follow. After about 2 km the trail crosses a bridge at a creek then carries on for another 2 km when it begins to climb. The grade is gentle at first but gradually the trail steepens. Just before reaching the Bryant Creek Shelter the trail climbs a steep, open hillside then continues a short distance through forest before descending to the meadows. You will see the shelter across the meadow to the left.

Cross the right flank of the meadow and enter the trees again. Ski past the Bryant Creek Warden Cabin. Follow the trail along the edge of the trees on the right side of the valley for 3 km then ski out left into the meadows. Cross the meadows to the left-centre of the valley. From here continue for 4 km to the hillside below the pass, sometimes following bits of trail through the trees, sometimes open meadows, and sometimes making your own trail.

The climb to Assiniboine Pass is steep and gains about 200 vertical-m. The trail follows the left side of the valley eventually making several switchbacks near the top. It works its way between two cliffbands then traverses out to the right to the lowest point in the pass.

Ski through the pass, following a groove and then descend gently for several hundred metres in a westerly direction until you reach a meadow. On your left along here is a steep wooded hillside — do not attempt to ski across it. Follow the meadow which soon begins to curve to the left (south-west) then ski through some trees for a short distance to O'Brians Meadow.

From O'Brians Meadow there are two ways to reach Assiniboine Lodge:

Either ski down and out to the right into the huge meadows below (Og Meadows). Then turn left and ski up these meadows and through a draw in the hillside to the lodge.

Or turn left and ski up O'Brians Meadow for about 150 m. Climb up onto the right hillside and ski around a little pond before entering the trees. From here the trail heads south to the lodge. It crosses meadows and traverses sections of forest. If you are new to the area and the trail has not recently been broken, it can be hard to follow.

Assiniboine Lodge is situated on a bench above Lake Magog. The Naiset Cabins are a short distance up the hillside to your left.

6 SUNSHINE TO ASSINIBOINE VIA CITADEL PASS   Ski touring

Grade Advanced
Distance 30 km one way
Time Most parties will take two days to ski this route
Height gain 730 m
Height loss 760 m
Max elevation 2,390 m
Maps Banff 82 O/4
Mount Assiniboine 82 J/13

The approach to Mount Assiniboine from Sunshine Village is not often used nowadays. It is hard for most of us to resist the appeal of the helicopter and if we do, we usually opt for the shortest route from Shark Mountain via Assiniboine Pass. However if you are looking for some adventure and a long hard tour this trip is for you.

Facilities There are two cabins located at Policeman's Meadow, about halfway along to Assiniboine (GR 907486). Note

that these cabins are incorrectly marked on the topo map. The cabins are in good shape and the stove is in good working order. These cabins are privately owned, but are left open for use in an emergency

Hazards There are a number of hazards on this tour. First of all you need good visibility to find your way across the meadows to Citadel Pass. The descent from the pass to the Simpson River is subject to avalanche hazard and good route finding skills are required. If you plan to stay at the Policeman's Meadow cabins you will find them tricky to locate so leave yourself some daylight to get settled in. Finally the route up Golden Valley and The Valley of the Rocks is famous for bottomless depth hoar and tricky route finding, so be prepared for hard trail breaking. This tour will offer a challenge to all ski tourers.

Early ski tourer on Quartz Ridge with Mount Assiniboine in the distance

Access This tour begins at Sunshine Village (see Citadel Pass page 61).

Ski 10 km from Sunshine Village to Citadel Pass. From the pass the route descends 600 m to the headwaters of the Simpson River. This descent is subject to avalanche threat from both sides, but the route itself is reasonably safe if you follow the best line. It is possible to stay on lower angled or treed slopes virtually all the way.

From the pass, the route descends very gently for the first kilometre, past a lake, then climbs briefly to the brow of a steep hill. As you descend from Citadel Pass be sure to follow the drainage out to the left and do not get drawn off to the right by an obvious line of meadows. Descend the steep hill using the safety of the trees wherever possible. There is some avalanche hazard at the top of the hill. From the bottom of this steep hill, the remainder of the descent to the valley bottom stays in the centre of the drainage. However, there are serious avalanche paths on both sides, so exercise caution.

As you descend you can look directly south across the valley to where, tucked into a side valley (actually named the Simpson River on the map), you will see a large meadow. This is Policeman's Meadow and you can likely spot the cabin on the right flank of the meadow. If you intend to stay at the cabin, the best route to follow in winter is along the left bank of the creek (serious bushwhacking) until it joins the Simpson River, then turn left and ski upstream along the river for about 1.5 km to reach the meadow.

It is possible to avoid the descent to the valley bottom by traversing to the left, high above Golden Valley, to reach The Valley of the Rocks directly. If conditions are perfectly stable and there is no risk of avalanche (i.e. early in the morning in the spring time when the snow is still well frozen) it is possible to traverse these slopes safely. However you have to cross some very large avalanche slopes and the risk is high if you try to cross them at the wrong time. If you choose this option you should be very sure that the snow is stable.

The route up Golden Valley is frustrating and is a series of hills and sinks. You are continually climbing hills, only to have to descend again on the other side. There is no proper drainage to follow. It is recommended that along here you work to the left (north-east) side of the valley and attempt to ski near the edge of the trees as much as possible. Higher up, in the Valley of the Rocks, the going gets easier. The trees are spread out, the terrain is uniform and it is possible to make reasonable headway.

About 1.5 km before Og Lake the trail leaves the trees behind and from here to Lake Magog it travels across open meadows. The route passes Og Lake and heads due south, passing through a narrow gap before continuing for about 3 km across flat, open meadows. The last 0.5 km climbs an open draw through the forest and pops over the hill just 100 m to the west of the lodge.

Of interest In 1974, Donnie Gardner and his companions, Chris Shank and Larry Mason, left Sunshine Ski Resort at midnight on their way to Assiniboine. At 7:00 am they arrived at Assiniboine Lodge for breakfast. From there they continued down Bryant Creek to Spray Lakes, then skied along the road to a waiting car at Three Sisters Dam. An impressive feat; over 80 km in 17 hours.

7 BANFF TO ASSINIBOINE VIA ALLENBY PASS   Ski touring

Grade Advanced

Distance 44 km one way

Time 2 days are normally required for this tour

Height gain 1,070 m to Allenby Pass
260 m over Assiniboine Pass

Height loss 500 m from Allenby Pass to Bryant Creek

Max elevation 2,440 m at Allenby Pass

Maps Banff 82 O/4
Mount Assiniboine 82 J/13

The original route into Assiniboine. It is the route which was followed by Erling Strom and his first party in 1928, when they discovered the wonder of winter at Mount Assiniboine. It was used for many years afterwards as an access route to Assiniboine Lodge for the guests and their guides. It is not often used now as it is such a long way, but it is recommended for a backcountry adventure.

Facilities Banff Sundance Lodge (phone 762-4551) is located along Brewster Creek (GR 935614) and is open in winter.

Halfway Cabin is located along the creek, 3 km north of Allenby Pass (GR 995496). It is marked incorrectly on the map. It is on the opposite side of the creek.

Access Park your car 0.8 km along the Sunshine Village access road at the start of the Sundance trails (see page 51).

Follow trail #1 along the Old Healy Creek Road for about 2 km to its junction with Brewster Creek Road. Turn right, and work your way along the trail up Brewster Creek to Banff Sundance Lodge. Up to this point the skiing is easy and the trail will quite likely be packed, but beyond here it is a backcountry route and you should be prepared to break trail.

The trail continues up Brewster Creek for about 12 km then turns right up a side valley. Several kilometres up this side valley you will find the Halfway Cabin. From here the trail climbs steeply through the trees to the high meadows of Allenby Pass. Follow Allenby Creek down from the pass and descend to Bryant Creek. Join the Shark Mountain/Bryant Creek trail to Assiniboine (see page 28). Skiers sometimes cut the corner above Bryant Creek, if the snow conditions are stable, and angle around the corner for Assiniboine Pass. Be careful however as these slopes are exposed to serious avalanche risk.

Of interest Erling Strom was born in 1897 in Norway and emigrated to the U.S.A. in 1919. For years he was a ski instructor at Lake Placid and ran a lodge at Stowe in Vermont. He is noted for having made the second ascent of Denali (North America's highest peak) in 1932. However, he will be forever associated with Mount Assiniboine and the beautiful lodge that he built in the meadows below.

8 MOOSE BATH

Ski touring

Grade Easy/intermediate
Distance 8 km return
Time 4 hrs
Height gain The trail climbs 140 m as far as the pass above Elizabeth Lake, then descends 150 m to Moose Bath. On the return to Assiniboine Lodge the trail climbs about 100 m to reach Cerulean Lake.
Max elevation 2,290 m
Map Mount Assiniboine 82 J/13

This is a varied and pleasant excursion. There are meadows, hills, and forests to travel through. It is not a difficult tour but you really get the feeling of exploring around. The scenery is beautiful, particularly at Sunburst Lake.

Facilities The tour passes by the Sunburst Lake Cabin, but it will be locked. There is an outhouse here.

Hazards The hillside descending to Elizabeth Lake has glades in the trees, which could pose an avalanche threat in certain conditions. Straying too far to the right as you climb from Moose Bath up to Cerulean Lake could expose you to avalanche from the slopes of Sunburst Peak.

Options For the really hardy and adventurous this tour starts you on a long tour via the Mitchell River to Settlers Road near Kootenay Park. It can also be tied in with Ferro Pass, Surprise Creek and the Simpson River.

From Assiniboine Lodge work southwest along the brow of the hill above Magog Lake. After a bit more than 1 km work your way right, through some trees, into a shallow drainage. Follow this drainage north-west for about 0.5 km until it pops over the crest of a hill to reach Sunburst Lake. About 100 m along the right shore of the Lake, you will find the Sunburst Lake Cabin, tucked in the trees. This is a pleasant spot for a break.

Continue north-west along the edge of the lake, then cross a short neck of land to the shore of Cerulean Lake. Traverse the east (right) edge of this lake for a short distance, then climb the hillside directly above its north corner. About 100 m of reasonably steep climbing through the trees brings you to the top. Down the other side you will see Elizabeth Lake. Descend to the lake taking a line a bit to your left. There is an opportunity for a few turns here, so have some fun. Cross Elizabeth Lake

and descend the creek that runs southwest. For most of the descent stay on the left bank of the creek, then work your way left (south) to a small pond shown on the map (Moose Bath!).

Cross the pond and work your way up the hillside above, through the trees, to reach Cerulean Lake. Cross the lake to the north-east to rejoin your earlier tracks, which are then followed back to the lodge.

Of interest The Sunburst Lake Cabin was operated by Lizzie Rummel for 20 years from 1951 to 1970. As well as the cabin, there were several tent cabins and her famous tipi. Lizzie became a legend in the Canadian Rockies and eventually had a school, two lakes, and a street in Canmore named after her. People would journey from around the world to spend time with her on the shores of Sunburst Lake. She could always remind us of what was really important and beautiful in life.

Looking across Lake Magog to Mount Magog, Mount Assiniboine and Mount Strom   Photo Vance Hanna

9 OG PASS

Ski touring

Grade Easy/ntermediate
Distance 10 km return
Time 4-5 hrs return
Height gain 300 m
Max elevation 2,300 m
Map Mount Assiniboine 82 J/13

A pleasant day trip through varied terrain. There are excellent views of Mount Assiniboine and a fun run down from the pass.

Access The trail begins at Assiniboine Lodge.

The trail starts just 100 m north-west of the lodge. Descend the draw for about 0.5 km until the trail breaks out into Og Meadows. Ski across the meadows heading north, for about 2 km, then just before the meadows narrow into a short 'canyon' turn right. From here follow the drainage up to Og Pass. On your return you can ski back down the creek from the pass then, for variation, just before reaching the meadows turn south and follow another drainage to Assiniboine Pass. From Assiniboine Pass work your way back through the meadows and forests to Assiniboine Lodge (see page 29).

10 DEAD HORSE CANYON

Ski touring

Grade Easy
Distance 5 km loop
Time 2-3 hrs
Height gain 120 m
Max elevation 2,290 m
Map Mount Assiniboine 82 J/13

A short, entertaining and easy day, with some climbing, a bit of a downhill run and some travelling through the forest.

Hazards The walls of the creekbed can be potentially dangerous during unstable conditions.

From Assiniboine Lodge ski south-east, past the cabins. Cross the little creek and continue up the hillside in front of the rangers cabin. Continue climbing up the open hillside above, and after about 0.5 km angle up and left through some open trees to gain the bench at the edge of treeline. Ski across this bench for a short distance , now travelling north-east, until you reach a prominent drainage which descends the hill to the north. The tour follows the creekbed, losing about 120 m in elevation. It is a fun run but never steep. Continue down the creek bed until you reach a large meadow (O'Brian's Meadow). Cross the meadow in a north-west direction until you gain the trail from Assiniboine Pass heading south to Assiniboine Lodge. Return along this trail (see page 29).

11 JONES BENCH

Grade Easy
Distance 10 km loop
Time 4-5 hrs
Height gain 180 m
Max elevation 2,350 m
Map Mount Assiniboine 82 J/13

This is a superb trip. It very quickly climbs above timberline and traverses above the meadows for several kilometres. The views are excellent and there is opportunity to make a few turns along the way. Highly recommended!

Hazards Although this tour is through moderate terrain, there are many little rolls and hills that can pose an avalanche threat.

Options A short side trip to the top of the Nublet is possible for the more adventurous skier.

From Assiniboine Lodge ski north-west across the meadows for about 0.5 km, then curve left (west). Follow more meadows for a few hundred metres until they begin to pinch out into the trees. Ski up the drainage that curves up to your right towards the Nublet. Climb at a gradual angle up the creek for about 120 m (vertical gain) until it reaches the edge of timberline. From here work your way out right, above timberline, to a rounded shoulder. The little peak above you is called the Nublet and the adventurous can climb on skis and occasionally on foot to its rounded and gentle summit. The leeward side of this shoulder offers an excellent place to make a few telemark turns.

Carry on traversing the bench, in a northerly direction, for 3 km. After you pass beneath Jones Hill on your left, you begin to descend gradually. To reach the valley bottom near Og Lake, it is necessary to ski all the way to a sink that is marked on the map (GR 951444) before descending to your right. Do not cut down into the valley before this point as you will encounter very steep terrain. Just beyond the sink you can descend easily to the valley floor.

Return to the lodge across the meadows along the valley bottom. Just before reaching the lodge it is necessary to climb a creek drainage, ski through a section of trees, then pop through a little 'pass' to the lodge.

Of interest Ken Jones was the first home-grown Canadian to receive all the National Parks guides badges — for skiing, mountain climbing, river and bush craft. For years he guided around Skoki, Lake Louise and Assiniboine. He was really a professional log builder who was responsible for Num-ti-jah lodge on the Icefields Parkway and worked on Skoki Lodge in 1936. Throughout the 1960's and 70's he was the Ranger at Mount Assiniboine Park. One of the Naiset Cabins is, in fact, his old ranger cabin and is now called Jones's Cabin.

Jones Hill, Jones Bench and Jones Pass (at Skoki) are all named for Ken. He can often be found working quietly around Mount Assiniboine Lodge. Don't be afraid to talk to him because he loves to tell stories.

12 WONDER PASS

Grade Easy
Distance 7 km return
Time 3 hrs
Height gain 210 m
Max elevation 2,360 m
Map Mount Assiniboine 82 J/13

Wonder Pass is another pleasant, short day trip; perfect for that lazy day. The trail leads you high above the trees into beautiful alpine terrain. The views are great.

Facilities The trail passes by the rangers cabin where you can stop for a chat and a check on snow conditions. Across from the rangers cabin are the Naiset Huts.

Options The tour can be extended beyond Wonder Pass. You can carry on south-east, along a bench, to a promontory high above Marvel Lake. There are some fine views here.

From Assiniboine Lodge, ski south-east past the cabins, then cross the little creek. Begin climbing the hill past the rangers cabin and carry on up the hillside above. The trail follows open terrain along the left bank of Magog Creek. After crossing the creek (where it turns east) the route stays high up on the left for the last kilometre and traverses into the pass. On the return trip you can come back the same way if you choose, or you can take a more direct line straight down the drainage below Wonder Pass. Both ways offer the opportunity to make a few turns.

Early days at Mount Assiniboine. Looking across Lake Magog from Assiniboine Lodge

Photo Whyte Museum of the Canadian Rockies

13 ELY'S DOME
Ski touring

Grade Intermediate/advanced
Distance 8 km return
Time A full day tour
Height gain 650 m
Max Elevation 2,830 m
Map Mount Assiniboine 82 J/13

A wonderful tour for that sunny spring day. The skiing can be excellent and there are marvellous views of Mount Assiniboine.

Hazards There is avalanche potential on this tour so use caution.

Access This tour begins at Assiniboine Lodge.

A route which allows you to climb the unnamed peak between Mount Cautley and Wonder Peak (GR 012389). Ski up the hill past the ranger's cabin and then work your way left across the meadows above towards the peak. The mountain is climbed by skiing up a ramp which traverses from right to left. If the proper line is followed throughout the ascent is safe and offers enjoyable telemark skiing on the way down. However there are steeper slopes nearby which could be dangerous in certain conditions.

Of interest The peak is named after the sister of Sam Evans. Sam was an early packer and guide who worked in the 1930's and 40's around Mount Assiniboine and Skoki. He came from Montana and was reputed to be enormously wealthy. They say he was an heir to the Dupont fortune, but he worked along with the rest of the guides and never let on. Well into his 80's now, he is still occasionally seen at both of the lodges.

TELEMARK AREAS
Ski touring

The Nublet
Some excellent telemark terrain can be found on the shoulder below the Nublet. See the Jones Bench tour (page 36) for the approach.

These south-east facing slopes are set at a fairly gentle angle and in the sun all day. Highly recommended!

The Cerulean Lake Hillside
The hillside above the north shore of Cerulean Lake offers some good telemark skiing.

This is glade skiing, in the trees, so it is an excellent area for those snowy and cloudy days. See the Moose Bath tour (page 33) for the approach.

BANFF AREA

Access Banff is located along the Trans-Canada Highway (Highway #1), 130 km west of Calgary. The other major road in this area is the Bow Valley Parkway (Highway 1A) which begins 6 km west of Banff and runs for 50 km along the north side of the Bow Valley, past Castle Junction to Lake Louise. The Kootenay Parkway (Highway #93) intersects the Trans-Canada at Castle Junction and leads south-west to Radium, BC. Just 20 km east of Banff along the Trans Canada Highway is the town of Canmore. It is rapidly becoming Canada's centre for nordic skiing. The Canmore Nordic Centre offers a premier quality training and racing facility and was the site of the cross country events during the 1988 winter Olympics. The town is much less crowded and more pleasant than Banff.

Facilities In Banff you will be able to find everything that you are likely to need on a skiing trip. There are a large number of grocery stores and shops with all manner of goods. There are a number of gas stations some of which remain open 24 hrs. Catering to your needs for ski touring equipment are two large outdoor stores, Mountain Magic (762-2591) and Monod's (762-4571). In the event that they cannot help you then Mountain Equipment Co-op (269-2420) in Calgary will likely have what you require. All modern amenities are also available in Canmore. There are numerous good restaurants, bed and breakfast establishments, as well as groceries, shops and gas stations. Spoke and Edge (678-2838) or Altitude Sports (678-6272) can help you with your nordic ski equipment needs.

Accommodation Banff has accommodation to suit almost all budgets, ranging from small bed and breakfast establishments all the way up to grand hotels like the Banff Springs Hotel. There is a large, modern Youth Hostel located in Banff (762-1470). Accommodation of all types is also available in Canmore. The Alpine Club of Canada runs two excellent and inexpensive facilities in this town — the ACC Clubhouse (678-3222) and the ACC Canmore Group Centre (678-3200)

Information Information about snow conditions, weather, trails, etc. as well as backcountry permits and registration may be obtained from the Park Information Centre at 224 Banff Avenue (762-4256). The centre is open 10:00 to 18:00 in winter.

Banff Sundance Lodge

This is the old Ten Mile Cabin which was used by skiers in the 1930's to reach Mount Assiniboine. It has been completely renovated and now has solar power, and indoor plumbing with showers. It will accommodate up to 30 guests at about $90 per person, meals included. Phone 762-4551 for information. GR 935614

Wardens The Banff Warden Office (762-1470) is located just east of the townsite on the north side of Banff Avenue at the Parks Compound. Specific information about current mountain conditions and up to date trail reports can be obtained here. You can also obtain backcountry permits and register out at this office.

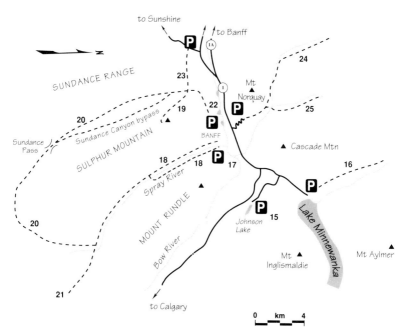

14 CARROT CREEK TRAIL

Nordic skiing

Grade Easy
Distance 5 km return
Time 1-2 hrs
Height gain 90 m
Max elevation 1,480 m
Map Canmore 82 0/3

This is a short and easily accessed ski tour. It is ideal for an afternoons exercise. It requires about 40 cm of snow to be skiable and in some years this area does not receive adequate snow.

Access A large parking lot is located on the north-east side of the Trans Canada Highway (Highway #1), 15 km east of Banff and 2.3 km west of the Park Gates. It is necessary to be driving in the west-bound lane to turn into the parking area. East-bound traffic must continue to the Banff Park Gate and turn around to get into the west-bound lane.

At the west end of the parking lot there is stairway gate through the fence. Climb through the gate then put on your skis. Ski for about 50 m north, towards the creek, then turn right. Continue north-east, towards the Fairholme Range, generally parallel to the creek. The trail passes through open aspen woods and is marked occasionally with a number sign or a piece of flagging. Much of the way the trail is an old roadway. Towards the end, the trail becomes narrow and eventually curves down to the edge of the creek where it stops.

For the return to the parking lot, come back along the narrow final portion of the trail and after about 0.6 km branch right along another trail, in the direction of the creek. From here continue through the open forest along a trail which is located a short distance south of Carrot Creek. The trail is at times a little hard to follow due to the open nature of the trees. As you near the road the trail turns back left (south) for several hundred metres to reach the parking area.

15 JOHNSON LAKE TRAILS

Nordic skiing

Grade All trails are easy except for one intermediate section.
Distance 11.4 km of trails
Time You can ski for the whole day here, or for a few hours if you choose.
Height gain 50 m elevation change throughout the trail network
Max elevation 1,425 m
Map Canmore 82 O/3

An excellent trail system offering pleasant skiing in a beautiful location. The trails are all quite easy with the exception of the portion of trail #1 between its junction with trail #3 and trail #4. You can spend a very pleasant day skiing through a mixture of terrain — open forest of aspen and spruce, beautiful meadows and dense forests of lodgepole pine. Trail #4 runs along the hillside above the Trans Canada Highway through stands of Douglas Fir and offers marvellous views of Mount Rundle across the valley.

Facilities Picnic tables, telephone and washrooms at the trailhead.

Hazards The area often is short of snow. While the trails do not require a lot of snow to be skiable, a minimum of 30-40 cm is recommended. This area was heavily mined in the late 19th century and there are a number of old mine shafts. Some are fenced off but some may not be. Stay well back from these hazards.

Access From the town of Banff drive to the interchange on the Trans Canada Highway (Highway #1) north-east of Banff, then continue up the Lake Minnewanka road beyond the interchange for 1 km and turn right. After another 4 km turn right again on another side road. Continue to the end of the road where there is a large parking area at the trailhead.

The trails are arranged so that they can be skied in larger or smaller loops. The biggest outing is to ski the full loop of trail #1 which is 8.2 km. The far end of the trail beyond the junction with trail #3 has a moderately challenging downhill, then a short uphill climb which could be a problem for novice skiers. For the return leg of this loop you can follow trail #4 which is a very scenic option. For a shorter alternative trail #2 and trail #3 are cutoffs which allow you to avoid the hills previously mentioned, and to reduce the distance by half. Simply ski the first part of trail #1

then take either of the cutoffs to gain the returning leg of trail #1.

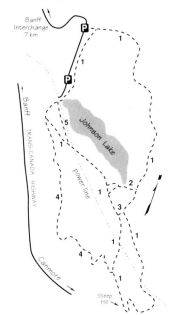

16 CASCADE FIRE ROAD

Nordic Skiing

Grade Easy
Distance The road is normally track-set for 13 km to Stony Creek
Time A few hours or all day if you choose
Height gain 180 m
Max elevation 1,480 m
Maps Banff 82 O/4
Castle Mountain 82 O/5

One of the most popular trails in the Rocky Mountains. The snow is usually good and this trail is one of the first to be track-set. Highly recommended.

Access There is a large parking lot on the left (north) side of the road, about 4 km along towards Lake Minnewanka. To reach this drive east from the town of Banff for several kilometres, pass under the Trans-Canada Highway (Highway #1), then head up the Lake Minnewanka Road.

The start of the Cascade Fire Road is not quite as straightforward as it might be. The parking lot is actually a short distance west of the start of the road and it is necessary to work your way to the road along a trail. This trail is well maintained and is marked with trail number signs (#1). It climbs up for a short distance then descends to the road. Beyond this follow the fire road for as far as you like. It climbs a bit but only just enough to give you a thrill on the way back down.

Photo Chic Scott

43

17 GOLF COURSE TRAILS
Nordic Skiing

Grade Easy
Distance Potentially about 10 km.
Time As long as you wish.
Max elevation 1,370 m
Map Banff 82 O/4

A very popular area with novices who want to get the feel of nordic skiing. It is safe, easy and close to the road. There are little hills that skiers can try their wings on. A recommended place to start. Some years it can be short of snow.

Facilities The Banff Springs Golf Course Clubhouse has made an effort in the past to be a nordic skiing centre.

Access Drive up Spray Avenue and turn left before you reach the Banff Springs Hotel. Drive down the hill, past Bow Falls and continue across the bridge over the Spray River. In another 1 km park on your left at the Golf Course Clubhouse.

There are officially four trails around the golf course numbered 4,5,6 and 7. (Trails #1,2 and 3 are along the Spray River and are dealt with on page 45) These trails however are rarely used and the only ones that regularly have adequate snow are #6 and #7. Most folks who ski on the golf course just wander at will on the fairways. This is truly a novice area where new skiers can try the sport in a safe environment. There is a small hill in front of the clubhouse that is fun to practice on.

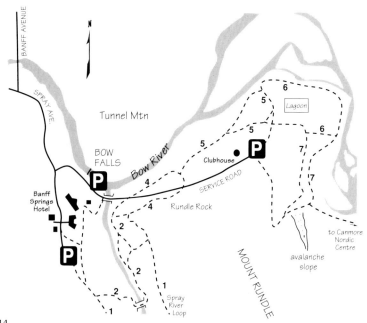

18 SPRAY RIVER LOOP

Grade Easy
Distance 10 km return
Time 3-4 hrs return
Height gain 200 m
Max elevation 1,390 m
Map Banff 82 O/4

This easy tour is one of the most popular in Banff National Park. The trail is always well groomed and because it is along a road it requires little snow. It makes an pleasant outing for all levels of ability.

Facilities At the end of the trail, where it crosses the Spray River there are picnic tables.

Hazards Trail #2 which descends back down to the Spray River from the west side of the loop can be tricky when it is icy. Beware!

Options The Spray loop serves as an integral part of two other trails: the Goat Creek Trail and the Sundance Pass/Spray River Loop

Access You can start either from the Banff Springs Hotel or from the Banff Springs Golf Course, a short distance away. Both parking lots are described.
Bow Falls Parking (Banff Springs Golf Course). Turn left off Spray Avenue towards the Banff Springs Golf Course. Park at the bottom of the hill, a hundred metres or so beyond Bow Falls, just before the bridge across the Spray River.
Banff Springs Hotel Drive up Spray Avenue to the Banff Springs Hotel. Go past the statue of the gentleman pointing very seriously (Cornelius Van Horne), and carry on underneath the CPR version of the Arc de Triomphe. Continue past the parking structure to a small parking lot at the trailhead.

The trail is described starting from the Golf Course. From the parking lot, walk across the bridge over the Spray River and put on your skis near the unusual statue of the Rocky Mountain Sheep, beside the first fairway. Ski across the fairway angling to your right towards the trees. Look for the trail about 100 metres down the fairway on the right side where it enters the trees. The trail climbs quite steeply for the first few hundred metres

then the angle begins to ease off. The wide trail climbs at a more gentle angle for the next couple of kilometres and there are nice views through the trees across the river to the right. Carry on along pleasant undulating terrain until a short downhill run leads you to the Spray River. Cross the footbridge to the picnic tables on the far side. This turn-around point is an excellent place for lunch in the sunshine.

For the return journey, ski back along the west side of the river. There are lovely views over the Spray River and down towards Cascade Mountain. There are as well several climbs of perhaps 60-70 m (vertical gain) but they are all quite manageable even for novice skiers. The trail continues without problems to the parking area at the Banff Springs Hotel. To return to your car at the Golf Course/Bow Falls parking lot, turn right on a side trail (trail #2), about 0.5 km before reaching the Banff Springs Hotel. This short trail winds its way moderately steeply down to the Spray River and can be tricky, particularly if icy. It crosses the river to the east bank via a footbridge, and continues back along the river to the first fairway of the golf course.

Photo Alf Skrastins

The Sulphur Mountain Fire Road offers a long descent which can be exciting if snow conditions are fast

19 SULPHUR MOUNTAIN ROAD

Ski touring

Grade Intermediate
Distance 5 km one way
Time 3 hrs up, 30 min down
Height gain 850 m
Max elevation 2,290 m
Map Banff 82 O/4

This is hardly a nordic ski tour, but is included because many folks still ski it. There is an excellent view from the top and, in good conditions, the run down is a lot of fun.

Hazards In icy conditions the ski down can be very fast and in cold weather the wind chill on the long descent may be very high.

Access Park at the Cave and Basin parking lot at the end of Cave Avenue. Follow trail #1 (see page 50) along the Sundance road for 2 km to where the Sulphur Mountain Road joins it from the left.

The tour simply follows the road all the way to the top. Put on a good climbing wax or skins and start climbing. Take a long rest at the top, then bundle up well for the chilling descent.

20 SUNDANCE PASS

Ski touring

Grade Advanced
Distance 28 km loop
Time A very full day trip
Height gain 350 m
Max elevation 1,740 m
Map Banff 82 O/4

A long and challenging trip which is not often skied, so you might be breaking trail. Although it starts at the outskirts of Banff townsite it is not long before you feel as though you are really in the wilderness.

The routefinding from Sundance Pass down to the Spray River is tricky and the skiing is not easy. There should be at least 60-70 cm of snow to make this trip enjoyable so wait until later in the season. Due to the north/south orientation of the valley it gets a lot of sun during the day.

Facilities There are camp shelters and picnic tables at Sundance Canyon, near the start of the tour, and there are picnic tables along the Spray River.

Access Park at the Cave and Basin parking lot at the end of Cave Avenue. A second car should be left at the Banff Springs Hotel parking lot (see page 45). Otherwise it is a long walk back to the Cave and Basin at the end of the day.

From the parking lot walk around the Cave and Basin to the start of the Sundance Road. Put on your skis here and ski along the road (Trail #1). The skiing is easy and the views across the Bow Valley are excellent. There are two options for negotiating Sundance Canyon itself.

You can ski up the Sundance Road then follow the summer trail directly up Sundance Canyon. This trail starts by crossing a footbridge to the left bank of the creek, then climbs without difficulty for a short distance. The terrain steepens and it is necessary to take your skis off. For the next 50 vertical metres you climb some steps with a railing, cross a little bridge, then climb steeply above, to reach easier ground. Beyond here you put on your skis and follow the creek and the trail again. Just beyond the end of the right-hand cliffs, you cross to the right side of the creek. The trail climbs a short distance through the trees before it begins to turn right, back towards Banff. At this point leave the trail to the left and carry on straight up the valley. The way through the woods is quite open. Carry on, trending slightly left until you reach the creek again. Follow the creek for 4 or 5 km until near the area of the pass. Following the creek is occasionally difficult and it is necessary to travel through the woods on the right or left bank for a distance, until it is possible to return to the creek again. When you are near the pass there is a large meadow off to your right which is a scenic place to sit in the sun and have lunch. Above you is the summit of Sulphur Mountain and to the west is the Sundance Range.

Alternatively you can follow the canyon bypass trail which avoids Sundance Canyon completely. It starts on the left side of the Sundance Road between the Old Healy Creek Road and Sundance Canyon itself.

The bypass trail is an excellent alternative. After a steep start, it climbs gradually through the forest and is clear to follow. It soon levels out and runs back into the valley for several kilometres.

Eventually it becomes more difficult to follow as the forest opens. If you lose the trail traverse out to the right to the creek bed and continue along the valley bottom to the meadow near the pass.

Not far beyond this meadow, the creek peters out and it is necessary to ski through the forest. There is a great deal of dead fall here and it is absolutely imperative to work your way to the left (east) side of the valley bottom, until you locate the trail which runs through the woods. This is the only reasonable way through the forest, so take a little time to search for it. Follow the trail for 2-3 km.

Eventually the trail breaks out into a series of long thin clearings. Follow the clearings, trending downhill and staying on the left side. At the end of the clearings it is necessary to find the trail again. A creek also appears at this point and for the next kilometre the trail is never far from the creek. The trail initially starts on the left bank of the creek then quickly it crosses to the right bank. It climbs high on a ridge then drops steeply down and swings back left again into the creek. The trail crosses the creek one more time to the left bank and climbs very steeply up a hill. From the top of this hill the rest of the descent becomes more reasonable. The trail now stays in the forest and does not return back to the creek. The descent begins steeply but soon becomes more moderate. It is a fun glide down the trail to the Spray River Road.

Turn left and ski along the Spray River Road. It is 2.2 km to the junction with the Goat Creek tour (Canmore to Banff) (see page 49) and then an additional 9.5 km to the Banff Springs Hotel and your waiting car (see the Spray River Loop, page 45).

21 CANMORE TO BANFF VIA GOAT CREEK · Nordic Skiing

Grade Intermediate
Distance 18 km one way
Time 3-4 hrs one way - downhill
4-6 hrs one way - uphill
Height gain One loses (or gains) about 270 m in elevation.
Max elevation 1,640 m
Maps Banff 82 O/4
Canmore 82 O/3

This trail is usually skied as a downhill run. You can cover 18 km pretty quickly. Most people leave a car at the Golf Course/Bow Falls parking lot in Banff, then drive back to the Canmore end and ski the trip one way.

Facilities There are washrooms at the parking lot at the trailhead (Canmore end) and picnic tables at the bridge across the Spray River, 5 km from Banff.

Hazards The descents into Goat Creek and later into the Spray River can be tricky if icy. Although this is really track skiing, you should be prepared for emergencies. It is a long way back to your car if you have trouble with a binding or break a cable. The nights can be very long and cold out there if something goes wrong.

Options You can also begin from the Banff end and ski the trail up and back in a day.

Access There is a large parking area at the trail head which is located on the right (west) side of the Smith-Dorrien Trail about 8 km from Canmore. To reach it drive through the town of Canmore and follow the signs for the Nordic Centre. When you are through town, do not turn into the Nordic Centre, but continue up the steep hill to Whiteman Pass. Follow the road around the reservoir and down a short hill. The parking lot is on your right.

Most people leave a second car at the Golf Course/Bow Falls parking area in Banff (see Spray River Loop, page 45).

From the parking lot ski down a few metres to the creek and cross it via a footbridge. The trail then angles up onto the right bank above the creek and contours around the hillside for about 1.5 km and enters Banff National Park. From here the trail gradually descends towards Banff for another 5 km, until it crosses Goat Creek. The trail is quite

wide and the skiing is easy. The last part of this section of the trip is a short, moderately steep downhill section which descends to Goat Creek.

Cross the creek on a footbridge and climb the hill on the other side. The trail ascends for about 50 m (vertical gain), contours around the hillside and in about 1 km descends, this time to the Spray River. Cross the Spray River via a footbridge and ski up the other side for a short distance to join the Spray River Fire Road. Turn right up the road and climb the hill. From the top of this uphill you get a long and gentle downhill for several kilometres to the Spray River picnic site. From here you can either continue down the left side of the Spray River or cross the river via the footbridge and continue back to your car along the right bank.

49

22 CAVE AND BASIN TRAILS

Nordic skiing

Grade The trails are easy with the exception of trail #3 which is intermediate/advanced
Distance 8.3 km of trails
Time You can ski on these trails for several hours or for most of the day if you chose.
Height gain Negligible with the exception of trail #3 where there is about 100 m of climb.
Max elevation 1,470 m
Map Banff 82 O/4

These trails are readily accessible and offer some pleasant skiing. With the ex-ception of trail #3 they offer easy skiing and do not require a lot of snow to be skiable. The views across the Bow Valley towards Mount Norquay and Mount Edith and west towards Mount Bourgeau and Mount Brett are excellent.

Facilities At Sundance Canyon, at the end of trail #1, there is a camp shelter and picnic tables where it is possible to have lunch and a warm fire (bring an axe).

Options The trails link up with both the Sundance Pass ski tour and the Sundance trails along the Old Healy Creek Road.

Access Parking is available at the Cave and Basin parking lot at the end of Cave Avenue or at the recreation grounds near the Sundance and Martin Stables (turn right about half way down Cave Avenue).

There are three trails in this network. They are intertwined and you can be creative and use your imagination to ski them.

Trail #1 begins at the recreation grounds and over 4.6 km (one way) of easy skiing, works its way to Sundance Canyon. The trail starts by skiing back for a short distance, on the right side of the entrance road, to reach the trail beside Cave Avenue. It continues, through the trees, along the right edge of Cave Avenue, beneath the Cave and Basin parking lot (you can park here too), then though a fascinating area of gurgling hot springs and singing birds! The trail meets the Sundance Road which it follows to Sundance Canyon. Along here the views are great but for much of the way the road can be windblown and bare of snow. About 1 km before reaching Sundance Canyon you will see, on the right, the start of the Old Healy Creek Road.

Trail #2 is really a branch which swings off from trail #1 at the Cave and Basin parking lot, and heads north along an old dike to reach the Bow River. It continues pleasantly along the edge of the river for another kilometre until it reaches the Sundance Road. This trail can be skied as a loop of 2.7 km (incorporating a portion of trail #1) from the Cave and Basin parking lot. It can also be incorporated into a ski along trail #1 to Sundance Canyon, either on the way there or back.

Trail #3 is a variation on the Sundance Road trail. It is a much more challenging way to reach Sundance Canyon or the Old Healy Creek Road. It begins where trail #1 meets the Sundance Road and climbs steeply, through the trees, above the road. It continues west, on the side of Sulphur Mountain for 1.6 km until it reaches the Sulphur Mountain road, then descends to the Sundance road, directly opposite the Old Healy Creek Road.

23 SUNDANCE TRAILS

Ski touring/nordic skiing

Grade Trail #1 (the Old Healy Creek Road) is easy. Trail #7 is advanced. All the other trails are intermediate.
Distance Trail #1 is 4.8 km one way. Trail #8 is 12 km one way. There are another 12 km of assorted trails in this network.
Time As long as you wish.
Height gain Minimal on all the trails except #8 where there is a 150 m elevation gain to the lodge.
Max Elevation 1,580 m
Map Banff 82 O/4

A varied and interesting set of trails. They are a real mixture. Some are flat and often track-set (Trail #1 the Old Healy Creek Road). Others are complex and usually require trail breaking (Trails #2-7) while Trail #8 will most likely be packed by snowmobile traffic taking supplies to the Banff Sundance Lodge.

Access This group of trails can be reached from two different ways. You can park at the Cave and Basin (see page 50) and follow trail #1 along the Sundance Canyon Road to its junction with the Old Healy Creek Road. There is also a parking lot 0.8 km along the Sunshine Village access road. To reach the latter, drive west of Banff about 9 km along the Trans-Canada Highway (Highway #1) and take the turnoff to the Sunshine Village Ski Resort.

The most popular trail is the Healy Creek Road (Trail #1) which can be skied one way or return. It is a broad, wide road and is often track-set. It crosses Healy Creek on a bridge not far from the Sunshine Road.

Trail #8 to Banff Sundance Lodge is a wide road which will likely be packed by lodge traffic. You might consider staying overnight and enjoying the stars and the wood smoke.

The other trails are rarely used and it is likely that you will be breaking trail. They can be tricky to follow and it is easy to get lost in the woods so take a compass.

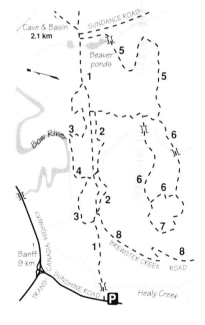

24 FORTY MILE CREEK

Grade Intermediate
Distance 10 km return to Edith Pass fork
34 km return to Mystic Warden Cabin
Time 4-5 hrs to the Edith Pass fork
All day to the Mystic Warden Cabin
Height loss 150 m from Mount Norquay
to Forty Mile Creek
Height gain 270 m gain along Forty
Mile Creek to Mystic Warden Cabin
Max elevation 1,830 m
Maps Banff 82 O/4
Castle Mountain 82 O/5

This trail offers some interesting skiing. You can take a few hours to ski a short distance along the creek, or take a whole day to ski as far as the Mystic Warden Cabin. Leave yourself plenty of time for the return trip - it is a long way.

Facilities Mount Norquay Ski Area. Outhouse at the Mystic Warden Cabin.

Options Beyond the Mystic Warden Cabin you can ski for another 3 km to Mystic Lake. You can also carry on over Mystic Pass (page 54) and back down Johnston Creek to the 1A highway (page 76).

Access Drive up the access road to the Mount Norquay Ski Area from the Trans-Canada Highway (Highway #1). Park in the large parking lot on the right.

From the parking lot ski past the lodge and across the ski slopes. Pass below the Lone Pine and Wishbone lifts and work your way down past the Spirit Chairlift and the Mystic Chairlift, until you are finally clear of the noise and rush of the resort. Follow the trail which descends gradually down the hill — it is generally wide and has no sharp corners. At one point a steep trail branches off to the right. Do not follow this trail — it is normally roped off. At another point the trail climbs up for a few metres but soon it begins its descent again. After about 2 km and a drop of about 120 m the trail reaches Forty Mile Creek.

Turn left and ski up the left side of the creek on a narrow trail which works its way up and down through the trees for about 1.5 km until it reaches a bridge across the creek. Although the views are good here, this is not the place to stop for lunch, as you are below a giant ava-

lanche path. Cross the bridge and continue up the right side of the creek for another 1.5 km until you reach the Edith Pass Trail fork. The very impressive mountain that you have been admiring along the trail is Mount Louis and is one of the great climbs in the area.

From here take the right branch which continues up Forty Mile Creek. For the next 12 km the trail stays on the right side of the creek and climbs very gradually as it works its way up the valley. It is generally easy to follow. Sometimes it is a few metres above the valley bottom and sometimes it drops down near the creek. The trail crosses some small creeks which can be a nuisance early in the season. It also crosses some large slide paths — do not linger here. Towards the end the trail descends to the left for a short distance to a fork. Follow the branch to the left which descends to the creek. Cross the bridge to the Mystic Warden Cabin on the far side.

The cabin steps are a great place to sit and have a drink and eat lunch. Return the same way back to Mount Norquay.

25 ELK LAKE SUMMIT

Ski touring

Grade Intermediate/advanced
Distance 20 km return
Time A full day tour
Height loss 150 m to Forty Mile Creek
Height gain 500 m from Forty Mile Creek
Max elevation 2,060 m
Map Banff 82 O/4
Castle Mountain 82 O/5

A challenging trail, particularly on the return trip. It offers an entertaining ski tour without having to drive too far from Banff.

Options It is possible to carry on beyond Elk Lake Summit to the Cascade Fire Road, then to return along the road

Access This tour begins at the Mount Norquay Ski Resort and follow the Forty Mile Creek Trail to the point where it meets the creek (see page 52).

After you descend the trail from the Norquay Ski Area and reach Forty Mile Creek, cross the creek on a footbridge in an easterly direction towards Cascade Mountain. Follow the trail on the other side which soon begins to climb. The trail climbs and switchbacks quite steeply for several hundred metres until it reaches a junction. Follow the trail which heads left, up the valley. The trail from here climbs at a much less steep angle and is quite enjoyable. It continues for 6 km without difficulty along the hillside to Elk Lake Summit.

to a second car. This trail is rarely skied and there is not much of a trail to follow. It is a long trip so get an early start. The route basically follows the creek bed north for 5 km beyond the summit then turns east and follows a gap in the mountains down to the Cascade River. It may be a problem getting across the river to reach the fire road. Ski south along the fire road for 13 km back to the Lake Minnewanka Road (see the Cascade Fire Road, page 43).

It is also possible to visit Elk Lake. The best bet is to continue through the pass down to the drainage which flows from Elk Lake then climb back up the creek to the lake.

Of interest The Mount Norquay Ski Resort began as a humble log cabin. It was built in 1929 by a group of Banff citizens who called themselves the Mount Norquay Ski Club. This group became The Ski Club of the Canadian Rockies and went on to build Skoki, Temple Chalet and the Post Hotel. The original Mount Norquay ski hut burned down in 1938.

26 MYSTIC PASS

Ski touring

Grade Advanced
Distance 13 km from Forty Mile Creek
to Johnston Creek.
The circuit from the Mount Norquay Ski
Area to the Bow Valley Parkway near
Johnston Canyon, is 37 km
Time 2 days to ski the complete circuit.
Height gain 430 m from Forty Mile
Creek to Mystic Pass
Height loss 730 m from Mystic Pass to
Johnston Creek
Max elevation 2,250 m
Map Castle Mountain 82 O/5

This tour begins at the Mystic Warden
Cabin and connects Forty Mile Creek with
Johnston Creek. It is a long adventure and
it is likely that you will be breaking trail,
Only very strong skiers will do this tour in
one day. If visibility is poor, it is tricky to find
your way over this pass, so be sure to
bring your map and compass.

Hazards Much of this tour is threatened
by avalanche slopes. It is recommended
to undertake this adventure only when the
hazard is low.

Access This connector starts at Mystic
Warden Cabin.

The trail begins on the north side of the
cabin. After a short, flat section through
the woods the trail climbs quite steeply
for about 75 m then levels off and heads
back left into the valley. It runs along
horizontally for several kilometres,
crossing some large avalanche slopes.
Eventually at a huge avalanche slope
you angle down left to the creek where
you will find a camping area and some
picnic tables. It is also possible to ski
along the creek for much of this section
and avoid the avalanche hazard.

From here the way to the pass is tricky.
It is possible to follow the trail most of
the way to the pass, if you have sharp
eyes. The trail begins straight up the hill
above the camp site. It is also possible to
work your way up the drainages coming
down from the pass. Either way is not
easy and requires good route finding
skills. Once you are above timberline
follow the drainage back for about 2 km
to the pass which is at the far end.

The descent down the other side is
quite good. Start by descending a groove
from the pass which soon steepens into
a creek drainage. The slope continues to
steepen and it is best to traverse left and
descend open timber to the valley below.
Once you are in the valley, work your
way along as best you can, following the
creek at times, or through the open
woods and even skirting the forest on the
right or left flank.

After 1.5 km the valley bottom opens
up beneath a large rock tower high on
your right. After another kilometre the
trees begin again but the way is easy
down the creek or through open timber
on either side of the creek. At the point
where a large avalanche path descends
from the left (south) side of the valley,
the summer trail climbs up onto the right
bank of the creek and traverses along
about 60 m above the creek. It is possible
to follow this trail, which may be broken,
or else to carry on down the creek bed.
The last kilometre of descent down the
creek is easy, either along the creek or
following the trail along the right bank.
Continue past the junction with the
Johnston Creek Trail, and follows the
creek for several hundred metres down
to Johnston Creek. Turn left and continue towards the Ink Pots.

BANFF TO CASTLE JUNCTION

The section of the Bow Valley between Banff and Castle Junction is a popular ski touring area due to its proximity to Banff. There are two parallel highways, the Trans-Canada Highway (Highway #1) and the Bow Valley Parkway (Highway #1A), both of which have trailheads for some excellent tours. Approximately 9 km west of Banff is the turnoff for the Sunshine Ski Area parking, also a ski touring trailhead.

Bow Valley Parkway This is the 'Old Highway' and it is a much more pleasant route along the Bow Valley. The road is narrow and curvy and requires a much slower rate of speed. It is well maintained but during storms it is advised to keep to the Trans-Canada Highway as it will be plowed and sanded more promptly. During winter there are limited facilities.

Facilities At Castle Junction there is the Castle Mountain Hostel which offers rustic but comfortable accommodation. Just across the road is the Castle Mountain Village Motel (762-3868) which offers more upscale accommodation, a gas station and a small general store. Further west along the road are the Baker Creek Chalets (522-2270) which offer cozy cabins, a fine restaurant and lounge and ski trails which start right at the door.

In Emergency Contact the Banff Warden Office at 762-4506.

There are two possibilities for back-country accommodation in this area. The Egypt Lake Shelter is primitive with no equipment apart from stove, woodpile and axe, while Shadow Lake Lodge is operated as a full service back-country lodge.

Egypt Lake Shelter

Map 82 O/4 Banff
Location In meadow above true left bank of Pharaoh Creek, 0.5 km NE of Egypt Lake GR 772621
Reservations Hut permit required from Canadian Park Service, Banff
Capacity 16
Facilities Wood Stove, woodpile, axe
Water Snowmelt, Pharaoh Creek

Shadow Lake Lodge

Originally constructed in 1928, Shadow Lake Lodge was completely refurbished in 1991. Meals are served in a main dining building and six log cabins provide accommodation for 24. There is propane heating and outdoor plumbing. The lodge is located about 0.5 km north-east of Shadow Lake, a 13.5 km ski from the Trans-Canada Highway. GR 736687
The season is Dec. 18 to Jan. 3 and from Feb. 15 to April 15.
Accommodation is about $100 per person (double occupancy) with all meals included. Afternoon tea is also available. Phone (403) 762-5454 for information and reservations.

Sunshine Village The meadows near the Sunshine Village Ski Resort provide one of the finest locations in the Rockies for ski touring. The meadows are large, stretching 10 kilometres out to Citadel Pass. On a sunny day it is paradise up here. The terrain is open and rolling and provides perfect ski touring opportunities. However when the clouds roll in and visibility is poor, navigation becomes very difficult. So save this area for that beautiful day in the spring, when you can sit in the sunshine and marvel at the tower of Mount Assiniboine in the distance.

Access is now difficult. It is no longer possible to purchase a one ride ticket for the gondola to Sunshine village. The only alternatives are to either ski up the ski-out to the ski resort or purchase a full day ticket, for about $40. Either way the touring on the Sunshine Meadows, on a beautiful spring day, is more than worth it.

To reach the Sunshine Ski Area, turn off the Trans-Canada Highway (Highway #1) about 9 km west of Banff and drive up the Sunshine access road to the Bourgeau Parking Lot. Walk across the parking lot to the gondola terminal building. If you choose to ski up 'the ski out', this trail begins just in front of the building. The climb to the ski area takes 2-3 hours and climbs 480 m over 4 km. If your pocketbook can afford it, you can purchase a lift ticket inside the terminal building. You can always combine a few runs on the lifts, with a tour.

History The Sunshine area had become popular as a summer destination long before its merits as a ski centre were discovered. One of the earliest visitors to Sunshine was the legendary Bill Peyto who led his clients into Assiniboine via this route. Amongst these was James Outram who made the first ascent of

Relaxing inside the original Sunshine Ski Lodge

Mount Assiniboine in 1901. A.O Wheeler (of Alpine Club of Canada fame) and the Brewsters also used this route to conduct their guests into the Assiniboine area. In 1928 the CPR built a cabin at Sunshine for the Trail Riders of the Canadian Rockies.

Cliff White and Cyril Paris were amongst the first to show an interest in the area as a winter destination. They skied through Sunshine in 1929 on their way into Assiniboine via Citadel Pass. They were looking for a location for a ski lodge and the next year struck upon Skoki. However in 1933 the two Brewster brothers Jim and Pat, Jim's wife Dell, Austin Standish and several others skied to Sunshine from the Bow Valley via Egypt Lake. They were impressed with the area, in particular the depth of snow, and the following winter they leased the cabin from the CPR and Sun-

shine hosted its first paying guests. In 1936 Brewster Transport bought the cabin for $300.

In the early days skiing at Sunshine was ski touring. Waxes, climbing skins and hard work were used to get up the hill. However in 1942 a portable lift was first used at Sunshine and by 1945 a permanent rope tow powered by a Mercury V-8 engine was installed. Since then the area has undergone a never ending spiral of growth, always asking for a just a little more. Over the years the number of lifts has escalated and the beauty that once attracted the ski adventurer must now be found by skiing well beyond the ski resort out into the silence and peace of the meadows. It is encouraging to note that the last application for yet another expansion was turned down by Parks Canada.

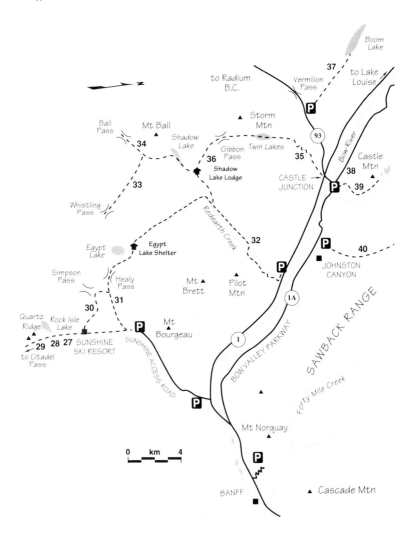

27 ROCK ISLE LAKE

Ski touring

Grade Easy
Distance 4 km return
Time 2 hrs
Height gain 110 m
Max elevation 2,290 m
Map Banff 82 O/4

The tour to Rock Isle Lake is short and easy. It is a perfect introduction for a novice to the joys of ski touring. It is hard not to notice the change, leaving the hectic pace of the ski resort behind, and skiing into the solitude and peace, only a few kilometres away. Many have discovered themselves and the mountains on the Sunshine Meadows.

Facilities There are washrooms, telephones and restaurants both at the lower terminal of the gondola (Bourgeau Parking Lot), and at the ski resort itself. The most peaceful spot at the ski resort is the public lounge in the old log structure at the centre of the resort. Few know of this lounge and you can sit here in peace, eat your lunch, and dream of the days when mechanized skiing was unknown and when this old building sat alone in the wilderness.

Hazards The meadows are not recommended when the visibility is poor, unless you are expert at map and compass navigation. The hillside on the south side of Rock Isle Lake offers good skiing, but the slopes present avalanche potential. Ski with caution!

Options From Rock Isle Lake you can carry on to Quartz Ridge (see page 60) or Citadel Pass (see page 61). The adventurous can ski to the Mount Assiniboine area from here, via Citadel Pass, Golden Valley and the Valley of the Rocks (see page 29).

Access See introduction above for access to the Sunshine area.

The trail to Rock Isle Lake begins at the bottom of the Strawberry Chairlift. Ski up the run to the left of the lift (Rock Isle Road). You can stop at the Parks Canada Snow Research Station for an avalanche forecast if you like. This is the log building just to the left of the lift, about 50 m up the hill. Carry on beyond the research station, climb to the top of the run and continue through the broad pass out into the meadows. There is a good view from here, of Mount Assiniboine on the horizon straight ahead. There will often be a snowmobile track along here. The lake is about 0.5 km ahead and down slightly to the right. From the lake you can carry on further or you can simply spend the day exploring where you chose.

28 QUARTZ RIDGE
Ski touring

Grade Intermediate
Distance 10 km return
Time 4 hrs
Height gain 350 m
Max elevation 2,530 m
Map Banff 82 O/4

A tour up Quartz Ridge is special indeed. The trail takes you up high above the meadows and the view is outstanding. Clear visibility is required to do this tour safely. The tour described takes you up the lower peak. The higher peak is more challenging and is not described.

Access See introduction above for access to the Sunshine area.

The first section of the trail to Quartz Ridge is identical to the tour to Rock Isle Lake (see page 59). When the trail turns down to the right to Rock Isle Lake, carry on straight south towards the twin summits of Quartz Ridge and Quartz Hill which can be seen clearly on the horizon. From this point you can attain Quartz Ridge by two routes:

You can ascend the small hill on the right above Rock Isle Lake, continuing along the crest of the ridge and rounding problem areas on the left, over to the base of Quartz Ridge.

Alternatively, you can follow a groove to the left side of this ridge crest, until near Quartz Ridge, then turn up to the right to gain the start of the mountain. Either way you end up at the base of the broad open north slope of Quartz Ridge. Work your way easily up for about 200 vertical-m to the top of the mountain. Skis can be worn right to the top.

Facilities There are washrooms, restaurants and telephones at the bottom terminal of the gondola lift. All of these facilities are also available at the Sunshine Ski Resort.

Hazards Be sure to follow a safe line throughout this trip as there are little slopes and rolls along the way which can be deceptive and which offer avalanche potential.

Options This trip can be combined with a tour to Citadel Pass (see page 61).

To return to Sunshine Village you can head back down the same trail, or if you feel adventurous, you can descend carefully down the other side of the peak to the notch between the two summits of Quartz Ridge and Quartz Hill. It may be easiest to take your skis off and walk the short distance down to the notch. The climb to the high summit of Quartz Hill is steep. Step kicking is required and there are large drops down the west face. This climb is ski mountaineering and is recommended only for those with some experience. However the descent from the notch down the north-east side of Quartz Ridge is fun and not too steep. Stay right to avoid steep slopes lower down. From the bottom of this descent you can work your way back north across the meadows to rejoin your trail from earlier in the day. This necessitates a short climb through a notch where you may have to herringbone or wax up.

Opposite: Looking across the meadows towards Citadel Pass (centre) from the high point of the tour

29 CITADEL PASS

Ski touring

Grade Easy/intermediate
Distance 20 km return
Time A full day tour
Height gain 430 m
Max elevation 2,390 m
Map Banff 82 O/4

A perennial favorite amongst local skiers. On a fine, sunny day the tour across the meadows to Citadel Pass, with the summit of Mount Assiniboine dominating the horizon, is highly recommended.

Options It is possible to carry on to Mount Assiniboine.

Hazards If visibility is poor, route finding can be very difficult.

Access Begin at Sunshine Village

Ski up the run to the left of the Strawberry Chairlift (Rock Isle Road). Just above the lower terminal of the lift is the Parks Canada Snow Research Station. It is a good idea to drop by and obtain the snow stability and weather forecast for the day. At the top of the Rock Isle Road run the angle lays back and you ski through a gentle pass. Far to the south, Mount Assiniboine can be seen on the skyline. Beyond the pass the tour heads out due south across the meadows. The normal route that most skiers follow stays on the right side of the meadow. Eventually the route passes under the lower Quartz Ridge then climbs for about 100 m (vertical) to cross a ridge that runs out from the higher Quartz Hill; the high point on the tour. Descend the other side of the ridge for about 2 km, losing about 150 m and passing Sundown Lake. The trail then levels out, crosses a drainage and begins to climb again, gaining about 120 m over the next 1.5 km to Citadel Pass.

Photo Rudi Setz Collection

Photo Whyte Museum of the Canadian Rockies

An early photograph from the Sunshine Meadows showing Quartz Hill and Quartz Ridge (right) with Mount Assiniboine in the background. The skier is Norm Knight

TELEMARK AREAS

The slopes around the Sunshine Meadows offers some short but very pleasant telemark skiing. Some of the best places to ski are:

Twin Cairns

The peak just west of the top of the Standish Chairlift is Twin Cairns. It is an entertaining ski ascent and on the way back down you can make a few turns. It is not possible to ski right to the top; you must scramble up the rocks the last few metres along the ridge.

Quartz Ridge

The northeast slopes of Quartz Ridge offer excellent skiing. In some places the slopes are gentle and in others the angle is quite steep. The whole slope is open and you must ski with caution. At the highest point the run would be about 200 m.

Opposite: Removing skins on Healy Pass. Pharaoh Peaks in the background

30 HEALY CREEK TRAIL FROM SUNSHINE

Ski touring

Grade Intermediate/advanced
Distance 10 km
Time An easy day trip
Height gain 170 m
Height loss 650 m
Max elevation 2,360 m
Map Banff 82 O/4

A fun trip which is almost completely downhill.

Options You can combine this trip with the tour to Healy Pass.

Hazards There is a cliff band which blocks the descent to Simpson Pass. Scout around until you find a safe route.

Access Begin at Sunshine village.

From Sunshine Village ski or ride to the top of the Wa-Wa lift. Angle off northeast to the notch in the ridge, north of Twin Cairns. From the notch curve around left, heading west across the open meadows. Very quickly you encounter a very steep escarpment which you can bypass by staying well to the left. The meadows roll with short little hills and after 1.5 km lead you to the top of a long descent down to the valley, just north of Simpson Pass. The descent is for the most part straightforward and much of it is through open forest, however there is one cliffband and you should scout around to find a safe line through it. Even at the most reasonable point the descent is steep and offers avalanche risk. If you stay far enough to the left you can avoid the cliff altogether.

Once through the cliff band, descend into the valley and angle right to gain the drainage of Healy Creek. The trail along here will be hard to follow but eventually you should reach the well packed Healy Pass trail which is followed back down to the Bourgeau Parking Lot. Beware — this is a steep and tricky descent. See the Healy Pass Trail on page 64 for more information.

Photo Gillean Daffern

31 EGYPT LAKE VIA HEALY PASS

Ski Touring

Grade Intermediate
Distance About 7 km to Healy Pass one way, and an additional 3 km down to the Egypt Lake Shelter.
Time Most people treat the trip to Healy Pass as a full day trip. With a packed trail however, you can reach the pass in 2 hours if you are fast.
It is an additional hour down the hillside to the Egypt Lake Shelter
Height gain 620 m to pass
Height loss 340 m to shelter
Max elevation 2,320 m
Map Banff 82 O/4

The ski tour to Healy Pass is very popular and for good reason. It is accessible and it gets you up high without too much difficulty. The views from the pass are outstanding — Mount Assiniboine can be seen very clearly to the south, Monarch Mountain is very imposing and the views of the Egypt Lake group of peaks and Mount Ball to the north-west, are very impressive. Some good telemarking can

be found in the vicinity of the pass. If you want to continue down the west side of the pass to the Egypt Lake Shelter, you can treat yourself to a marvelous Canadian Rockies night under the stars, complete with the smell of wood smoke.

Facilities There are washrooms, telephones and refreshments at the bottom terminal of the gondola at the Bourgeau Parking Lot. There is a camping area with picnic tables and an outhouse about half way along the trail to the pass.

Hazards The trail crosses major avalanche paths. Take note of the steepness of the trail up to Healy Pass and be sure that you will be able to ski back down it.

Options This trip is often linked up with the tour along Pharaoh and Redearth Creeks. The loop is usually done by strong skiers in one day. However, it can also be done as a two day trip with an overnight at the Egypt Lake Shelter.

Access About 9 km west of Banff on the Trans-Canada Highway, follow signs to Sunshine Ski Area. Drive another 9 km to the Bourgeau Parking Lot and park along with the hoards of downhill skiers. Walk beyond the terminal of the gondola lift to the trailhead, which is the bottom of the old ski out trail (most everyone uses a new ski-out trail now).

If you intend to ski to Healy Pass or Egypt Lake and return to your cars the same way, then you will only need one car. However many people make a two day trip of this, staying overnight at the Egypt Lake shelter, then skiing down Pharaoh and Redearth Creeks the second day, to the Trans-Canada Highway. In this case you will need to leave a

second car at the Redearth Creek parking lot (on the south-west side of the highway 20 km west of Banff).

Begin by skiing up the old ski out above the Bourgeau Parking Lot. Be sure you have a good grip wax on your skis because it is pretty much uphill almost all the way to the pass. Some people even like to use climbing skins to make it a little easier. The trail climbs up the broad ski-out for about 0.5 km and then turns off on a smaller trail to the right. Along this section of trail you can admire the waterfall frozen to the side of the cliff on the right across the valley. It is called Bourgeau Left Hand and is a well-known and populer ice climb.

The trail descends for a short distance, then crosses a creek. It climbs steadily for several kilometres until it reaches Healy Creek. This section of the trail is narrow, fast and tricky to negotiate on the way down.

Cross the creek and continue along the north bank through the woods, gradually gaining height. The trail crosses several large avalanche paths where it is not advisable to stop. After about 4 km there is a camping area on the left with some picnic tables and an outhouse. A short distance farther along the trail branches. The left fork heads up to Simpson Pass and the right fork heads up towards Healy Pass. Beyond this point the trail climbs steeply again and after some distance actually climbs almost straight up the hill. Just as the trail reaches tree line it begins to level off making a traverse to the left out into the open where the drainage comes down from the pass.

If it is a cold and blustery day this is your last point for shelter so it is a good place to have a drink and a bite to eat before heading up to the pass. Once into the drainage you can follow it straight west to the pass. On a sunny day this section in the meadows, high above the trees, is very beautiful — looking back you can see the striking summit of Mount Assiniboine on the horizon.

If you are returning to the Bourgeau Parking Lot the way down is steep and tricky. It is an advanced trail. Stay in control and ski safely.

If you are going on to Egypt Lake you can either attempt to follow the summer trail down (difficult to find and not recommended) or you can head directly down the meadows ahead of you and through the trees until you gain the valley. If you choose this route, it is likely that you will reach Pharaoh Creek upstream from the shelter. Turn right, down the creek for a short distance until the creek opens up dramatically into a broad meadow. There is a very obvious bridge across the creek, sticking up in the meadow, and the shelter is on a bench on the left (west) bank in the direction of the Pharaoh Peaks about 20 m above the creek.

Egypt Lake Shelter in a good snowfall year

Skiing Redearth Creek   Photo Alan Kane

32 REDEARTH CREEK
Nordic skiing/Ski touring

Grade The trail along the fire road, as far as the turn off to Shadow Lake, is easy. The short section into Shadow Lake is very steep and is a difficult trail to descend. The section up Pharaoh Creek from the warden cabin to Egypt Lake is intermediate, but is fast and tricky on the way back down.

Distance 11 km to turnoff to Shadow L.
2.5 km from turnoff to Shadow Lake
9 km from here to Egypt Lake Shelter

Time For most people it is a full day to get to the Egypt Lake Shelter (one way) via Redearth and Pharaoh Creeks. The trip to Shadow Lake and back out again is usually a full day.
For a shorter day you can ski to the picnic site about 6 km up the fire road, where the road crosses the creek.

Height gain 425 m to Shadow Lake
600 m to Egypt Lake

Max elevation 1,820 m at Shadow Lake
1,995 m at Egypt Lake

Map Banff 82 O/4

The Redearth Creek trail is very popular. The first part is a fire road and is easy and often trackset. It is a good place to practice your skills in a safe environment. The tour

all the way to Shadow Lake is popular as well. The full tour up to Egypt Lake, with an overnight at the shelter, is a great adventure and is highly recommended.

Hazards The descent down Pharaoh Creek has some sharp turns at the bridges. Ski carefully! The climb towards Shadow Lake, from the cutoff, is difficult, particularly to descend. If it is at all icy it is advisable to walk down.

Options You can continue to Egypt Lake and then over Healy Pass to the Bourgeau parking lot near Sunshine. Most people ski this tour in the opposite direction. The tour up to Twin Lakes can be continued over Gibbon Pass to Shadow Lake and exit via Redearth Creek.

Facilities Toilets at the Redearth Creek parking area. Picnic tables and an outhouse at the 6 km bridge where the fire road crosses Redearth Creek. There is a ski lodge at Shadow Lake.
The trail passes picnic benches on the east side of Pharaoh Creek about two thirds of the way up the creek, from the Shadow Lake cutoff.

Access There is a large parking lot on the south side of the road about 20.0 km west of Banff.

From the Redearth Creek parking lot you are immediately faced with two choices. You can ski back south-east (towards Banff), along the edge of the trees, parallel to the road, for 2-300 m, to pick up the fire road where it heads up right into the trees. Alternatively you can follow a trail which heads up into the trees from the corner of the parking area near the toi-

lets. Both trails come together after a short distance and then continue up the fire road. This section may be track set. The road is wide the skiing easy. After 6 km the road descends gently to the creek and crosses it. There are picnic tables and an outhouse on the far (north) side.

The road continues up the right bank of the creek for another 5 km to the Shadow Lake cutoff. From here it is challenging to get into Shadow Lake. The trail climbs very steeply for about 100 vertical metres before it levels off

Relaxing outside Shadow Lake Lodge   Photo Chic Scott

and turns to the left for another 2 km to Shadow Lake Lodge. A few hundred metres before the lodge the trees begin to open up into a meadow. The lodge is on the right at the edge of the trees.

If you are going to Egypt Lake then stay on the fire road for several hundred metres beyond the Shadow Lake cutoff. The road descends to Redearth Creek and crosses it to a warden cabin and a corral. The road ends here and a trail crosses Pharaoh Creek to the far side and heads up the left bank. For about 5 km the trail follows next to the creek, sometimes on one bank and sometimes on the other, crossing the creek perhaps eight times on small bridges. After 5 km the trail crosses to the east bank (left side) of Pharaoh Creek and begins to angle up the hillside. For the next 2-3 km the trail stays on the east bank of the creek and climbs perhaps 100 vertical-m above the creek before descending to the creek again.

For the rest of the way, the valley bottom is wide and open and it is best to follow the creek bed. After about 1.5 km the warden cabin can be seen in the edge of the trees on the left. Just a few hundred metres beyond, on a bench on the right above the creek, is the Egypt Lake Shelter. Beyond this point the creek pinches off and becomes quite narrow, so it should be easy to ascertain if you have missed the shelter.

33 HAIDUK LAKE

Ski touring

Grade Intermediate
Distance 14 km return from Shadow Lake Lodge
Time A moderate day trip
Height gain 250 m
Max elevation 2,060 m
Map Banff 82 O/4

This is a popular tour with visitors at the Shadow Lake Lodge. It is a very pleasant way to spend the day and the tour takes you to a lovely lake tucked away into the mountains.

Options If you wish to continue to Whistling Pass, ski across Haiduk Lake then climb steeply, gaining about 100 vertical metres, to reach a higher bench. Soon the trees disappear and you can ski straight up the valley to the pass, avoiding a small band of cliffs on the left.

From the pass it is possible to descend a short distance to Scarab Lake.

The descent to Egypt Lake is steep, difficult and is not recommended.

Access This tour begins from the Shadow Lake Lodge.

From the lodge, follow the right bank of the river up to Shadow Lake. Ski along the left side of the lake to the point where Haiduk Creek enters the lake (this point is normally obvious because the incoming stream melts a pool out into the lake).

From here the route follows Haiduk Creek upstream for 2.5 km. At the start the ascent is a bit steep and forested, but it soon opens up into meadows. After about 1 km you reach a large meadow. Angle out to the right corner where the way continues up the open drainage of the creek.

Note: Many people leave Shadow Lake before they reach the true creekbed. They follow a false creekbed which appears to be the obvious way. However, the forest soon pinches in and the way becomes very narrow. After about 1 km this route pops over a hill and descends to the meadow mentioned above.

After another 2 km you cross a second large meadow to its end where a huge avalanche path can be seen sweeping down. Just before reaching the end of the meadow look for a trail on the left (GR 724654) normally marked with flagging which climbs to Haiduk Lake

The trail now climbs steeply for about 150 vertical metres then meanders through forest for a short distance until it breaks out into more open country. Continue along the right side of the creek. It is sometimes hard to stay on the trail as it makes its way through meadows, glades and open forest. The way is often marked with flagging.

Eventually you arrive at a large, open meadow which you cross to reach the lake about halfway along the left shore.

34 SHADOW LAKE TO BALL PASS

Ski touring

Grade Advanced
Distance 12 km return from Shadow Lake Lodge
Time An easy day trip
Height gain 380 m
Max elevation 2,200 m
Maps Banff 82 O/4

An adventurous trip that takes you to a high and remote pass.

Facilities There are picnic tables before the trail begins its steep climb to Ball Pass.

Hazards The last climb up to the pass itself is subject to avalanche risk. Retreat if you doubt the stability of the snowpack.

Options It is possible to descend the other side of Ball Pass, down Hawk Creek to the Kootenay Parkway.

Access Begin at Shadow Lake Lodge.

Follow the Whistling Pass Trail to RE21 (GR 724653) along the west fork of Haiduk Creek which descends from Ball Pass (see page 69). From here the trail climbs steeply, close alongside the right bank of the creek. At some points the route follows the creek. After about 0.5 km the angle eases and after 1.5 km a band of cliffs looms straight ahead. Ski along the creek which curves to the right under the cliffs. Gradually the cliffs peter out and after 0.5 km disappear completely.

Swing left and begin climbing the treed slope above the creek. Soon another set of cliffs will appear straight ahead. Climb diagonally up and to the left under the base of the cliffs, to the highest larch trees, then climb the slopes above them, angling back to the right into the pass. This last section of about 75 m (vertical), above the final larch trees is steep and potentially dangerous. Take care!

Photo Gillean Daffern

35 TWIN LAKES

Ski touring

Grade Advanced
Distance 15 km return
Time This is a full day tour
Height gain 630 m
Max Elevation 2,060 m
Maps Banff 82 O/4
Castle Mountain 82 O/5

A challenging and very steep trail, which can often be icy.

Hazards The descent from Twin Lakes can be very difficult. Take care!

Options This makes a good, long tour when combined with Gibbon Pass, and Redearth Creek.

Access There is a summer parking lot at the trailhead which is just a few hundred metres south of the large interchange on the Trans-Canada Highway (Highway #1) at Castle Junction. You must find your way through the high elk fence at this point. This lot may not be plowed, so you may have to park some distance away along the highway.

From the parking lot ski across a bridge to the south-east side of the creek. Turn right and follow a wide trail along the creek. After less than 1 km the trail narrows then crosses a bridge, back to the north-west bank.

From the bridge, make several switchbacks up the steep hillside above, then continue along over rolling terrain high above the right bank of the creek. The trail is hard to follow as it climbs and descends and meanders along. After about 0.5 km the trail begins to climb steeply. It does not switchback much but just climbs straight up the hillside. Over the next few kilometres the trail gains about 400 m vertical.

At the 2,000 m level the angle lays back and over the next 2 km the trail traverses south, climbing gradually into the Twin Lakes drainage. Ski up the river bed for another 2 km to reach lower Twin Lake.

Photo Alf Skrastins

Opposite: A touring party at Ball Pass preparing for the run down

36 GIBBON PASS

Ski touring

Grade Advanced
Distance 5 km from Twin Lakes to
Shadow Lake
Time 4 hours
Height gain 230 m
Max elevation 2,290 m
Map Banff 82 O/4

An interesting pass to traverse. The climb up from Twin Lakes gives excellent touring, but the descent to Shadow Lake will tax the most experienced skier.

Hazard There is some avalanche hazard off the slopes of Storm Mountain.

Access This trail connects the Twin Lakes tour and the Redearth Creek/Shadow Lake tour.

Ski across the south Twin Lake to the far end then ski up a shallow draw to the right of the trees under the impressive cliffs of Storm Mountain. Follow the draw for about 1.5 km until it begins to get much steeper. Climb up and left through open forest for about 75 m (vertical) until you break out into open meadows. Follow the meadows easily to the pass. There are great views here with the massive bulk of Mount Assiniboine looming to the south.

From the pass head across open meadows towards the south-east. The trees begin very quickly and you must follow the best line possible, dropping straight down the hillside below for 460 vertical-m to Shadow Lake Lodge. The hill is steep and skiing is tricky — many switchbacks will be necessary. At times it may be possible to follow the summer trail but normally it will be hard to find. The lodge is located on the edge of a meadow right at the bottom of the hill.

37 BOOM LAKE

Nordic skiing

Grade Easy
Distance 10 km return
Time 3-4 hrs return
Height gain 180 m
Max elevation 1,890 m
Map Lake Louise 82 N/8

The Boom Lake trail is deservedly one of the most popular in the Rocky Mountains. Due to its high location near Vermilion Pass, it gets snow early and keeps the snow well into the spring. It takes little snow to make the trail skiable and you can

often find keen skiers here as early as November. In addition to good early season snow conditions, the trail is very pleasant and makes a nice easy outing.

Facilities Toilets are located at the trailhead.

Hazards The steep initial sections of this trail can prove difficult for beginner skiers on the return journey, and can provide an exciting ride in icy conditions. Beware!

Access There is a large parking lot at the trail head which is located 6 km southwest of Castle Junction on the Kootenay Highway (Highway #93). The parking lot is on the right (north) side of the road.

The trail starts at the north end of the parking lot. It immediately crosses a bridge and very soon starts to climb. For the next 0.5 km the trail climbs fairly steeply, then for another kilometre it continues to climb but at a lesser angle. For the next 3 km, until just short of the lake, the trail rolls up and down through mature forest. The last several hundred metres is a run down to the lake, arriving on the lakeshore about one quarter of the way along the north bank. The trail is usually well packed and sometimes groomed

Photo Alan Kane

38 TRAILS NEAR CASTLE JUNCTION
Nordic skiing

Grade Easy
Distance 13.7 km of trails
Time You can ski here for a few hours or all day if you choose
Height gain Nil
Max elevation 1,450 m
Map Castle Mountain 82 O/5

One can pass some pleasant hours skiing here. The three trails are normally track set by the management of the Castle Mountain Motel.

Options You can also ski the trail to Tower and Rockbound Lakes (see page 75) from here.

Facilities The Castle Mountain Hostel is located within a few metres of these trails. Across the road is the Castle Mountain Village motel which offers a general store, gas pumps and telephones.

Access All three trails begin at Castle Mountain Junction where the connector road from the Trans-Canada Highway (Highway #1) intersects with Bow Valley Parkway (1A Highway). Turn to the right (east) at this junction and immediately you will see a parking lot on the left (north) side of the highway. You can leave your car here and make your way to the trails either by skis or on foot, as required.

Trail #1
Starts from the junction and runs west along the north side of the highway. Just beyond the Castle Mountain Village the trail angles right and gets away from the road. You can follow this trail easily for 10 km.

Trail #2
Is short and easy. From the parking lot it heads through the woods for a short distance and crosses a bridge over Silverton Creek. It works its way east and reaches the campground where it does a loop.

Trail #3
Makes a loop on the south side of the highway. It begins near the access road into the hostel, and heads south until it reaches the power line, which it follows to the east for about 1 km. The trail then turns north and works its way back to Castle Junction.

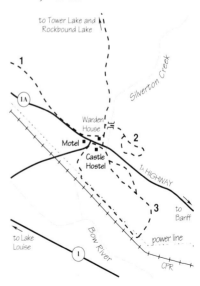

Photo Alf Skrastins

Rockbound Lake

39 TOWER LAKE AND ROCKBOUND LAKE   Ski touring

Grade Intermediate/advanced
Distance 14 km return
Time A full day trip.
Height gain 760 m
Max elevation 2,200 m
Map Castle Mountain 82 O/5

A steep climb much of the way but you are rewarded at the top with a beautiful valley tucked in behind Castle Mountain. The views are exceptional and the two lakes are in a beautiful setting. The ski down at the end of the day can be very hard on the legs, particularly if the trail is icy.

Access The parking lot is on the north side of the road beside the warden's house at Castle Junction. It is located just a few metres east along the Bow Valley Parkway from the junction with the connector road to the Trans Canada Highway (Highway #1).

The trail heads straight into the woods from the parking area. It begins climbing immediately and it is best to either wear skins or have a very good climbing wax

on your skis. As you work your way up through the trees there are occasional views out over the Bow Valley. Over the next 3 km the trail climbs 500 m. About half way up the climb the trail splits. Follow the branch that swings steeply up and back to the right. Eventually the trail reaches the shoulder of Castle mountain and begins to lay back. It swings to the left quite sharply and heads north-west back into the valley behind the mountain. For another 3 km, as far as Tower Lake, the trail rolls pleasantly up and down, gradually gaining elevation. On your left are impressive views of the Eisenhower Tower, looming high above. Near Tower Lake, in the open meadows, is a lovely place to stop and have lunch, however the sun leaves this valley early in the day, so bundle up.

If you want to continue up to Rockbound Lake it is not too difficult, but skins are a real asset. The route climbs up the treed slopes through the cliffs, directly across Tower Lake. Although it looks unlikely, the way is reasonable and there is only 100 vertical m of steep climbing. Just over the top the route

descends a short distance to Rockbound Lake. There is very impressive scenery all around. An outstanding viewpoint can be found, over to the right, where the stream leaves the lake and plunges over a cliff. On the promontory, over the edge of the chasm cut by the stream, there is a great view back down the Bow Valley, all the way to Banff.

The return to your car can be a challenge. It follows the exact same route but now it is almost all downhill. Keep your speed under control. The trail down from the shoulder is quite wide but in icy or crusty conditions can be dangerous.

---

40 JOHNSTONS CREEK

Ski touring

Grade Intermediate/advanced
Distance 10 km to the Ink Pots return
34 km to Luellen Lake return
Time 4-5 hrs to the Ink Pots return
A very full day tour to Luellen Lake.
Height gain 200 m to the Ink Pots
520 m to Luellen Lake
Max elevation 1,620 m at the Ink Pots
1,950 m at Luellen Lake
Map Castle Mountain 82 O/5

This trail offers a fairly steep ascent, crossing a high shoulder before descending steeply to the Ink Pots. If icy or crusty,

the skiing will be challenging. The Ink Pots themselves are a lovely destination. The continuation up Johnston Creek to Luellen Lake is not a difficult tour but it is long, so leave yourself lots of time for the return journey.

Options For the really adventurous you can continue up Johnston Creek, beyond Luellen Lake, to Pulsatilla Pass, down Wildflower Creek into Baker Creek. You can descend Baker Creek to the highway or even carry on to Baker Lake, Skoki and Lake Louise.

Access There is a parking lot, on the right (north) side of the Bow Valley Parkway (1A Highway), several kilometres west of the Johnston Creek Motel.

From the parking lot the trail climbs very gradually through the trees for the first 2 km. It works its way back to the east towards Johnston Canyon, then joins the summer canyon trail. From this point the grade begins to steepen and after

another kilometre climbs at a stiff angle up to the shoulder. You are now high above the creek and there is an excellent viewpoint down the Bow Valley. Up to this point the trail is very wide but beyond here the trail narrows.

The trail now descends, sometimes quite steeply, down to the valley bottom. It emerges from the trees and the Ink Pots are right there. This is a lovely spot to sit on a sunny day and contemplate.

If you choose to continue farther up the valley, ski a short distance and you will see a bridge which crosses the creek. You can either cross the creek and ski across the meadows along the right bank, or just follow the creek itself (if it is frozen and snow covered). After a kilometre both trails join and the route now follows the creek bed. Continue along the creek for another kilometre to where a small creek enters from the right (east). This is where you turn if you wish to ski to Mystic Pass.

To continue up to Luellen Lake you have two choices. You can turn up the small side creek for several hundred metres until you see a trail sign on the left bank. At this point you join up with the summer trail which continues up the valley through the forest. It is also possible to continue up Johnston Creek itself for 2 km, then at some clearings on the right side of the creek, work your way several hundred metres up to the right through the forest to the trail. From here just keep following the summer trail. It is never particularly steep and keeps climbing steadily. After a few more kilo-

metres it passes a warden cabin. Carry on up the trail beyond the warden cabin for another 4-5 km to the cutoff for Luellen Lake. To this point the trail has stayed in the forest on the right (north-east) side of the creek.

To reach Luellen Lake turn left at the cutoff and ski straight downhill, following a trail, for a short distance to the creek. Cross the creek and climb a steep bank on the far side. Find the summer trail again, which climbs the hill above. There are many blazes. The trail climbs steeply up the hill for about 0.5 km, angles left and pops over a ridge, then descends a short distance to the lake.

Kaufmann Lake

KOOTENAY NATIONAL PARK

Kootenay National Park is the forgotten treasure amongst our wonderful Rocky Mountain Parks. It is almost completely wild, both along the highway and in the backcountry. It is also very little used, summer and winter.

Access The park is traversed from the north-east to the south-west by the Kootenay Parkway (Highway #93). Along the way there are only two facilities which are open in winter and those are the Kootenay Crossing Warden Station, and the Dolly Varden campground just west of there. The highway normally has a fair amount of traffic but it is all headed for the Columbia Valley, the Panorama Ski Resort and other destinations in BC or south of the border. If you find yourself stuck along the highway you will most likely be able to flag a ride quickly but you will have to go to Radium or back to Banff for help. The highway is well maintained and is rarely closed in winter due to snow or avalanches.

Facilities Radium itself, which is located just a few kilometres west of the park gates is a bustling little town where it is possible to find the modern amenities you might require. There are service stations, a Post Office, restaurants, grocery stores, a government liquor store and numerous motels. The famous Radium Hot Springs are located just east of town, along the highway into the park. The pool is actually just inside the park.

The backcountry has only one Alpine Club Hut, the Fay Hut. There are no other so-called 'improvements' beyond the highway.

The Kootenay National Park Administration Office (604-347-9615) is located in the town of Radium, on the hill above the Husky service station. The Warden Headquarters (604-347-9361) is just inside the park gates, on the hillside across the road from the Radium Hot Springs Aquacourt.

Fay Hut

Map 82 N/8 Lake Louise
82 N/1 Mount Goodsir (for approach)
Location On a forested bench overlooking Prospector's Valley
GR 553791
Reservations Alpine Club of Canada
Capacity 18
Facilities Foamies, Coleman stoves & lanterns
Water Snowmelt
Notes Final approach to hut up steep scree and cliffbands can be tricky in winter. Potential for avalanche danger

Kootenay Park Trails Trails 44 - 51 are recommended for cross country skiing by Kootenay National Park. They offer ski touring in a quiet, beautiful setting. It is unlikely that you will run into many folks on these trails. They are described here briefly from information provided by Kootenay Park. These trails are all considered to be easy by Park authorities, but note that there may be sections on each trail which require intermediate or even advanced skiing ability. Some of the trails parallel the highway on old fire roads, so it can be advantageous to have two cars to avoid having to return by the same route.

Further information can be obtained from the warden office at Kootenay Crossing or from the park headquarters near Radium. Note that nordic ski trails in Kootenay National Park are not track-set. You should be prepared to do your own trailbreaking.

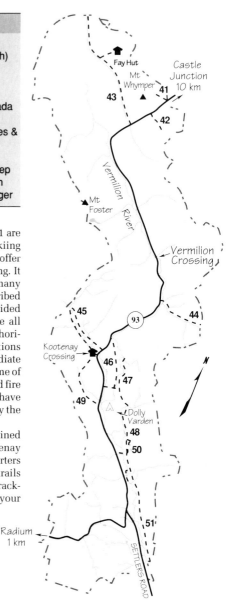

41 CHICKADEE VALLEY (WHYMPER VALLEY)

Ski touring

Grade Intermediate
Distance 10 km return
Time 3-4 hrs return
Height gain 200 m
Max elevation 1,860 m
Map Mount Goodsir 82 N/1

A pleasant half day outing. Snow is required to cover the creek bed, so wait until after Christmas. The scenery at the head of the valley is alpine and impressive. For those interested in making a few telemark turns, there are opportunities in this valley.

Hazards Several large avalanche paths reach the valley bottom.

Access Park at the Great Divide parking lot at Vermillion Pass, located 10.2 km south-west of Castle Junction on the Kootenay Highway (Highway #93). This parking lot is on the left (south) side of the highway.

From the parking lot walk directly across the highway and put on your skis. Head straight towards the Chickadee Valley through sparse trees which exist now as a result of the forest fire. The trail is a little unclear for the first several hundred metres until the creek bed becomes distinct. Follow the creek for the next 4 km to the end of the valley. The trail is fairly steep for the first kilometre, then it is very gentle for the rest of the tour. At the end of the valley there is a large open area where you can view the surrounding mountain walls and glaciers.

Excellent opportunities abound for making telemark turns in this valley and it is a popular destination for this purpose.

Of interest On this tour you can get a good view of the forest fire which burned the area in 1968. You can see how the forest has regenerated itself over the last twenty five years.

Looking north-west from the Stanley Glacier towards Mount Whymper   Photo Leon Kubbernus

42 STANLEY GLACIER VALLEY   Ski Touring

Grade Intermediate
Distance 10 km return
Time 4 hrs
Height gain 275 m
Max elevation 1,850 m
Map Mount Goodsir 82 N/1

The Stanley Glacier tour is a good one for a little later in the season. With a good base of snow, there is excellent potential for making turns at the head of the valley. The run back down to the car, following the creekbed rather than the trail, is excellent. The steep switchbacks at the start of the climb are a little daunting and you should have a good wax that really works or perhaps even use skins. The excellent skiing through the burned out forest that we have enjoyed has now disappeared as the new growth matures.

Hazards A number of large avalanche paths descend into this valley and you should not stop while exposed to the threat from above. There is a lot of deadfall on this tour resulting from the fire, so be careful of hitting a half buried tree.

Access There is a parking lot at the trailhead which is located about 13 km along the Kootenay Highway (Highway #93), south-west of Castle Junction. The parking lot is on the left (south) side of the highway.

The trail leaves the parking lot and immediately crosses the Vermilion River via a footbridge. From here it switchbacks steeply up the hillside above. Usually it is not too hard to follow, but often has deadfall across it (old burned trees) which can be a nuisance on the way up and a real danger on the way down (later in the season the deadfall will be well covered). After about 180 m of vertical gain the angle eases off and the trail meanders for 0.5 km across the flats, then dips down left to reach Stanley Creek.

Cross the creek on a small footbridge then head back up the valley on the left side of the drainage. Towards the end of the treed valley the trail climbs a few metres up onto the left (north-east) flank and is a bit hard to follow. Continue up the valley to the end of the trees. For those interested in making turns, there is good potential on the open slopes straight ahead.

To return, follow the trail back down as far as the crossing of Stanley Creek. From here there is an excellent descent straight down the creek bed. However this should only be done later in the season (after mid-January) when there is good snow cover and the creek is well frozen. Follow the creek down until almost at the valley bottom, then cut over the left bank and follow the hillside back down to the junction with the up trail.

History This area was burned by a large fire in the summer of 1968. It is interesting to see how rapidly the forest regenerates itself.

Along the south-west wall of the valley, high on the side of Mt. Stanley there are some very impressive frozen waterfalls. Farther up the valley is an impressive waterfall climb called Nemesis. See if you can spot any climbers on it.

43 TOKUMM CREEK (PROSPECTOR'S VALLEY) Ski touring

Grade Easy/Intermediate
Distance 14 km to Kaufmann Lake Junction one way
Time It normally takes a full day to ski to the Kaufmann Lake Junction and return, or to ski one way to the Fay Hut with full packs
Height gain 340 m to Kaufmann Lake Junction
Max elevation 1,830 m at Kaufmann Lake Junction
Map Mount Goodsir 82 N/1
Lake Louise 82 N/8

A long tour up a wild valley. You can make a short day of it or go as far as you like. This trail is not recommended early in the season as there are many creek crossings which are bridged by single logs only.

Facilities Toilets at the parking lot.

Hazards There are many avalanche paths which descend to the valley floor. Do not linger in these areas.

Options The adventurous can continue up the valley, beyond the Kaufmann Lake turnoff, and ski to the Eagle Eyrie near Opabin Pass. There is no trail much of the way and you should follow the creek bed where possible. Travel is not too difficult if you wait until later in the year when the creek is well frozen and covered with snow.

This tour is often skied in reverse in a long, hard day by strong skiers. You begin by skiing up the road to Lake O'Hara (see page 131), then continue to Opabin Pass (see page 133) and finally you complete the tour by skiing down Tokumm Creek to the Kootenay Parkway. It is probably no advantage to overnight at the Elizabeth Parker Hut if it means that you will be carrying a sleeping bag. Get an early start and carry a headlamp!

Access Park at the Marble Canyon parking lot which is on the right (north) side of the Kootenay Parkway (Highway #93) 7 km west of the Alberta/B.C. Border.

Begin by skiing back north-east up a large swath through the trees for about 150 m to gain the Tokumm Creek Trail which is found up on the left bank. This route bypasses the Marble Canyon portion of the trail. Follow the trail through thick forest, with a few short climbs. After about 3 km the trail emerges from the trees onto the open flats beside Tokumm Creek. For the rest of the way follow the trail which is found along the right bank of the creek. The ski up to Kaufmann Lake is sometimes done by nordic skiers, but it is not highly recommended — it is steep and narrow.

Fay Hut Approach Elevation gain 430 m. The turn-off to the hut is sometimes difficult to locate. After about 9 km of skiing along Tokumm Creek you cross a large, obvious drainage coming in from the right. Shortly after this drainage Tokumm Creek starts to narrow (either ski along the creek or along the trail which is up on the right bank). In another 1.5 km there is another open area — there is a large avalanche path on the left and a creek comes in from the right. This is the turn-off.

From the turnoff ski up the drainage along the left side or if there is enough snow, along the creek itself. In about 1.5 km, a wall of grey and black streaked rock about 20 m high and 50 m wide is encountered where the stream turns left. Cross the stream to the right bank.

The going gets steep here. Trend up and right, zig-zagging through light trees. You are heading towards a cliff band above with an obvious break just to the right of straight above you. The route lies through this break and is a skis-off affair. It can be a very strenuous struggle but there is a thick rope hanging down to help you get up.

Once the top of the cliff is gained the hut is a few minutes away to the right and slightly uphill.

The Fay Hut was the first hut to be built by the Alpine Club of Canada. It was built in 1927. Over the years the hut fell into disrepair, however the ACC has now completely refurbished it and it is in excellent condition. Perched high above the valley it is easy to feel like the "King of the Universe" on a starry night. The hut gives access to the back sides of the Ten Peaks, and it is possible to ski from the Fay Hut to the higher Colgan Hut.

44 SIMPSON RIVER

Ski touring

Grade Easy
Distance 16 km to park boundary return
Time A full day
Height gain 120 m
Max elevation 1370 m
Map Mount Assiniboine 82 J/13

Facilities The Surprise Creek cabin in Mount Assiniboine Provincial Park is 2 km beyond the Kootenay National Park boundary. Use of this cabin is on a first-come, first-served basis. Firewood is not provided.

Options The Simpson River can be followed all the way up to Simpson Pass then down Healy Creek to the Sunshine Ski Resort parking lot.

Access Park 0.7 km north of the Simpson Monument at the bridge, 6 km south of Vermillion River Crossing.

This tour is a gradual climb following the left bank of the Simpson River, as far as the park boundary. Return by the same route.

45 WEST KOOTENAY

Ski touring

Grade Easy
Distance 19.2 km round trip
Time A full day
Height gain 40 m
Max elevation 1230 m
Map Spillimacheen 82 K/16

The West Kootenay tour follows an old fire road winding through mixed coniferous forest to the park boundary. You can either return the way you came or cross the Kootenay River and return on the summer hiking trail.

Access Park at the Kootenay River Crossing Warden Station, 61 km south of Castle Junction.

From the warden station ski up the steep hill (the steepest hill on the entire tour) to a fork at about 0.4 km. The left-hand fork leads south to Dolly Varden Campground (see page 87). Follow the right-hand fork north-west along the south side of the Kootenay River. After 9.5 km, near the park boundary, take the right-hand fork leading to a bridge across the Kootenay River. Cross the bridge and return to the highway along the hiking trail on the north side of the river.

46 HECTOR GORGE

Ski touring

Grade Easy
Distance 11.2 km one way to the
highway 600 m south of Hector Gorge
Time 3 - 5 hours
Height gain 150 m
Max elevation 1280 m
Maps Spillimacheen 82 K/16
Mount Assiniboine 82 J/13

Access Park on the road (Highway #93), 5.5 km south of Kootenay River Crossing and 1 km north of Dolly Varden Winter Campground. You may choose to leave a second car at the top of the hill at the end of the passing lane, 2 km north of Kootenay River Crossing and about 0.6 km south of Hector Gorge.

Leave the highway at the fire road gate. After crossing one bridge, turn left just before a second bridge (about 1.3 km) and follow the trail until it returns to the highway between Kootenay Pond and Hector Gorge.

47 SPLIT PEAK

Ski touring

Grade Easy
Distance 6.4 km to end of the trail
below Split Peak
Time 3 hours one way
Height gain 150 m
Max elevation 1370 m
Maps Spillimacheen 82 K/16
Mount Assiniboine 82 J/13

Access Park on the road (Highway #93), 5.5 km south of Kootenay River Crossing and 1 km north of Dolly Varden Winter Campground.

Leave the highway at the fire road gate and cross two bridges. Take a left turn approximately 90 m past the second bridge at about 1.5 km from the highway, and follow the trail to its terminus.

48 EAST KOOTENAY

Ski touring

Grade Easy
Distance 11 km to Dog Lake
14 km to McLeod Meadows picnic area.
18 km to Cross River trailhead
Time A full day
Height loss 75 m
Max elevation 1210 m
Maps Spillimacheen 82 K/16
Mount Assiniboine 82 J/13
Tangle Peak 82 J/12

A pleasant, easy ski following the East Kootenay Fire Road on the east side of the Kootenay River. The northern section is a pleasant valley-bottom road winding through pine forest, while the southern section stays close to the river with its broad alluvial flats. The trail can be skied in either direction using a combination of three different trailheads.

Access There are 3 possible trailheads. On the road 1 km north of Dolly Varden Winter Campground (see opposite page), at McLeod Meadows picnic area 16 south of Kootenay River Crossing, or at the Kootenay River picnic site 3.5 km farther south.

From the northernmost trailhead, Leave the highway at the fire road gate and cross two bridges. Take a right turn at the fork 90 m from the second bridge. Ski the relativelt flat fireroad south towards Dog Lake (possible side trip). You can either exit to McLeod Meadows by turning right after 12 km or continue a further 4 km to Kootenay River picnic site.

49 DOLLY VARDEN

Ski touring

Grade Easy
Distance 11 km one way from either direction or 12 km to Crook's Meadows.
Loop section 3 km.
Time An easy day
Height gain 50 m
Max elevation 1280 m
Map Spillimacheen 82 K/16

This tour follows the southern section of the West Kootenay fire road through mature forest from Kootenay River Crossing warden station to Crooks Meadow.

Facilities Picnic shelters and firewood are available at Dolly Varden and Crook's Meadows.

Access Park at the Kootenay Crossing Warden Station, Dolly Varden Winter Campground, or at the gate to Crook's Meadows. A second car may be an asset.

From the Kootenay Crossing Warden Station, ski up the Kootenay River Fire Road for 400 m, then take the left fork and follow the road to Dolly Varden

Creek. Continue on out to the highway through Crook's Meadows or cut off to Dolly Varden through blazed trail at sign 1 km north of Crook's Meadows. This section can also form a pleasant loopl if you ski on the highway right of way between Dolly Varden Winter Campground and Crook's Meadows gate.

50 DOG LAKE

Ski touring

Grade Easy
Distance 6 km return
Time 3 hours
Height gain 75 m
Max elevation 1210 m
Maps Mount Assiniboine 82 J/13
Tangle Peak 82 J/12

Facilities A picnic shelter and firewood is available at McLeod Meadows picnic site.

Access Park at the McLeod Meadows picnic area 16 south of Kootenay River Crossing.

Leave the picnic site and campground and ski over the foot bridge continuing to the East Kootenay Fire Road. Turn left and follow the trail to Dog Lake. Ski across the lake to its north-west end and return via Dog Creek to the East Kootenay Fire Road, turn left and ski south on the fire road to rejoin your outgoing route. Return to McLeod Meadows via the foot bridge.

51 CROSS RIVER

Ski touring

Grade Easy
Distance 14 km one way to the park boundary
Time A full day
Max elevation 1150 m
Map Tangle Peak 82 J/12

Another section of the East Kootenay Fire Road which parallels the Kootenay River and later, Settlers Road to the Kootenay Park boundary. This easy valley road winds its way through mixed, mature forest and can be followed as far as you wish.

Access Park at the Kootenay River Picnic Site 20 km south of Kootenay River Crossing, or on the road 0.6 km north of Nixon Creek.

From the picnic site, ski north along the river bank to a bridge crossing the river. Ski across the bridge and continue for about 1 km to the East Kootenay Fire Road. Turn left for McLeod Meadows and the East Kootenay/Dog Lake trails or turn right for the Cross River trail and the park boundary.

LAKE LOUISE AREA

Lake Louise is known world wide as a mountaineering centre and as a downhill ski resort. It also offers extensive opportunities for cross-country skiing — nordic skiing along set tracks or ski touring into a wilderness setting. The scenery is simply outstanding and the area gets lots of snow. It is the perfect centre for a ski holiday.

Facilities The facilities at Lake Louise are spread out. There are three main centres which are collectively referred to as Lake Louise. These are: the Lake Louise Townsite, Upper Lake Louise and the Lake Louise Ski Resort. Virtually all amenities that you might require can be found at one of these three locations.

Lake Louise Townsite There are two service stations here, two major hotels — the luxurious Post Hotel (522-3989), the Lake Louise Inn (522-3791) and numerous restaurants and lounges. Wilson's Sports (522-3636) can help you with your equipment needs. In addition there is a post office, government liquor store, bank, art gallery, book store, grocery store and an outstanding bakery and delicatessen called Laggans. Most of these are located in the Samson Mall. Finally there is a medical centre and a

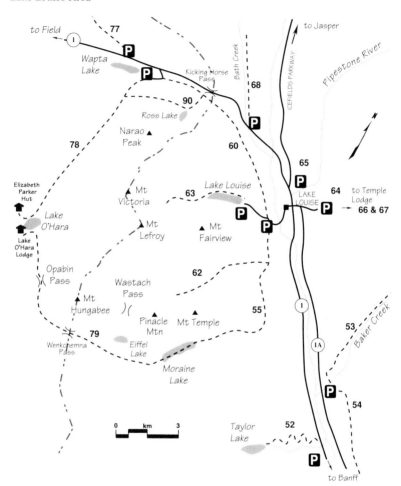

Parks Information Centre. At the west end of town, almost as far along the road as you can drive is the Warden Office. The Lake Louise Alpine Centre (522-2200) offers excellent low cost accommodation with a lovely ambiance

Upper Lake Louise On the shores of Lake Louise itself, about 3 km up the hill from the townsite is the famous CPR Hotel, The Chateau Lake Louise. It is luxurious but surprisingly, during the winter is not as expensive as it looks. Just a short distance down the road is Deer Lodge which is a little less grand but perhaps more homey. Many trails begin near here and are referred to collectively as the Upper Lake Louise Trails.

Lake Louise Ski Resort Is located across the other side of the Trans-Canada Highway, about 2.5 km north-east of the townsite. The lifts all begin here and the main centre is the Whiskey Jack Lodge. The Whitehorn trails are near here and the access to Skoki starts nearby.

In Emergency The Warden Office (522-3866) is located at the west end of town, but is only open regular office hours. Outside of these hours phone the Banff Warden Office (762-4506). There is an RCMP Office (522-3811) just east of the Petro Canada service station.

History Lake Louise was not the original home of mountaineering in Canada — that honour rests with the Rogers Pass, where there was a luxurious hotel called Glacier House. However, the focus shifted over the years and when Glacier House closed in 1926 (the railway had been re-routed) Lake Louise became the Alpine Centre of Canada.

For years, illustrious mountaineers from around the world would meet at the Chateau to climb the glittering peaks above, or to prepare for their trips to the backcountry. Today, Lake Louise is still a great climbing centre — the massive North Face of Mount Temple, the airy ridge of Mount Victoria and the steep quartzite cliffs at the end of the lake draw adventure seekers from around the world.

Lake Louise has also grown in stature as a ski destination. Skoki Lodge opened its doors in the spring of 1931 and has now grown to a downhill skiing giant known as Skiing Louise.

An extensive array of nordic skiing trails has developed all around the valley. The Chateau, which for years was only open in summer, now does a healthy business in the winter and the rustic Post Hotel has grown into the luxurious and sophisticated operation we see today.

---

52 TAYLOR LAKE
Ski touring

Grade Advanced
Distance 10 km return
Time 5-6 hrs return
Height gain 600 m
Max elevation 2,070 m
Map Lake Louise 82 N/8

Steep and tricky, this is hardly a cross country ski trail at all. However, many people still ski it. To be avoided when conditions are icy.

Options It is possible to traverse southeast to reach O'Brian Lake.

Access A parking lot is located on the south-west side of the Trans-Canada Highway (Highway #1), 8 km west of Castle Junction.

The first 2 km of this trail are reasonable as they work their way up the hill through the trees. The trail then steepens and is a continuous climb to the lake. Be careful on your way back down the hill, as the trail is narrow and the corners are tight.

53 BAKER CREEK
Ski touring

Grade Intermediate
Distance 12 km to the meadows return
Time 4-5 hrs to the meadows return
Height gain 210 m
Max elevation 1,700 m
Map Lake Louise 82 N/8

A popular trail with pleasant views of Protection and Lipalian Mountains and the meadows make a superb place to sit in the sun and have lunch.

Facilities Toilets at the parking lot.

Options You can continue skiing farther up this valley. The trail crosses the meadow, gradually climbing, staying above the creek, then continues another 5 km to a campground. Really keen skiers can carry on for another 12 km to Baker Lake then descend via Boulder Pass to Lake Louise, or continue via Skoki and the Pipestone River to Lake Louise.

Access Park across the road from the Baker Creek Chalets on the Bow Valley Parkway (1A Highway), about 14 km west of Castle Junction. The parking lot is on the south side of the bridge.

From the parking lot ski about 75 m along the creek then cross a bridge to the north side. From here ski back to the left, under the hill, away from the creek, for about 100 m, then turn right into a draw and start climbing. The trail climbs

steeply for a short distance angling up to the left, then makes a long switchback back to the right and crosses under the power lines. It continues to climb through a mature forest of lodgepole pine at a moderate angle for several kilometres. Keep your eye open for some viewpoints on the right, high on the hillside above Baker Creek. Eventually the trail flattens out for several more kilometres as far as a beautiful meadow under the slopes of Lipalian Mountain.

54 BAKER CREEK POWER LINE TRAIL
Nordic skiing/ski touring

Grade Easy
Distance 7 km return
Time 2 hrs
Height gain Nil
Max elevation 1,480 m
Map Lake Louise 82 N/8

Although not one of the most scenic trails around it does have one good view of the peaks surrounding the Bow Valley. It is easy and accessible and may be packed.

Facilities Toilets at the parking lot.

Access Park across the road from the Baker Creek Chalets on the Bow Valley Parkway (1A Highway) about 14 km west of Castle Junction. The parking lot is on the south side of the bridge.

This trail heads straight back into the woods from the parking lot. It is occasionally marked by signs with a #2.

After about 100 m it reaches a clearing, turns right, and for the next few kilometres follows the power lines. Eventually the power lines run up a steep hillside to the left and the trail turns down right into the trees. Ski through the trees to a campground. You can do a circuit of the campground on roads, then return to your car the way you came.

UPPER LAKE LOUISE TRAILS

There are seven trails in this network. They are all well maintained and are normally either packed or trackset. They provide wonderful nordic skiing opportunities for all levels of ability. They are easily accessible, and are located in the heart of very beautiful country. There are amenities nearby, such as washrooms, telephones and restaurants. In short these trails are perfect for a pleasurable day of fresh air and exercise for families and for those who are new to the sport. After a days skiing it is pleasant to visit the Chateau for a cup of hot chocolate or a beer in luxurious surroundings.

Many of these trails are accessed from the large parking lot on your left just before you reach the Chateau Lake Louise. There are heated washrooms at the west end of the lot (nearest to the Chateau).

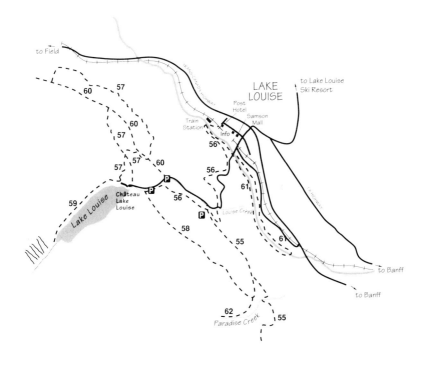

55 MORAINE LAKE ROAD

Nordic Skiing

Grade Easy

Distance 22 km to Moraine Lake return
16 km to viewpoint return

Time This tour can vary from an hour or two, if you are fast, to a full-days' outing if you choose.

Height gain Elevation gain on the trip out is about 250 m (to the viewpoint). Elevation gain on the return from Moraine Lake is about 60 m (to the viewpoint).

Max elevation 1,880 m

Map Lake Louise 82 N/8

The trail follows a paved road which is not plowed in the winter. Consequently it requires little snow to be in shape and is one of the first trails to be skiable each season. The grade is always gentle and it is a perfect trail for beginners to start on. It also is a popular trail for more experienced skiers to get a good workout on, and to push their heart rate up a bit. Because the trail contours around the shoulder of Mount Temple, high above the valley, the views down the Bow Valley and then later into Consolation Valley and the Moraine Lake Valley, are excellent.

Facilities At Moraine Lake there are picnic shelters and picnic tables.

Hazards Be sure to leave enough time and energy for the return trip. Do not stop while crossing the avalanche paths near Moraine Lake.

Options You can tie into more advanced tours such as the traverse of Wenkchemna Pass and Opabin Pass to Lake O'Hara.

Access A large parking lot is available at the trailhead. It is located on your left about halfway up the hill from the townsite of Lake Louise, towards the Chateau Lake Louise.

From the end of the parking lot, ski around the road closure gate, then simply head up the road. The track is usually set and on a weekend there will be plenty of company on this trail. After about 2.5 km the trail crosses Paradise Creek, then it begins to climb gently for another kilometre. The trail levels out again as far as the viewpoint overlooking Consolation Valley. This is a fine place for lunch and is often as far as most people go. For the more adventurous another 3 km, gently downhill, takes you right to Moraine Lake (this portion of the trail crosses major avalanche paths and should be traversed without stopping).

56 THE TRAMLINE TRAIL

Nordic skiing

Grade Easy
Distance 4.4 km one way
Time 30-45 minutes downhill, 1.5 hours uphill
Height gain 180 m
Max elevation 1,730 m
Map Lake Louise 82 N/8

A fun trail and an interesting way to connect upper and lower Lake Louise. If you are staying in a hotel at Lake Louise it is entertaining to ski the trail in one direction, have a cup of tea and a rest, then return along the trail to your starting point. The trail is virtually downhill (or uphill) all the way so it can be a lot of fun to ski down but a bit of a bore to ski back up again. The trail is wide and has a gentle grade all the way. Halfway down the hill there is a beautiful view along the Bow Valley. A portion of this trail is excellent to start even very young children on — they can ski easily downhill from parking lot C and you can have a car waiting to pick them up at the Moraine Lake Road parking area.

Facilities There are public, heated washrooms at the west end of the parking lot nearest the Chateau. All services are available at both ends of the trail (the Chateau and the Post Hotel/Samson Mall).

Hazards The trail can be challenging when it is icy. Beware!

Options This trail links up very nicely with the Bow River (Riverside) Loop.

Access A large parking lot is located on the left, just before reaching the Chateau. Park at the east end of lot C (farthest from the Chateau) for the start to this trail.

From the end of parking lot C the trail heads gently downhill, parallel to the road (follow trails with sign #3). After 1.6 km it crosses the Moraine Lake Road then descends into the forest. After a short distance it curves around left, back to the Lake Louise road. You must take off your skis and cross the road (Attention!). The trail crosses Louise Creek then descends to the Bow River, directly across from Laggan Station (the VIA Rail station). From here the trail is a little complex and contrived but it can be skied virtually all the way. Cross the Bow River on a footbridge, and immediately across the bridge turn right and follow a trail along the river. After about 0.5 km the trail crosses a road to the left then continues down to the right (east), parallel to the railway tracks. Finally the trail goes underneath the railway tracks at the railway bridge over the Pipestone River, and you are now on the doorstep of the Post Hotel. The Samson Mall is not far away, a few hundred metres east, down the valley.

Of interest The Tramline trail is an old tram bed. During the period from 1912 to 1930 this tramway was the access route for tourists to the Chateau Lake Louise.

"Touring folks" skiing in an early Telemark Loppet when it used to start from the Wapta end of Highway 1A. The modern Lake Louise Loppet starts on the lake in front of Chateau Lake Louise

57 TELEMARK TRAIL

Nordic skiing

Grade Intermediate
Distance 9.3 km loop
Time 2-3 hours
Height gain 120 m
Max elevation 1,760 m
Map Lake Louise 82 N/8

This trail is really composed of two distinct parts - the upper trail above the 1A highway and the lower trail below the 1A Highway. The upper trail is steep, tricky and in many places confusing. There are several trails in this area and sometimes it is difficult to know which one to choose. The lower trail is excellent, offering varied, rolling terrain

Access On the left side of the road, just before the Chateau Lake Louise is a large parking area. Park at the west end of the parking lot nearest to the Chateau.

with hills, turns and open meadows. It is ideal for beginners. The two components are combined to form a figure-8.

Facilities There are public, heated washrooms at the west end of the parking lot nearest to the Chateau. Full services are available at the Chateau Lake Louise.

Hazards The upper Telemark Trail can be tricky to follow. It can also be very challenging when icy. Ski with caution.

Options This trail could be combined with a trip along the Great Divide trail.

Ski or walk around to the front of the Chateau. Cross in front of the Chateau and just beyond the building, turn up to your right (the start of the Lake Agnes trail). The trail is marked with signs with a #5 on them. The Telemark Trail turns up immediately behind the Chateau, and then makes a sharp left turn at the Hillside Cottage. From here it winds its way steeply down to the snow-covered 1A Highway.

Cross the highway and ski along an old access road for a few hundred metres. The trail then turns into the woods and follows lovely, rolling terrain for about 4 km. The trail makes a sharp turn to the left on the brow of a hill and ascends gently to the 1A Highway

Turn left and ski back along the almost flat highway for 1.7 km. Turn right into the woods and climb gradually up a winding trail to the junction you crossed on your way down from the Chateau. Continue straight up an old road to where the trail ends near the Chateau Staff quarters. From here you can carry your skis back to the car.

Of interest The Telemark Trail is the site, every March, of the Lake Louise Loppet (formerly called the Telemark Loppet) cross-country race. This citizen's race has been held every year since 1973.

58 FAIRVIEW LOOP
Nordic Skiing

Grade Easy
Distance 7.5 km to complete the loop back to the parking area.
Time 2 hrs
Height gain 50 m
Max elevation 1,730 m
Map Lake Louise 82 N/8

Highly recommended, it traverses through forest and clearings giving a nice open feeling, variety and good views. There are moderate little uphills, downhills and turns which help to make the trail entertaining and interesting.

Access A large parking lot is located on the left, just before reaching the Chateau. Park at the east end of lot C (farthest from the Chateau) for the start to this trail.

From the end of the parking lot the trail (marked with a #1) goes up to the right for a short distance, then turns left into the trees. It rolls up and down for several kilometres underneath Fairview Mountain before reaching an exhilarating

Facilities Heated washrooms at the west end of the parking lot nearest the Chateau. Full services are available at the Chateau Lake Louise and nearby Deer Lodge.

Options This trail forms a pleasant alternate start to the ski trip along the Moraine Lake Road to Moraine Lake. It can also be tied in with a trip along the Tramline Trail to the lower townsite of Lake Louise.

downhill run; enjoyable even for beginners. After about 3 km the trail turns sharply back to the left and descends to the Moraine Lake Road. Turn left and follow the road (Trail #2) back to its junction with the Tramline Trail (Trail #3) at the edge of the parking area for the Moraine Lake Road Trail. Turn left again and ski up the gradual grade of the Tramline Trail back to parking lot C.

An early photo of a well-dressed tourer on the shore of Lake Louise.
Mount Lefroy (left) and Mount Victoria in the background.
Photo Whyte Museum of the Canadian Rockies

59 LAKE LOUISE SHORELINE TRAIL
Nordic skiing

Grade Easy
Distance 6.0 km return
Time 2 hrs return
Height gain 30 m
Max elevation 1,760 m
Map Lake Louise 82 N/8

A pleasant trail in beautiful surroundings. There are few hills to speak of and it is well suited for beginners.

Facilities There are public, heated washrooms at the west end of the parking lot nearest the Chateau. Full services are available at the Chateau Lake Louise.

Hazards Do not ski across the lake unless it is well frozen and covered with a substantial cushion of snow.

Options This trail joins up with the Plain of Six Glaciers Trail (see page 104)

Access On the left side of the road just before the Chateau Lake Louise is a large parking area. Park at the west end of the lot nearest to the Chateau.

From the parking lot ski or walk around to the front of the Chateau. Cross in front of the Chateau and just beyond the building take the trail up to the right to Lake Agnes. After only 100 m turn left onto a trail through the trees. This is the Shoreline Trail and is marked with the signs #4. The trail parallels the lake about 20-40 m up the hillside. It climbs very gently for a ways, then it descends for the second half to join the main trail just beneath the prominent frozen waterfall which can be seen up on your right. You can carry on for another 0.5 km, underneath the very impressive quartzite cliffs. Beyond this the trail becomes more challenging. You can return to your car the same way or for variety you can ski across the lake.

Of interest Lake Louise was discovered by Tom WIlson in 1882. In 1885 the railway was completed and the CPR saw tourism as an integral part of their business. Over the years they have constructed a succession of chalets and grand hotels on the shore of Lake Louise.

The first chalet was constructed in 1890, but was destroyed by fire in 1893. In 1894 a more luxurious chalet was built and a second storey was added in about 1898. The chalet was substantially enlarged between 1904 and 1911. By 1920 the first concrete wing was added. In 1924 a fire consumed all of the wooden structure, leaving only the concrete wing standing.

The nucleus of the present structure was built on the ruins. In the 1970's it was renovated to allow opening in winter, and in more recent years a new wing, entrance and parking structure were built.

60 GREAT DIVIDE TRAIL
Nordic Skiing

Grade Easy
Distance 15 km return
Time 3-4 hrs
Height gain 30 m
Max elevation 1,670 m
Map Lake Louise 82 N/8

This trail is a snow covered highway. It is flat and usually trackset and is an excellent place for a novice skier to practice or for an expert skier to train. The snow comes early here and the road only requires 20-30 cm to be skiable.

Facilities At the Great Divide there are toilets, picnic tables, camp shelters and stoves

Options It is possible to carry on beyond the Great Divide for another 3 km to the start of the Lake O'Hara Fire Road (see page 131). You can leave a car here and ski just one way (11 km) or for the really hardy you can ski return (22 km), or even combine it with a trip up to Lake O'Hara (an additional 24 km!).

A enjoyable combination is to ski the Great Divide trail for 3.6 km to the turnoff onto the Lower Telemark Trail (see page 96) and then return to your car along this lovely trail.

Access Follow the road which climbs from the lower townsite of Lake Louise up to the Chateau. After several kilometres the road takes a sharp turn to the left to make its final climb up to the Chateau. At this point proceed straight ahead and park in a plowed out area. This, in the summer, is the start of a section of the 1A Highway (also known as the Bow Valley Parkway) which crosses the Great Divide into British Columbia.

From the parking area climb up and over the snow bank to gain the road. Put your skis on and head down the road for as far as you like. The road is virtually flat all the way except for a slight hill just before the Great Divide.

History The Great Divide is on the Alberta/B.C. border. It is also on the backbone of the continent and water will flow west from here into the Pacific ocean or east into the Atlantic ocean.

61 BOW RIVER (RIVERSIDE) LOOP

Nordic skiing

Grade Easy
Distance 6.9 km loop
Time 2 hrs
Height gain None
Max elevation 1,550 m
Map Lake Louise 82 N/8

This loop travels along the edge of the Bow River and the views are excellent. There are numerous self guiding information displays which are fun to stop and read. The drawback of this trail is that it crosses several roads and these require the removal of skis. Because the trail is so near to town there will likely have been pedestrian traffic, causing damage to the ski track.

Facilities The trail is near to all amenities at the Samson Mall and the Post Hotel.

Hazards Be careful crossing roads. Take your skis off - it is hard to avoid a racing car with your skis on!

Options The Tramline Trail and the Bow River Loop make a good combination.

Access Parking is available at the Samson Mall, the Post Hotel, the tent and trailer campground and Laggan Station (the VIA Rail station). The trail is accessible from any of these locations. The trail is described from Laggan Station.

From Laggan Station cross the Bow River on the footbridge. Turn left and continue east along the river. Several cleared paths follow above the river, but the trail actually drops below these into the trees in an unobvious way and follows a trail close to the river. Take off your skis and cross the upper Lake Louise access road then continue along the edge of the river. The following section down to what is called the Island Bridges is 2.5 km and crosses another road at the campground, then skirts the trailer village. At the Island Bridges the trail crosses the river then returns along the north-west bank. This section crosses another road and may be a bit beat up by pedestrian traffic. Back at the upper Lake Louise access road you can cross the bridge over the Bow River and return along the previously described trail to Laggan Station or you can cross the road and work your way on foot through bits of civilization into the Samson Mall.

The upper end of Paradise Valley beyond the Giant Steps   Photo Leon Kubbernus

62 PARADISE VALLEY

Ski touring

Grade Intermediate
Distance 20 km return from the
Moraine Lake Road trailhead
Time An easy day trip for most parties
Height gain 410 m to the meadows at
the head of the valley
Max elevation
2,090 m at the meadows
Map Lake Louise 82 N/8

A classic tour which is very popular, offering interesting skiing and some of the most impressive mountain scenery in the Canadian Rockies.

Options The traverse through Wastach Pass to the west of Eiffel Peak is possible, in the proper conditions. Some parties combine this pass with Opabin and Wenkchemna Passes, when they do the traverse from Lake O'Hara to Lake Louise, finishing their adventure along Paradise Valley.

Access The tour begins along the Moraine Lake Road trail. There is a large parking lot about halfway up the hill, between the town of Lake Louise and the Chateau. It is located to the left at the turnoff for Moraine Lake.

From the parking lot ski around the road closure barrier and head up the road. The trail will usually be track set for the 2 km to your turn off to Paradise Valley. Angle right and climb up a hill through the woods. After a short distance another trail (the Fairview trail) will branch off to the right again, and curve back to the north-west. Do not follow this trail. Instead, carry on ahead and climb a steep bank to gain the crest of a forested ridge. Continue climbing through the trees, for about 0.5 km, until the trail intersects with the main trail between Lake Louise and Moraine Lake.

Turn back to the right towards lake Louise and ascend for a short distance until there is another trail intersection. You now turn to the left into Paradise Valley. The trail continues to climb for a

short distance, then makes a long descent down into the valley to break out of the trees at Paradise Creek. This is a lovely spot to rest and admire the impressive north face of Mount Temple towering 1,500 m above.

The trail now crosses the creek on a bridge and continues over rolling terrain along the south bank. After 0.5 km the trail again crosses the creek to the north side and continues working its way up the valley through mature forest. After several kilometres the trail makes its way back to the left to the creek.

The trail works its way up a steep hillside, in the area between the two arms of the creek, eventually following along the north bank of the south arm to a large meadow. There are views of the imposing face of Mount Hungabee at the end of the valley and high above you to the south can be seen the solitary needle called the Grand Sentinel.

63 PLAIN OF SIX GLACIERS

Ski touring

Grade Intermediate
Distance 10 km return
Time This is a moderate day trip (4-6 hours) for most skiers.
Height gain 200 m
Max elevation 1,900 m
Map Lake Louise 82 N/8

A truly outstanding tour which takes you into the heart of one of the most impressive mountain settings in North America. The skiing is not difficult and the tour is not long, however the setting, below Mount Victoria at the Plain of Six Glaciers, is awe inspiring. The last half of the tour follows a creekbed so wait until after Christmas when there is adequate snow.

Facilities Public heated washrooms are available at the parking lot. The Chateau Lake Louise is open all winter and a hot drink in the lounge or coffee shop at the end of the day, is a most welcome treat.

Hazards Beyond the end of the lake you should not follow the summer trail high on the north-west side of the valley as it is extremely exposed to avalanches from above. The valley bottom is crossed by several giant avalanche paths. Care should always be taken in choosing rest stops and lunch stops, so that you are not in one of these paths. This tour is not recommended when the avalanche hazard is high.

Access On the left side of the road just before the Chateau Lake Louise is a large parking area. Park at the west end of the lot nearest to the Chateau.

From the north-west end of the parking lot, walk or ski to the front of the Chateau Lake Louise. You can either follow the Lake Louise Shoreline trail (see page 99) or head directly across the lake (be certain that it is well frozen). At the end of the lake the trail passes beneath some large quartzite cliffs which can be seen on the right. Just beyond this point the summer trail starts to climb steeply, angling up to the right. At this point however, a short jog of a few metres to the left puts you into the creekbed. Follow the creek for about 2 km, climbing gently most of the time, until you reach a large open, flat meadow, surrounded by some of the most impressive peaks in the world. It is best to stop here since travel any further will take you into terrain requiring glacier travel experience and technique. This meadow is a lovely place to break out the thermos and sandwiches and enjoy the view. Skiing back down the creekbed is fun but the plod across the lake at the end of the day can be a little tedious.

Of interest The Plain of Six Glaciers sits in the centre of some of the greatest mountain peaks in the world. Above you tower Mount Lefroy and Mount Victoria. These two peaks were first climbed in August 1897 by a strong international team of climbers led by Swiss guide, Peter Sarbach — the beginning of mountain guiding in Canada. The upper walls of Lefroy and Victoria are graced with formidable glaciers and ice walls. Perhaps you will be lucky enough to see an ice avalanche break off and thunder its way to the valley bottom.

64 WHITEHORN TRAILS

Nordic Skiing

Grade Easy/intermediate
Distance 6.4 km of trails
Time The loops can be skied in several hours
Height gain 75 m
Max elevation 1,670 m
Map Lake Louise 82 N/8

These trails are a short pleasant diversion. They meander through the forest and are quite easy. They provide an option if all your friends have gone lift skiing and you are looking for somewhere near at hand to do a little cross country skiing. The noise emanating from the ski resort spoils the experience somewhat.

Facilities There are no man made facilities on the trails, however it is a short distance to the Whiskey Jack Lodge at the ski area where there are restaurants, washrooms and telephones.

Hazards Be careful not to lose the trail or lose your bearings in the woods — it all looks much the same once you get started.

Access From the Trans-Canada Highway (Highway #1) take the turn off and follow the signs to the Lake Louise Ski Area. Park at the furthest end (north-east corner) of parking lot #4.

The trail starts at the extreme right hand (north-east) end of the parking lot. It initially descends for a few metres then divides into two branches - you can choose either the right or the left branch, it makes little difference. You can do the loop of trail #1 which is an easy trail or you can combine this loop with trail #2 to make a longer loop. Trail #2 is only marginally harder and barely deserves the intermediate designation. The trail is almost completely in the trees and only occasionally does one get a glimpse of Mount Whitehorn above. The trails are well marked with numbers and care should be taken in following them, particularly after a heavy snowfall, as it all looks much the same once you are in the woods. The trails are usually packed and are sometimes trackset.

Of interest The roots of the mammoth ski development near here begin at Skoki in 1931. The first ski touring guests skied all the way to Skoki from the train station at Lake Louise. Temple Lodge hosted its first guests in 1939 and the following year the Lake Louise Ski Lodge (now the Post Hotel) opened its doors. To this point skiing was self-propelled.

In the 1950's all this began to change. In 1952 the first lift was installed near Temple Lodge and in 1954 the Gondola lift to Whitehorn was built. Since then the growth of the ski area has been phenomenal. It is heartening to note that it now requires an act of parliament to extend the boundaries of ski resorts within the National Parks.

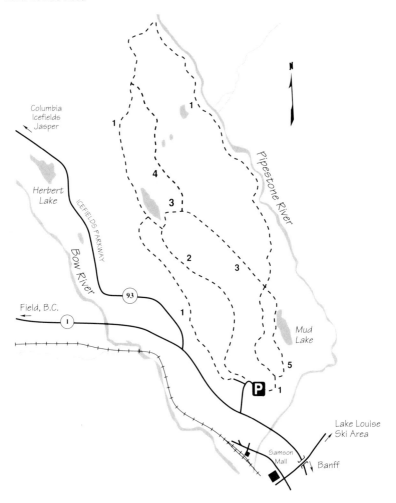

65 PIPESTONE TRAILS

Nordic skiing

Grade Mainly easy trails, with one intermediate section
Distance 21 km of trails
Time One can ski for a few minutes or all day if you choose.
Height gain 120 m between the low point and high point of the trail system
Max elevation 1,670 m.
Map Lake Louise 82 N/8

The Pipestone trails offer a good days' skiing for beginners and experts alike. It is a great place to get in a few hours of fresh air if you have limited time. The trails are all easy with the exception of trail #5 which has some steep hills and is graded inter-mediate. Normally the trails are packed and groomed. The experience is some-what marred by the background noise emanating from the Lake Louise Ski Area.

Hazards Trail #5 should be avoided if you are not a strong skier or if conditions are icy. It is easy to get turned around when skiing these trails, and to find that you are going the opposite way to what you think, so keep a close check on your progress at each intersection.

Options One can ski these trails in any direction and in any combination, to get the outing of your choosing.

Access To reach the parking lot, turn north off the Trans-Canada Highway (Highway #1) 0.7 km west of the Lake Louise overpass and follow the signs. The road climbs uphill for several hundred metres before turning right into the parking lot.

The Pipestone network comprises five numbered trails. With the exception of trail #5 they are all graded easy. Trail #1 is 12.6 km, trail #2 is 2.8 km, trail #3 is 2.1 km, trail #4 is 1.9 km and trail #5 is 1.5 km. The trails run through a mixture of forest and clearings. The open area around the unnamed lake along the west arm of trail #1 is an excellent area for a sunny lunch break. There are few hills of any steepness on trails #1 to #4, however the way the trails are laid out it is almost continuously uphill when skiing north (away from the parking lot) and then the return journey is a thrilling but not ex-cessively steep downhill run. The trails are well marked with numbers and are easy to follow. The last portion of trail #1 (west branch) is a little confusing where it works its way through the government horse barns, but this should present only minor route finding problems. For the more adventurous the view of the great Lake Louise peaks across Mud Lake on trail #5 is excellent.

History Some old, tumbled-down cab-ins, remnants of an old logging camp, can be seen along trail #4.

The parking lot is on the brow of a hill overlooking the Bow Valley. Tom Wilson camped near here in 1882 when he was led by native guides to "the lake of the little fishes", now known as Lake Louise.

66 HIDDEN BOWL

Ski Touring

Grade Easy
Distance 8 km return
Time 4-6 hrs return
Height gain 250 m to Hidden Lake
Max elevation 2,270 m
Map Lake Louise 82 N/8

The tour to Hidden Valley is a short and pleasant trip in beautiful surroundings. It passes the historic Ptarmigan Hut, sometimes known as the Halfway Hut. Once in Hidden Valley there is opportunity to make a few telemark turns on the slopes of Richardson Ridge on the west side. The view of the giant Lake Louise peaks down the valley is outstanding.

Facilities Washrooms, telephones and restaurant facilities can be found at Temple Lodge. A snow stability report can be optained at the Canadian Parks Service Snow Research Station near Temple Lodge.

The Ptarmigan Hut is located at the entrance to Hidden Valley. It was built in 1931 and now is rumoured to be the home of the ghost of "Kit" Paley, who was the first ski fatality in the Rockies. He was avalanched on the slopes of Fossil Mountain in April 1933.

Access Park at Fish Creek parking area which can be reached by taking the exit from the Trans-Canada Highway (Highway #1) at Lake Louise and proceeding up the road towards the Lake Louise Ski Area. After 1.5 km another road branches right. Take this and follow it for 1 km to the Fish Creek parking area. From here you catch a bus which will take you up the road to Temple Lodge. The bus is operated by the Lake Louise Ski Area and you should check on the schedule and fee with the ski resort (522-3555). If you miss the bus or if it is not running you can ski up the ski-out to the Temple Ski Area. This 'ski out trail' crosses the road beside the Fish Creek parking area. It is about 3 km to Temple Lodge.

The trail starts just beyond the bus drop-off point at the Temple Ski Area, about 100 m up the hill above the ski lodge. It heads back north-east, through the trees, along the east flank of the valley. It should be obvious if you are clearly on the correct trail. The trail is usually quite well packed because the snowmobile travels along here taking supplies into Skoki Lodge. The trail runs for about 2.0 km through the trees then it breaks out into the open valley bottom. After a short distance the Ptarmigan Hut can be seen about 100 m off to your left, across the other side of Corral Creek (marked incorrectly on the map — it is really on the north side of Corral Creek, in the angle formed with Hidden Creek).

From the hut head north-west up Hidden Creek. Ski directly up the creek bed. After about 0.5 km the terrain starts to open up and there is some pleasant skiing on moderately angled slopes to your left. From these slopes (called Richardson Ridge) you can get good views of Mount Richardson, Pika Peak and Ptarmigan Peak.

The return trip is a fun downhill run. You can make it all the way back to the cars in the Fish Creek parking area with only the occasional section of uphill work.

67 PURPLE BOWL

Ski touring

Grade Intermediate
Distance 6 km return
Time 4-6 hrs return
Height gain 500 m
Max elevation 2,500 m
Map Lake Louise 82 N/8

The Purple Bowl tour is an excellent way to get away from it all and up into alpine terrain in a few short hours. A perennial classic which is not to be missed.

Facilities There are no man made facilities on this tour, however washrooms, telephones and restaurant facilities are available at Temple Lodge.

Hazards The slopes on the southwest side of Purple Valley are attractive and can offer some good skiing, however they are sufficiently large enough and steep enough to offer serious avalanche possibilities. They should be avoided unless you have a good background in snow stability evaluation.

Access The trail begins from the Temple Ski Lodge. See the Hidden Bowl entry for details on how to reach the lodge.

The route begins about 100 m up the hillside from Temple Ski Lodge, along the trail which goes to Ptarmigan Hut and on to Skoki. Follow the trail for several hundred metres then angle up to the right on a man made cut through the trees (there are often tracks here and the trail may be packed). The trail angles up and curves around to the right, heading almost due east into Purple Valley. It runs high above a stream, and after about 1 km breaks out of the trees into the open. You can now meander up the open valley towards the high alpine terrain at the end. It is possible to ski for another 1 or 2 km to attain a high pass from where you can look down into Baker Creek far below. There are some gentle slopes up here to make turns on. This is indeed a glorious place on a warm, sunny day.

On the ridge above Purple Bowl
Photo Alf Skrastins

68 BATH CREEK

Ski touring

Grade Easy/intermediate
Distance 14 km return
Time This trip is a full day tour.
Height gain 210 m
Max elevation 1,820 m
Map Lake Louise 82 N/8

The tour up Bath Creek follows the creek-bed and so requires a fair amount of snow. There are good views of Mount Bosworth and Mount Daly.

Access The parking lot is on the right (north) side of the Trans-Canada Highway (Highway #1), 9 km west of Lake Louise. Park in the first of two plowed lots, just before the highway crosses the bridge over Bath Creek.

From the parking lot head north towards the railway tracks, skiing just beside Bath Creek. Take off your skis and cross both sets of tracks. From here you have two choices for the first portion of this tour.

You can either follow a trail along the bank of the creek, just into the edge of the trees, or you can follow the trail which heads through the forest straight ahead. After 100 m or so, take a branch to the left which brings you down to the creek. From here both trails connect and follow along the edge of the forest, beside the creek, for about 1 km. The trail now breaks out into the creek bed and for 3 km travels easily and pleasantly up the creek. It then opens up and the tour continues across the flats for another 2 km.

Gradually the flats narrow and the route takes the right bank of the creek for a short distance before crossing to the left bank where it stays for the remainder of the trip. About 1 km up the creek from the gravel flats, you reach a canyon. This can be avoided by climbing up on the left into the trees, then descending back to the creek after a short distance. Follow the creek for another kilometre until it becomes a canyon again. This gorge is much larger and is a good place to have lunch and end the tour.

SKOKI AREA

The Skoki area is perhaps the heart of backcountry skiing in the Canadian Rockies. The Lodge has been in continuous operation for over 60 years. Skoki is the start of what today has become Skiing Louise. In fact Skoki is still owned and operated by Skiing Louise.

Access From the overpass at the Lake Louise townsite on the Trans-Canada Highway (Highway #1), drive 1.6 km towards the Lake Louise Ski Area. Turn right onto the Temple Lodge access road and continue for 1 km to the Fish Creek parking lot. From here a small bus takes you to the Temple Lodge (phone 522-3555 for reservations and information) or you can ski 3 km up the 'ski out'.

From Temple Lodge it is possible to ski to Skoki in the morning, have a cup of tea, then return to your cars before dark. It is better to stay for a night or two at the lodge and savour the ambiance. There is a camping area about 1 km beyond the lodge for those with limited pocketbooks.

History The history of the Skoki area is worthy of a book. Skoki Lodge was one of the earliest ski lodges in the Rockies. It was built in the autumn of 1930 by Earl Spencer for Cliff White and Cyril Paris, and opened for business the following spring. The lodge was enlarged to its present form in 1936. During its heyday throughout the 30's and 40's the world came to Skoki to experience the magic of winter in the Canadian Rockies. In those days people skied all the way from Laggan Station (at the Lake Louise townsite) into Skoki, sometimes overnighting at Halfway Hut.

Skoki Lodge

This historic lodge has played a major role in the development of skiing in the Rockies. It has operated continuously since 1930 and today is not much changed; offering a remarkable opportunity to step back in time and experience our romantic past.. Heating is still by wood stove, lighting with coal oil lanterns and plumbing is outdoors. A central lodge and cabins provide accommodation for 22 skiers. Gourmet meals are served by candle light in the main building. The lodge is reached by an 11 km ski from the Lake Louise Ski Area. The season is from Christmas to April. Accommodation is about $100 per person with all meals included. Phone (403) 522-3555 for information.

111

Skoki Area

Halfway Hut in its heyday. Ptarmigan Peak in the background

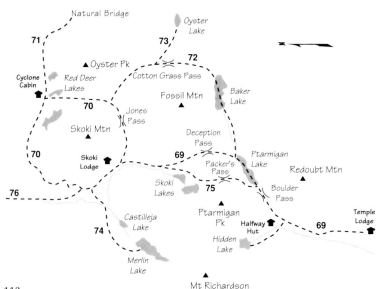

Natural Bridge

71

Oyster Lake

73

72

▲ Oyster Pk

Cotton Grass Pass

Cyclone Cabin

Red Deer Lakes

Fossil Mtn ▲

Baker Lake

70

Jones Pass

Skoki Mtn ▲

Deception Pass

70

Skoki Lodge

69

Packer's Pass

Ptarmigan Lake

Redoubt Mtn ▲

76

Skoki Lakes

75

Boulder Pass

Castilleja Lake

Temple Lodge

74

Ptarmigan Pk ▲

Halfway Hut

69

Hidden Lake

Merlin Lake

▲ Mt Richardson

69 SKOKI VIA BOULDER AND DECEPTION PASSES   Ski touring

Grade Intermediate
Distance 11 km one way
Time 4-5 hrs one way
It is a bit faster on the return trip, back to Temple Lodge.
Height gain 540 m
Max elevation 2,510 m
Maps Lake Louise 82 N/8
Hector Lake 82 N/9

The ski tour to Skoki is a classic and local skiers find that they repeat this trip over and over as the years pass by. The scenery is outstanding, the trail is interesting but not too difficult and the lodge at Skoki is a marvellous place, rich in history. You can get a hot drink here before skiing back to your cars. It is highly recommended that you consider spending a night here, to discover the roots of our skiing heritage. Crossing Ptarmigan Lake on your return journey can be difficult if the wind is blowing in your face.

Facilities There are toilets, telephones and a restaurant at the Temple Lodge. Skoki Lodge is rustic and has no telephone. Tea is served all afternoon to the public and if you are interested in staying overnight reservations can be made at the

Lake Louise Ski Area (phone 403-522-3555). Halfway hut (Ptarmigan Hut) is located several kilometres up the trail from Temple Lodge. It is a bare bones structure which has no stove. It can provide shelter for lunch on a windy day but it is not intended for overnight use.

Hazards This tour takes you through avalanche country. Although there is little danger if you stay on the correct trail, you must be careful not to stray onto surrounding terrain which may not be as safe. This is back country skiing and you should be prepared to deal with emergencies.

Options There are a number of lovely trails in the vicinity of Skoki Lodge. It is worth staying a night or two at the lodge to try a few of them.

On the return trip it is a pleasant change to ski through Jones Pass and around Fossil Mountain, through Cottongrass Pass and back across Baker Lake to regain the trail at Ptarmigan Lake.

If you are really ambitious it is possible to descend Skoki Creek to Little Pipestone Creek and then down to the Pipestone River, which can be followed back to Lake Louise (see page 123).

Access Park at the Fish Creek parking lot. This can be reached by taking the exit from the Trans-Canada Highway (Highway #1) at Lake Louise and proceeding up the road towards the Lake Louise Ski Area. After 1.5 km the Temple Lodge access road branches right. Turn right and follow it for 1 km to the Fish Creek parking lot. From here you catch a bus which will take you up the road to the Temple Lodge. This bus is operated by the Lake Louise Ski Area and you should check on the schedule and the fee with the ski resort

(522-3555). If you miss the bus or it is not running you can ski up 'the ski out' to the Temple Lodge. The ski out trail crosses the road beside the Fish Creek parking area and it is 3 km to Temple Lodge.

From the bus drop off point near Temple Lodge, continue up the snow covered road. You will pass the Parks Canada snow research station. It is a good idea to stop a moment and read the snow stability report, posted just inside the front door. Ski past a maintenance

Fossil Mountain from just above Deception Pass

Photo Alan Kane

shack and across the Larch run, about 100 m up the hill above Temple Lodge.

The trail to Skoki heads into the woods on the far side of the run, and it will have a prominent sign. Just a few metres after starting along the trail, another trail branches down to the left — do not take this trail. Continue straight ahead, crossing some open areas, and carry on for about 2 km, gradually gaining height. The trail is normally well packed and easy to follow because of the passage of the snowmobile transporting supplies into Skoki. Eventually the trail breaks out of the woods into a large open meadow with beautiful views all around. Over on the left of the clearing is Ptarmigan Hut, on a small hill above the creek (It is marked incorrectly on the map — it is actually on the far side of Corral Creek above its junction with Hidden Creek).

Continue up the valley, staying generally towards the left side and at the end climb moderately steeply up to Boulder Pass. The giant boulders, strewn quite liberally all around, can provide a sheltered place to sit in the sun and have lunch. Beyond Boulder Pass cross the lake, following the giant stakes driven into the snow to mark the trail. On the far side of the lake climb to Deception Pass which is about 180 vertical-m above, on the left. It is usually a good idea to stop and put on your climbing skins, unless your wax is working really well.

From Deception Pass it is a fun run down to Skoki Lodge. The trail is well marked at the start with large marker stakes and later with pieces of Day-glo flagging. From the pass ski north across the slopes of Fossil Mountain following open terrain then the trail begins to angle down to the left into the trees. The trail through the trees to the lodge is often packed by snowmobile traffic and easy to follow. The lodge is located on the right bank of Skoki Creek beneath the slopes of Skoki Mountain.

Skier at Deception Pass. Redoubt Mtn. in background

Photo Alan Kane

Skoki Lodge in the 1930's,   Photo Whyte Museum of the Canadian Rockies

70 SKOKI MOUNTAIN LOOP

Ski touring

Grade Easy
Distance 9 km loop
Time 3-4 hrs
Height gain 80 m
Max elevation 2,200 m
Map Hector Lake 82 N/9

This is an interesting trail that can be started after a leisurely breakfast and still bring you back to the lodge for afternoon tea. The trail runs through dense forest and across wide meadows. The trail when done clockwise, as described, offers no difficult downhills, although there is some challenging uphill climbing near the start.

Facilities The Cyclone Wardens Cabin can be visited on this trip, however it will be locked. Unfortunately, the historic old Cyclone Cabin was removed by Parks Canada and a modern one left in its place.

Hazards Carry a map! A little experience at reading a map is helpful here because it requires judgement to know which valley is which.

Options This trail can be combined with a trip to the Natural Bridge (see page 118)

Access The trail begins and ends at Skoki Lodge.

From Skoki Lodge, ski north down the trail for about 1 km to the point where the trail levels out at the campground on the edge of the meadows. The trail angles up to the right into the trees. It is marked with flagging and is generally easy to follow. There is some steepish climbing at the start. The trail works its way around the shoulder of Skoki Mountain and breaks out into the meadows along Little Pipestone Creek. Ski along the meadows and past one of the Red Deer Lakes. A nice little side trip is to visit the Cyclone Warden Cabin. To find this cabin, ski to the east end of the meadows where they begin to pinch off and the cabin is located to the left in the edge of the trees, below Pipestone Mountain.

To return to Skoki Lodge, ski straight south from the cabin across the meadows to the trees on the far side where you will find the trail. It is tricky to follow at the start. After a short distance it begins

to work its way to the right towards Skoki Mountain, then follows up the open draw to Jones Pass between Skoki and Fossil Mountains. Through the pass the trail crosses beneath some large avalanche paths. The last 0.5 km back to the lodge on the west side of the pass, is a gentle downhill run, curving back to the right, through some trees.

Of interest Often at Skoki, you will find old timer Ken Jones splitting wood or shovelling snow. Ken worked on the construction of the lodge in 1936 and worked as a guide during the 1930's, 40's and 50's. He loves to talk, so if you get a chance ask "Greybeard" for a story — you won't be dissapionted.

71 THE NATURAL BRIDGE

Ski touring

Grade Easy
Distance 16 km return
Time 5-6 hrs
Height gain 80 m
Max elevation 2,200 m
Map Hector Lake 82 N/9
Barrier Mountain 82 O/12

This trail is an extension of the tour round Skoki Mountain. It is a little longer and provides almost a full day's ski. The destination is a natural rock bridge at the end of a small valley behind Oyster Peak.

Access The trail begins and ends at Skoki Lodge.

This trip is really an extension of the tour round Skoki Mountain. Use this description as far as the Cyclone warden cabin. From this cabin continue east down the Red Deer River for several kilometres, then work your way to the right through

Facilities The Cyclone warden cabin can be visited on this trip, however it will be locked.

Hazards A map and some proficiency in reading it can be very helpful on this tour. In the vicinity of the Red Deer Lakes where several valleys meet, it can be difficult to decide which one to follow.

the woods and over into the drainage behind Oyster Mountain (there is a trail here but it is difficult to follow). Follow this unnamed creek bed for a short distance until you reach the natural bridge. Return the same way back to Cyclone Cabin then follow the Skoki Mountain Tour back to Skoki Lodge.

Ken Jones about to lead a group to Natural Bridge

Photo Chic Scott

72 FOSSIL MOUNTAIN LOOP

Ski touring

Grade Intermediate
Distance 11 km return
Time 5-6 hrs
Height gain 300 m
Max elevation 2,470 m
Maps Lake Louise 82 N/8
Hector Lake 82 N/9

This is perhaps the most challenging tour from Skoki Lodge and will take you a good part of the day to complete. Some experience at routefinding and map reading is a definite asset. There will probably be a fair amount of trail breaking across the open areas because they drift over easily in the wind. It can be skied in either direction but travelling anti-clockwise is the usual way.

Hazards There is some avalanche potential on this tour and you should be knowledgeable and prepared for emergencies.

Options This tour can be combined with a trip to Oyster Lake. Skied clockwise from Skoki to Baker Lake it can also be used as an optional return from Skoki back to your car at the Fish Creek parking area. Follow this tour in reverse through Jones Pass, over the shoulder of Fossil Mountain into Cottongrass Pass then around the corner and across Baker Lake to Ptarmigan Lake (to regain the standard route to and from Skoki).

Access The trail begins and ends at Skoki Lodge.

From Skoki Lodge ski south up the valley to the top of Deception Pass. The trail is normally easy to follow as there will most likely be snowmobile tracks, flagging on the trees, and near the top there are stakes driven in the ground. The trail stays well up on the left side of the drainage as you climb to the pass.

From the top of the pass it is safest to head more or less straight down to the flats at the north-east end of Ptarmigan Lake. Trying to cut the corner down to Baker Lake could get an inexperienced skier into trouble. Ski north-east across the flats then descend through a notch and down a slope to Baker Lake. Cross Baker Lake to its north-east corner and climb up onto the bank. Soon you should see evidence of a Parks Canada campsite. Descend an open groove in the trees for about 100 m until an obvious way opens up through the trees to the left. Work your way across to the left, gradu-

ally descending through open trees until you reach Cottongrass Pass at the head of Baker Creek.

Cross the meadows of Cottongrass Pass heading north, then work your way to Jones Pass. One possible route is to stay at treeline and cut around the corner of Fossil Mountain just below a little rock outcrop. If you choose this route be very careful of potential avalanche terrain. A safer choice is to round the corner lower down in the trees following a route which is normally flagged by the folks from Skoki Lodge.

After rounding the corner continue into the valley between Fossil Mountain and Skoki Mountain. Carry on easily up the valley, staying to the right and climbing gently to Jones Pass. Do not linger here on the large avalanche paths. Cross Jones Pass staying to the right then descend gently, angling to the right for a short distance to Skoki Lodge.

73 OYSTER LAKE

Ski touring

Grade Easy/intermediate
Distance 12 km return
Time 4-5 hrs
Height gain 150 m
Max elevation 2,290 m
Map Hector Lake 82 N/9

Hazards Rounding the shoulder of Fossil Mountain offers some avalanche risk. However this can be avoided, if you are unsure, by taking the lower path through the trees.

This is a very pleasant tour, through lovely open terrain. Oyster Lake itself makes a relatively scenic destination. There is even a thrilling bit of skiing coming back down the creek bed from the lake to Cottongrass Pass. A recommended tour.

Options This tour can be combined, with the trip around Fossil Mountain or your return journey to the Fish Creek parking lot, via the Fossil Mountain Loop.

Access The trail begins and ends at Skoki Lodge.

From Skoki Lodge head south back up the valley. Within a hundred metres the trail curves around to the left and climbs slightly, through some trees to Jones Pass. Continue at a very gentle angle down the other side staying to the left. Do not linger on these large avalanche paths. The most efficient trail then cuts high on the right around the corner of Fossil Mountain. There is some avalanche risk through here and if you are unsure of the safety of this section of the tour you can opt to stay a little lower and climb through the trees. There is a flagged trail which works its way through the trees around the shoulder, with very little climbing. The trail leaves the trees behind and crosses the open meadows of Cottongrass Pass. Ski across the meadows to the drainage coming down from Oyster Lake. You can either ski up this drainage or climb the sparsely

treed shoulder to the right. Near the top, climb the drainage itself up an open slope to the right, then cut back sharply to the left and over a little notch to the lake. Return by the same route back to the lodge.

Of interest Over the years many people have had the pleasure of managing Skoki Lodge. One of the most wonderful figures to have filled this role was Lizzie Rummel, who ran the lodge from 1943 to 1949 before going on to run Sunburst Lodge at Mount Assiniboine. Her personality, her love of the mountains and her overwhelming generosity was eventually rewarded with the Order of Canada in April of 1980.

74 MERLIN VALLEY

Ski touring

Grade Advanced
Distance 6 km
Time 3-4 hrs
Height gain 210 m
Max elevation 2,230 m
Map Hector Lake 82 N/9

A challenging trail which takes you up into a beautiful high valley. There is excellent terrain for telemark skiing once you reach the upper Merlin Valley. The climb from the meadows up to Lake Merlin is steep and difficult, and requires some route finding. The descent is equally challenging.

Hazards This trail is very demanding and only experienced skiers will be able to properly handle the descent back down from Lake Merlin.

If you plan on skiing on the slopes above Lake Merlin be aware that you are in potential avalanche terrain and should be prepared accordingly.

Access The trail begins and ends at Skoki Lodge.

Ski down the trail north of Skoki Lodge to the meadows. Turn left and cross the meadows in a south-west direction for several hundred metres then climb up on the right bank at a very large and tall tree. Continue across an open avalanche path, then work your way into the trees. After several hundred metres the trail begins to climb to the right up an open area with sparse trees. The angle is very steep but eventually eases off and the trail cuts left into the trees, where it continues to climb, but now at a more moderate rate. There are numerous blazes along here which makes it relatively easy to follow the trail. It climbs right up to the base of some cliffs then traverses left across very steep terrain (in the trees), just below them. After a few hundred metres the terrain flattens out. If you are only going to the lake you can reach it easily now by a short descent down to the left. If your destination is Merlin Ridge then continue climbing and angling up and to the right.

Alternative ascent route: Cross the meadows to the farthest south-west end, then climb an open slope on the right (this is a rock slide in the summer). From the top traverse left to Castilleja Lake. Climb the treed slope above the lake. Work your way up by traversing back and forth through the trees, then traverse back left (west) to Lake Merlin when you are high enough.

The real problem with both these very steep ascents is the descent back down the trails afterwards, to the meadows. They are not easy.

Of interest Sir Norman Watson was a colourful character in the history of Skoki. The British Baronet was an early shareholder in the Ski Club of the Canadian Rockies which owned Skoki Lodge, and by the late 1930's had become the major shareholder. He had great dreams of turning the Lake Louise, Temple and Skoki areas into a little Switzerland complete with cows and cowbells in the meadows.

75 PACKERS PASS

Grade Intermediate
Distance 11 km
Time 4 hrs from Skoki back to the Fish Creek parking lot
Height gain 300 m
Max elevation 2,470 m
Maps Lake Louise 82 N/8
Hector Lake 82 N/9

An interesting variation to the tour to Skoki. It takes the pass between Packers Peak and Ptarmigan Peak just west of Deception Pass. It is more difficult than Deception Pass and is subject to ava-lanche risk. It offers a slightly more direct route between the Fish Creek parking area and Skoki Lodge. It is described here as a return trip from Skoki.

Facilities There are facilities at either end of the trip (Lake Louise ski area and Skoki Lodge) and there is the rustic Ptarmigan Hut in the middle.

Hazards This variation is subject to sig-nificant avalanche hazard and should be undertaken only by experienced back country skiers.

Access This trail is actually a variation to the normal ski tour to and from Skoki Lodge.

From Skoki Lodge start up the trail to-wards Deception Pass. In less than a kilometre turn right up the creek that drains Skoki Lakes. Direct access to the lakes is blocked by cliffs so one must climb the small drainage to the left, be-low Packers Peak then cut back to the right above the cliffs. Rather than de-scending along the bench back down to Skoki Lakes angle up and over the shoul-der of Packers Peak, then make a rising traverse high on the north-west slope of Packers Peak up to Packers Pass. De-scend the other side easily, down a ramp to the south-west to Ptarmigan Lake, and regain the standard route back to the Fish Creek parking area.

History Throughout the 1930's, 40's and 50's all the supplies for Skoki were packed in on the backs of men. The loads were often very heavy, up to 35 kg, and the wages poor — a dollar a day at the start. But it was a good life out in the open air, skiing and enjoying all that beauty around you. Two of the early packers and guides were Ken Jones and his friend Sam Evans, from Montana. The legend says that they carried loads into Skoki from Lake Louise every day for 65 days straight one year. Packer's Pass is a more direct route into Skoki and it may be that these packers used it to save a little time.

76 SKOKI TO L. LOUISE VIA THE PIPESTONE RIVER Ski touring

Grade Intermediate
Distance 24 km
Time This tour normally takes all day
Height loss 600 m
Max elevation 2,160 m at Skoki Lodge
Maps Lake Louise 82 N/8
Hector Lake 82 N/9

This tour offers an alternative way to ski out from Skoki. It is long and trail breaking

will often be required. It is a full days trip for most of us and in deep snow might be difficult to complete in a day. The Pipestone Valley is wide and beautiful and the solitude is wonderful — it is unlikely that you will run into any other parties.

Hazards If the snow is deep and you anticipate that you will be breaking trail, give yourself lots of time.

Access The tour begins from Skoki Lodge and ends at the parking lot for the Pipestone Trails (see page 107)

From Skoki Lodge follow the trail heading north down Skoki Creek. After about 1 km, at the meadows, ski through the campground and carry on straight ahead (do not take the trail which climbs up and to the right over to the Red Deer Lakes). Carry on down Skoki Creek on a good trail which is well flagged at first. Stay on the right bank a short distance above the creek. The trail descends steeply for another kilometre and then flattens out again. Continue along the gentle valley bottom, through the trees on the right side of the creek. After about one more kilometre the valley begins to open up as

Photo Chic Scott

Rest stop in the remote Pipestone Valley

123

you reach Little Pipestone Creek and it is best to simply follow the creekbed.

Cross some large open meadows with huge avalanche paths above on the right and then climb up onto the right bank of the creek and find a very clear and well defined trail through the trees. Follow this trail easily for about 2 km until it starts to descend. The trail descends steeply for a short distance, then levels out and you leave the trees and enter an open meadow.

From here the trail is tricky to follow although there are a large number of blazes on the trees. Head west, doing your best to follow the blazes, through the trees, to the junction with the Pipestone River. You could also head for the Little Pipestone Creek and then follow it down to the junction with the Pipestone River. Across this section of the tour it might be advisable to pull your compass out and follow it if necessary. From the junction of the Little Pipestone Creek and the Pipestone River, head down the Pipestone River across beautiful open meadows for about 5 km. Eventually the trees close in and the meadows narrow but it is still best to follow the river itself for another 7 km. About 6 km before reaching the highway look for the Pipestone trails up on the right bank of the Pipestone River — they are easy to miss. Ski down the Pipestone trails back to your waiting car at the parking lot.

TELEMARK SKIING AT SKOKI

All of these areas present avalanche risk. Exercise caution at all times.

Packers Peak

The north-west flank of Packers Peak, above Zigadenus Lake offers excellent skiing on a slope of almost 300 m.

Merlin Ridge

The slopes above Lake Merlin offer excellent opportunities for telemark skiing on moderate terrain. The descent is about 360 m from top to bottom. This area is tricky to reach due to the steep climb from the valley up to the lake. See the tour to Merlin Lake (page 121).

Wolverine Slopes

These slopes are found low down on the west flank of Fossil Mountain. They are just above the path between Skoki Lodge and Deception Pass. They are short but offer some entertaining skiing.

Skoki Valley

Telemark skiing can be found in several locations near to the lodge itself:
- just above the lodge on the slopes of Skoki Mountain there are opportunities for tree skiing. In fact years ago runs were actually groomed and cleared up here.
- across from Skoki Lodge, in the trees at the base of the Wall of Jericho, some open glade skiing can be found.

YOHO NATIONAL PARK

Yoho Park offers some of the finest ski touring in the Rocky Mountains and sees a lot of activity. There are two backcountry huts (Elizabeth Parker and Stanley Mitchell) and one backcountry lodge (The Lake O'Hara Lodge). The park gets a lot of snow, has spectacular scenery and has a long tradition of ski activity. In fact the Alpine Club of Canada ran its first ski camp at Lake O'Hara in 1936 and almost every year through the 40's ran a ski camp in the Little Yoho Valley. These two areas are now amongst the most popular in the whole range. In addition the Wapta Icefields straddle the continental divide between Banff and Yoho Parks.

Access The Trans-Canada Highway (Highway #1) traverses Yoho Park as it makes its way from Lake Louise to Golden. The road is of course the main highway across Canada and is kept in top condition in all weather. The town of Field which is the only centre in the park is located along the highway, 26 km west of Lake Louise.

Facilities The town of Field offers very limited facilities. There is a service station and one small motel in town. There are several bed & breakfasts, a liquor store, post office and a small grocery store. The Emerald Lake Lodge (604-343-6321) offers luxurious accommodation with ski trails starting right from the door. It is reached via a spur road which turns off the highway, 2.5 km west of town. East of Field, 10 km along the highway, is the West Louise Lodge also known as Wapta Lodge, with a gas station, hotel, restaurant and lounge. For most of your needs however it is best to shop in Lake Louise or Banff.

Information There is a Parks Information Centre at the entrance to Field just off the highway. The Warden Office is located at the Boulder Creek maintenance compound 5.5 km west of town.

Lake O'Hara is world famous for its summer hiking trails. However these trails are not so suitable for winter skiing. Many of the classic hikes are steep and travel through avalanche prone terrain. The region is so beautiful that many people come here simply to look and enjoy the grandeur rather than do a lot of skiing. There are a few trails which can be skied safely.

The obvious and easy tour is to do a circuit of Lake O'Hara. Although this is a very easy trail it can be pleasant for skiers of all abilities. The scenery around you is truly outstanding. One of the most popular ski tours at Lake O'Hara is from the Elizabeth Parker Hut to MacArthur Pass. This trail is safe and the route is easy to follow. North-west of the pass, towards Mount Odaray, there are some slopes where you might make a few telemark turns. The trail from the ACC Hut to Morning Glory Lakes runs through the trees most of the way and is

Elizabeth Parker Hut

Map 82 N/8 Lake Louise
Location Alpine meadow west of Lake O'Hara. GR 457893
Reservations Alpine Club of Canada
Capacity 24 in two huts
Facilities Fully equipped
Water Creek 30 m north of hut
Notes Locked when custodian is not present. Combination required

Lake O'Hara Lodge

This luxurious lodge was built in the 1920's, and today offers all modern amenities. In the winter only the central building is open offering guest rooms, lounge area, dining rooms, indoor plumbing and central heating. The lodge is located on the shores of Lake O'Hara, an 11 km ski from the Trans-Canada Highway. GR 463895 The season is mid-January to mid-April. Accommodation is about $150 per person with meals included. A light lunch is available for non-guest from noon to 2:30 PM. Phone (403) 762-2118 from Oct. to May, and (604) 343-6418 from June to Sept. for information.

safe. From the meadows the trail heads north into the trees then makes a long descent to the lake. Novice skiers might find this challenging. It is also possible to ski up onto the Opabin Plateau, south of Lake O'Hara, but there is a very steep climb involved here which will be tricky on the way back down.

Opposite: Alpine Club of Canada Ski Camp group preparing for a trip outside the Stanley Mitchell Hut

Yoho Valley Trails There is great ski touring potential in the Little Yoho Valley. In fact this area has been the scene of ski camps, run by the ACC and by Hans Gmoser, for many years. Much of the skiing is up high, on glaciers, but there are also telemark areas lower down, and some nordic style tours.

One of the main locations for ski mountaineering is up on the President Range. You can ski to President Pass and perhaps even make ascents (on foot) of The President or The Vice President (this tour present serious avalanche potential). There are many other popular locations for ski mountaineering, which are the subject of another book however, and are not dealt with here.

The presence of the Stanley Mitchell Hut makes this valley the perfect location for a ski holiday. The cabin is very comfortable and is in good shape. It is in close proximity to all the good skiing. If the weather is good you will have no trouble entertaining yourself ski touring for a week. It is always a treat, at the end of a hard tour, to return to a comfortable huts and toast oneself around the fire.

The Yoho National Park Warden Service has designated several additional trails as cross country tours (#88-91). These are included here for completeness, with the descriptions provided by the Canadian Parks Service.

Stanley Mitchell Hut

Map 82 N/10 Blaeberry River
Location In Alpine meadow near head of Little Yoho Valley GR 303083
Reservations Alpine Club of Canada
Capacity 30
Facilities Fully equipped
Water River directly south of hut
Notes Locked when custodian is not present. Combination required

Photo Chic Scott

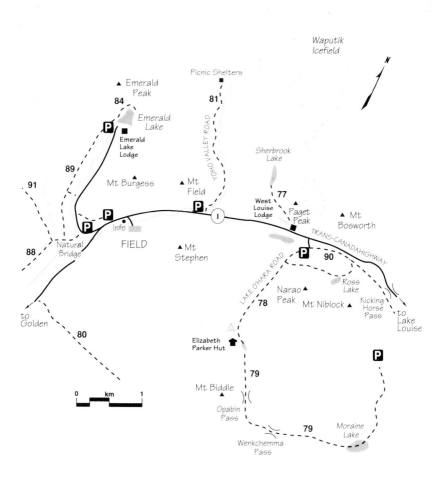

77 SHERBROOKE LAKE

Ski touring

Grade Intermediate/advanced
Distance 6 km return
Time 3 hrs return
Height gain 180 m
Max elevation 1,800 m
Map Lake Louise 82 N/8

A steep and challenging trail. If it is icy or rutted it is even more difficult. However it is popular due to its proximity to Wapta Lodge. Sherbrooke Lake is a beautiful destination.

Facilities The tour begins at Wapta Lodge and all amenities are available there.

Hazards The trail is marked incorrectly on the topographical map.

Options Sherbrooke Lake is the usual exit from the Wapta Icefields Traverse. The descent from the Scott Duncan Hut (see page 165) can of course be skied in reverse, to reach the icefields.

Access Park at West Louise Lodge which is located near the summit of the Kicking Horse Pass on the north side of the Trans-Canada Highway (Highway #1) 4.5 km west of the Alberta/B.C. border.

The trail begins behind the lodge and immediately climbs up and left through the trees. Most of the tour climbs at a fairly steep angle up the slopes of Paget Peak. The trail can be hard to find in some places, but because it is well used this is not normally too much of a problem. After 2 km the trail rounds the shoulder of the peak, breaks out of the trees and continues easily through the open area above the creek to the lake.

Neil Liske on the way down to Sherbrooke Lake after the first complete Jasper to Lake Louise high level traverse
Photo Don Gardner

Lake O'Hara Fire Road

Photo Rudi Setz Collection

78 LAKE O'HARA FIRE ROAD

Ski touring

Grade Easy
Distance 24 km return
Time 3 - 4 hours to Lake O'Hara. The run back out is about 2 hours.
Height gain 430 m
Max elevation 2,030 m
Map Lake Louise 82 N/8

A very popular day trip and of course many folks stay overnight at the Lake O'Hara Lodge or the Elizabeth Parker Hut. The tour requires little snow as it follows a road and the snow comes early. Often this tour can be skiable by late November! The route is very easy to follow and usually the trail is broken or packed by a snowmobile.

Facilities There are toilets at the parking lot. There is an outhouse about halfway along the trail, on the left.

Options From Lake O'Hara it is possible to continue on to Lake Louise, via Opabin Pass and Wenkchemna Pass. You can also carry on to Marble canyon on the Kootenay Parkway via Prospector's Valley or ski over McArthur Pass and out the Ottertail Fire Road.

Access Turn left (south) off the Trans-Canada Highway (Highway #1) 2.5 km west of the Alberta/BC Border (the Kicking Horse Pass) onto the 1A Highway. Continue across the railway tracks then immediately turn right and drive a short distance along the road to the parking lot.

The route to Lake O'Hara follows the snow covered summer road. To begin with the road climbs at a steady angle for about 2 km before levelling off. For the next 5 km the trail is gently uphill and all around you is impressive mountain scenery. Just after crossing the creek the road begins to climb again and gains altitude until just before the lake. The return trip can be quick and a lot of fun if the trail is packed and there are good tracks.

The first buildings you will see as you reach the lake are the warden cabin and the summer kiosk called "Le Relais" — they are log buildings and there is one on either side of the road. The lodge is just a few hundred metres beyond on the edge of the lake.

To reach the Elizabeth Parker Hut you must follow a trail to the right at "Le Relais", which climbs steeply up through the trees. After several hundred metres it breaks out of the trees and makes a zig-zag following a stream for a short distance before crossing the meadows to the hut.

Of interest The Elizabeth Parker Hut was named after on of the founders of the Alpine Club of Canada. This spirited woman was a great defender of our mountain environment. In 1906 she said *"It is the people's right to have primitive access to the remote places of safest retreat from the fever and fret of the market place and the beaten tracts of life."* and *"In time we ought to become a nation of mountaineers, loving our mountains with the patriot's passion".* Canadian Alpine Journal, 1907.

Skiing at Lake O'Hara

Photo Leon Kubbernus

79 OPABIN/WENKCHEMNA CIRCUIT   Ski touring/Ski mountaineering

Grade Advanced

Distance 24 km one way (Lake O'Hara to Lake Louise)

Time Most parties do this trip in a long, hard day after overnighting in the ACC hut at Lake O'Hara.

Height gain 610 m to Opabin Pass
340 m to Wenkchemna Pass
60 m along Moraine Lake Road

Height loss 330 m from Opabin Pass
730 m from Wenkchemna Pass

Max elevation 2,600 m at both Opabin and Wenkchemna Passes

Map Lake Louise 82 N/8

One of the best high mountain tours in the Rockies. It is long, challenging and takes you through superb mountain scenery. It is however a serious trip and there is some very real avalanche risk, so exercise caution.

Options It is possible to cross Wastach Pass to Paradise Valley, then exit via the Paradise Valley Trail. This makes for a longer and harder day. There is potential avalanche hazard on this pass as well.

Hazards The slopes below all three passes, Opabin, Wenkchemna and Wastach, have significant avalanche risk. You should know what you are doing and use all safety procedures. This trip is not recommended unless the avalanche hazard is low. There are small glaciers on both sides of Opabin Pass and there are some crevasses. It is advised to carry a rope just in case!

Access Begin this tour by skiing up the Lake O'Hara Fire Road (see page 131).

From the lodge ski around the south side of Lake O'Hara to the drainage coming down from the Opabin Plateau where you will find a trail junction. Ski up the steep trail (skins advised) to gain the hanging valley then head south along the valley towards Opabin Pass. The travel is open and in good visibility the way is not hard to find. The route ascends a small glacier with some large crevasses. The final climb to the pass is steep and may require step-kicking.

The descent from Opabin Pass is steep only for a short distance then becomes very pleasant for about 300 vertical metres down to the Eagles Eyrie. This run down can be a fun bit of skiing if the snow is good. The climb from near

Eagles Eyrie up to Wenkchemna Pass is also a risky slope. It is fairly steep, and underneath the ground surface is smooth scree. Once again use caution. The last part of the climb up to the pass is often windblown and bare and it can be a real pain climbing those last few metres over loose rocks.

The descent from Wenkchemna Pass to Moraine Lake is pleasant and follows an easy line across moraine and open meadows. Stay well south of Eiffel Lake and marvel at the walls of the Ten Peaks above you. Ski along the margin of the forest and the moraines until you reach the drainage which flows down to Moraine Lake. Descend this drainage, then ski across the lake itself to reach the lodge on the opposite side. Continue to Lake Louise along the Moraine Lake Road (see page 94).

Looking west from the Stanley Mitchell Hut to some fabulous ski touring terrain

Photo Rudi Setz Collection

80 OTTERTAIL VALLEY FIRE ROAD

Ski touring

Grade Easy
Distance 28 km round trip to McArthur Creek
Time It is a full day tour to ski to McArthur Creek and back, but you can ski as far along the road as you like
Height gain 300 m
Max elevation 1,500 m
Maps Golden 82 N/7
Lake Louise 82 N/8

An easy and enjoyable ski which is not often travelled. A pleasant way to get some fresh air and solitude.

Options Occasionally adventurous skiers will cross McArthur Pass from Lake O'Hara then descend McArthur Creek to the Ottertail Fire Road. A good adventure for those looking for something a little different.

Access Park at the trailhead on the south-east side of the Trans-Canada Highway (Highway #1), 8.5 km west of Field.

This tour follows a fire road so it is wide and the grade is gentle. The road does much of its climbing over the first 3 km

then levels off. Ski as far as you like then turn back when you've had enough. If you have the time and energy to make it all the way to the McArthur Creek Warden Cabin you will be treated to a spectacular view of the towers of the Goodsirs to the south.

81 YOHO VALLEY ROAD

Ski touring

Grade Easy
Distance 26 km return
Time This is normally a full day trip, to Takakkaw Falls and back
Height gain 150 m
Max elevation 1,480 m
Map Lake Louise 82 N/8

A straightforward and easy ski up a road, which is not plowed in the winter. Usually, the road is skied by folks who are continuing up the Yoho Valley to the ACC hut in the Little Yoho Valley. However you can ski the road for as far as you like — a few kilometres or right up to Takakkaw Falls. At the end of the road you get a great view of Takakkaw Falls, frozen into its winter splendor. You might even see some waterfall ice climbers on it.

Facilities There is a campground at Takakkaw Falls which has enclosed camp shelters and toilets.

Hazards The avalanche slopes off Wapta Mountain should be crossed quickly. This trail should be avoided in periods of extreme avalanche hazard!

Options The trail ties in with the tour up to the Little Yoho Valley (Stanley Mitchell Hut) and the continuation across the Wapta Icefields to Bow Hut.

Access There is a large parking area at the trailhead which is reached by taking the turn-off for the Yoho Valley, 4 km east of Field. If you are coming from Lake Louise, the turn is on your right, just after you descend the big hill from the Kicking Horse Pass and after crossing the bridge over the Kicking Horse River.

This tour follows a road throughout, to a campground located not far from Takakkaw Falls. The road begins from the east end of the parking area and is simple to follow. After about 5 km the road climbs several switchbacks. Just after the switchbacks, the road is threatened by giant avalanche slopes high on Wapta Mountain. In fact often the road is piled high with avalanche debris. You should proceed as quickly as possible across these areas, without stopping.

At the end of the road you can ski over to the right to get a better view of the falls, or carry on straight ahead into the campground and find a picnic shelter and table for lunch. Although the return journey should in fact be downhill and should give a fun glide back to the cars, it has been noted by many skiers that this road is unique in that it appears to be uphill in both directions!

Of interest Above the Yoho Valley Road, on the west side just before reaching Takakkaw Falls is Yoho Pass. In 1901, the famous mountaineer Edward Whymper camped here with his Swiss Guides and made a number of first ascents in the area. In 1906, the Alpine Club of Canada held its first climbing camp at Yoho Pass.

82 LITTLE YOHO VALLEY

Ski touring

Grade Intermediate/advanced
Distance 10 km one way from Takakkaw Falls to the Stanley Mitchell Hut. Note! The trip from the parking lot, to the hut in the Little Yoho Valley, and back to the cars is about 46 km.
Time From the highway, the hut can be reached in one day (depending on conditions), by strong skiers. Many skiers will find two days are necessary for the trip. The return journey, from the hut back to the highway, is normally done in one day.
Height gain 150 m from Highway #1 to Takakkaw Falls. 575 m from Takakkaw Falls to the Stanley Mitchell Hut
Max elevation 2,060 m
Maps Lake Louise 82 N/8
Hector Lake 82 N/9
Blaeberry River 82 N/10
Touring the Wapta Icefields (Murray Toft)

The trip into the Little Yoho Valley and a stay at the beautiful Stanley Mitchell Hut is one of the great experiences of the Canadian Rockies. The area abounds in superb skiing and one can easily spend a week here and see new terrain almost every day. The cabin is very beautiful and is the postcard picture of what a mountain hut in the Rockies is supposed to look like.

Facilities There is usually one camp shelter at the Takakkaw Falls campground that is completely enclosed. It is often used by parties who cannot make it to the Stanley Mitchell Hut in one day. There are toilets nearby and a pile of firewood will be hidden under the snow not far away. Check with the Yoho National Park Warden Service before starting out.

Hazards Watch out for the steep descents down the Laughing Falls Hill and the Hollingsworth Hill on your way out, particularly if conditions are icy.

Be sure to cross the Wapta Mountain slide paths quickly with no stopping.

Allow plenty of time to reach the hut when you leave the Takakkaw Falls shelter. If you are breaking trail you will find the going very slow, particularly up the headwall. It is best to spend a night at the shelter and be warm and comfortable, rather than to pushing, in one marathon day, and find yourself in the dark, under the stars, frantically trying to find the hut. It has happened many times!

Options A night at the Stanley Mitchell hut is a pleasant conclusion to the tour across the Wapta Icefields (see page 172)

Access One begins this tour by skiing the Yoho Valley Road (see page 135) as far as the campground at Takakkaw Falls. Overnight here if necessary.

The trail leaves from the far (north) end of the campground, crossing a large open area, which in summer is a stream outwash, then enters the woods on the opposite side. The trail is easy to follow to begin with as it follows a wide, straight cut through the forest. After several kilometres it climbs a long and uniform hill (Hollingsworth Hill) for a way, then continues through the woods beyond (the trail can be hard to follow along here).

After 4.5 km (from the campground) the route turns left, near Laughing Falls, and begins its climb out of the Yoho Valley into the Little Yoho Valley. The turnoff point is sometimes hard to find, particularly if the trail signs are buried deep under the snow. Nowadays there are enough people touring into this area that the trail may be easier to follow than in the past. The trail switchbacks through open, mature forest up the west wall of the valley, and can be hard to follow if you are new to the area.

After about 240 m of climb, when the angle begins to ease off, the trail angles over left towards the Little Yoho River. It continues above the river into the valley, along the hillside on the north bank. After a while the steep hillside that the trail is traversing levels off, and the trail meanders through the forest and open glades to the hut. Stay on the north bank of the river throughout. The trail can be hard to find at times because it crosses meadows, then re-enters the forest on the opposite side at points that are hard to locate. The hut is located in trees at the edge of a meadow, on the north side of the Little Yoho River, about 5 km from the Laughing Falls turnoff.

The return journey to the highway can be an exciting challenge for inexperienced skiers. This is particularly true in the springtime, when the trail can be icy. The descent of the steep hillside above Laughing Falls is not a laughing matter if you are unsure on your skis. Be careful here and take your time. The same holds true for the Hollingsworth Hill which is steep and long. For your return journey remember to get away early in the morning to allow plenty of time to return to the highway in one day.

83 KIWETINOK PASS   Ski touring

Grade Easy
Distance 7 km return
Time 3-4 hrs
Height gain 400 m
Max elevation 2,450 m
Map Blaeberry River 82 N/10

This is a very enjoyable short tour in beautiful surroundings. Highly recommended!

Access The tour begins at the Stanley Mitchell Hut.

This tour follows the Little Yoho River up to Kiwetinok Pass. There is little in the way of difficulties along the way and the route is usually obvious. Most of the tour is above treeline and you can ski where you please. You can ski through the pass and to the brow of the hill overlooking the Amiskwi Valley, and sit in the sun while you eat your lunch.

TELEMARK AREAS

One of the most popular telemark areas in the Little Yoho Valley is the hillside opposite the cabin and a short distance east, below the Vice President. For several kilometres along here, there are gladed runs through the trees which are ideal for those overcast and snowy days. The length of the runs is generally 100-150 m. There is a lot of terrain here and it can keep you amused for several days if necessary.

Skiing at Emerald Lake

Photo Tony Daffern

84 EMERALD LAKE TRAILS

Nordic skiing

Grade Easy
Distance The loop around the lake is 5 km and can be extended by another 2 or 3 km
Time 2 hrs
Height gain Nil
Max elevation 1,300 m
Map Golden 82 N/7

A lovely circuit in a very beautiful setting. The skiing is easy and the trail will almost always be packed or trackset. The valley is oriented south-west and gets sunshine most of the day. It is highly recommended.

Facilities There are toilets at the parking lot and the Emerald Lake Lodge is nearby with all amenities. There is a sports shop which rents cross country ski equipment at the start of the trail, near the bridge.

Hazards You should not linger on the large avalanche path on the south-west side of the lake.

Options It is possible, for the adventurous, to use Emerald Lake as a starting point to ski to the Little Yoho Valley. The route would traverse Yoho Pass and continue along the Iceline trail to the Little Yoho. This could prove to be an excellent approach to the Stanley Mitchell Hut.

Access Turn right (north) off the Trans-Canada Highway (Highway #1) 3 km west of Field. Follow the road for 6 km, passing the Natural Bridge parking area, to the end where there is a large parking lot.

The trail begins at the end of the parking lot, where the road crosses over a bridge, to the Lodge. Walk in front of the sports shop and put on your skis. The trail stays a few metres above the lake, in the trees, as it circles the lake in a clockwise direction. It is easy to follow. Near the start of the circuit the trail crosses the foot of a large avalanche path — do not linger here. At the end of the lake the trail cuts directly across the open area, heading east, entering the trees on the other side, and begins to make its way back towards the lodge. If you like you can make a loop back into Emerald Basin and ski several additional kilometres. The loop eventually rejoins the main trail which works its way back along the east shore of the

lake. It makes several short climbs and descents along here, which could be challenging for a novice skier. Eventually the trail returns to the farthest east corner of the lodge from where it is necessary to remove your skis and walk through the lodge area and back over the bridge to your car.

Of interest The Burgess Shales are located high above Emerald Lake on Wapta Mountain. These shales are deposits of fossils from the Cambrian era. They contain some of the most unique fossils in the world and scientists today are studying them closely. Their findings are re-writing the story of evolution on our planet.

85 CHANCELLOR PEAK CAMPGROUND

Ski touring

Grade Easy
Distance 4 km return
Time 1-2 hrs return
Height gain Nil
Max elevation 1,120 m
Map McMurdo 82 N/2

A short, easy tour into a campground, it is ideal for those who would like a very easy day or those who might like to try winter camping in a safe and accessible location.

Facilities At the campground there are picnic shelters and toilets.

Options There is a fire road which leaves from the back of the camp-ground. It is a nice option for a tour the next day (if you are camping) or as an extension to a day trip.

Access There is usually a small cleared area at the trailhead which is located 23 km west of Field on the Trans-Canada Highway (Highway #1), immediately across the Leanchoil Bridge over the Kicking Horse River. The parking area is on the right (north) side of the road.

From the parking area at the highway simply follow the easy and flat road for 2 km to the campground. There are very impressive views of Mount Chancellor and Mount Vaux along the way.

86 ICE RIVER FIRE ROAD

Ski touring

Grade Easy
Distance It is 32 km return if you ski all the way to the park boundary at the Ice River.
Time As long as you wish
Height gain 150 m
Max elevation 1,300
Maps Mount Goodsir 82 N/1
McMurdo 82 N/2

A long and easy plod along a straightfor-ward fire road. There are no hills or cor-ners to speak of but it is an opportunity to get out on a quiet trail and wander.

Access Park your car at the Hoodoo Creek Campground, on the left (south-east) side of the road, just before cross-ing the Leanchoil Bridge, 22.5 km west of Field.

Ski past the entrance into the camp-ground then head south down the fire road. The road follows the Beaverfoot River Valley, through heavy timber all the way to the park boundary. Put your mind in neutral, breathe deeply and listen to your skis as they swish through the snow.

87 WAPTA FALLS

Ski touring

Grade Intermediate
Distance 9 km return
Time 3-4 hrs return
Height gain 80 m
Max elevation 1,120 m
Map McMurdo 82 N/2

A pleasant afternoon trip. Although the tour is only graded intermediate, the trail is narrow towards the end and requires caution and skill. There is a limited view of the falls from the viewpoint at the top of the hill.

To see them properly one should really descend the hill to the river which can be tricky for inexperienced skiers.

Facilities There are picnic tables about 1.5 km along the way.

Hazards Take care on the steep and narrow downhill sections. If necessary, walk! Take care at the viewpoint above the falls. It's slippery and it's a long way down.

Access There is a small, cleared parking area at the trailhead which is located 25 km west of Field, on the Trans-Canada Highway (Highway #1), about 2 km beyond the Leanchoil Bridge over the Kicking Horse River. The parking lot is on the left (south) side of the road. Keep a sharp eye open for it, because it sneaks up quickly on you.

From the parking lot, ski around the road closure bar and head down to the road. For the first 1.5 km the trail is actually a summer road and is wide and easy. At the end of this section there are picnic tables. The trail carries on along the cut line for another 1.5 km, following the left side of the slash and once again is easy. Eventually, the slash peters out and the trail plunges into the woods.

For the next kilometre the trail is narrow and climbs at a moderate angle. This takes you to a viewpoint above the Kicking Horse River, overlooking Wapta Falls. Unfortunately it is not easy to see the falls and you must continue along the trail for another 0.5 km to get a good

look. The trail is steep, particularly at the start, and you should walk down it if you are unsteady on your skis. The trail initially angles out to the right then lower down traverses back to the left.

At the bottom of the hill you can ski a few metres back along the river up to the base of the falls. They are large and impressive from this vantage point.

88 NATURAL BRIDGE TO KICKING HORSE FIRE ROAD Ski touring

Grade Easy
Distance 13 km return
Time 4-5 hrs
Height gain 60 m
Max elevation 1,220 m
Map Golden 82 N/7

Options You can always continue farther south along the Kicking Horse Fire Road or north-west along the Otterhead Road.

Access Turn right onto the Emerald Lake access road, 4 km west of Field. Park at the Natural Bridge parking lot, 1.5 km along this road.

From the Natural Bridge. Ski 2.4 km along the road past the animal salt lick, to the Amiskwi River Bridge. Cross the bridge and continue left on the fire road for another 4.1 km to the junction with the Otterhead River.

89 TALLY-HO TO EMERALD LAKE Ski touring

Grade Intermediate
Distance 20 km return
Time It is a full day tour if you ski the trail return. About 3-4 hrs one way
Height gain 200 m
Max elevation 1,300 m
Map Golden 82 N/7

Facilities There are toilets at the Emerald Lake parking lot and the Emerald lake Lodge is nearby with all amenities.

Options You can combine this tour with the Emerald Lake Trail. You can leave a car at Emerald Lake and ski the trail one way.

Access Park at the picnic site, on the north side of the Trans-Canada Highway (Highway #1) 1 km west of Field.

From the picnic site, follow the old Tally-Ho Road for 3 km. Parallel the Emerald Lake Road for 0.8 km and take your skis off to cross the road. Continue on an old road which heads west to a bridge across the Emerald River. Cross the bridge and ski north along the Emerald River Trail. The trail has some short, steep sections before terminating at the Emerald Lake parking lot.

90 ROSS LAKE CIRCUIT
Ski touring

Grade Intermediate
Distance 9.5 km loop
Time 3 hrs
Height gain 200 m
Max elevation 1,830 m
Map Lake Louise 82 N/8

Facilities There are toilets at the Lake O'Hara Fire Road parking lot.

Access Park at the Lake O'Hara Fire Road parking lot. Turn left off the Trans-Canada Highway, 3 km west of the Alberta/B.C. Border (the Kicking Horse Pass). Drive a short distance, cross the railway tracks then turn right and drive a few hundred metres to the parking lot.

From the Lake O'Hara parking lot, follow the 1A highway until you reach the Ross Lake trailhead sign on your right. The trail climbs gradually for 1.3 km to this small lake bounded by a great rock wall. Turn west at the lake and continue for another 3.2 km to rejoin the Lake O'Hara Fire Road. Turn north (right) at the fire road to return to the parking lot. There are some narrow and fast sections.

91 AMISKWI FIRE ROAD TO AMISKWI PASS
Ski touring

Grade Easy to advanced
Distance 75.8 km return
Time You can ski along this road for several hours or for several days.
Height gain 800 m
Max elevation 1,960 m
Maps Golden 82 N/7
Blaeberry River 82 N/10

This 38 km fire road has little to offer the day skier. It is not groomed or trackset and is not particularly scenic for the first 25 km.

Facilities There is a private cabin just outside the park boundary at Amiskwi Pass. Call (604) 343-6397 evenings for information.

Access Turn right onto the Emerald Lake access road, 4 km west of Field. Park at the Natural Bridge parking lot, 1.5 km along this road.

From the Natural Bridge, ski 2.4 km along the road past the animal salt lick to the Amiskwi River Bridge. From the junction with the Kicking Horse Fire Road continue north along the Amiskwi Fire Road for another 35.5 km.

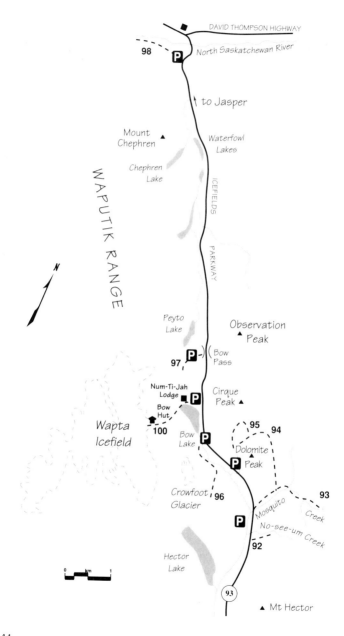

DAVID THOMPSON HIGHWAY

98

North Saskatchewan River

↑ to Jasper

Mount
Chephren ▲

Waterfowl
Lakes

Chephren
Lake

ICEFIELDS

WAPUTIK RANGE

N

PARKWAY

Peyto
Lake

Observation
▲ Peak

97

Bow
Pass

Num-Ti-Jah
Lodge

Cirque
Peak ▲

Bow
Hut

100

Wapta
Icefield

Bow
Lake

95   94

Dolomite
▲ Peak

Crowfoot
Glacier   96

93

Mosquito

Creek

No-see-um Creek

92

Hector
Lake

0   km   1

93

▲ Mt Hector

ICEFIELDS PARKWAY SOUTH

The Icefields Parkway (Highway #93), also known as the Banff-Jasper Highway, which stretches from Lake Louise to Jasper is one of the most scenic drives in the world. However, in winter it is a remote stretch of highway and there are no service stations for a distance of 230 km.

The southern portion of the highway from Lake Louise to Saskatchewan River Crossing, where the David Thompson Highway (Highway #11) comes in from Rocky Mountain House, is rarely closed in winter. It is well maintained although sanding is minimal and salt is not used, so expect some snow and ice on the road.

On the rare occasions when the highway is closed it may be possible to complete your journey by driving east on the David Thompson Highway to Rocky Mountain House or Red Deer and heading north or south from there. Whichever way you head it is a very long way around.

Be certain that you are prepared to deal with cold weather and snow. This includes a strong battery, good snow tires, jumper cables, survival gear and a shovel.

In emergency There is a warden station at Saskatchewan River Crossing which is the only evidence of civilization along this section of highway. There is a pay telephone at the tourist complex at Saskatchewan River Crossing.

Accommodation There is a Hostel which offers rustic, but comfortable, accommodation at Mosquito Creek. The campground at Mosquito Creek is normally plowed in the winter and there is a camp shelter and firewood available. Num-ti-jah Lodge, at Bow Lake, has not been open in winter for some years.

92 NO-SEE-UM CREEK

Ski touring

Grade Easy/intermediate
Distance 4 km return
Time 1-2 hrs
Height gain 180 m
Max elevation 2,000 m
Map Hector Lake 82 N/9

A short and easy tour with impressive mountain scenery at the head of the valley

Hazards Stay well back from the avalanche slopes at the end of the valley.

Access It is necessary to park along the side of the highway. The creek intersects the road 23 km north along the Icefields Parkway (Highway #93) from its junction with the Trans-Canada Highway (Highway #1).

The tour simply follows the open drainage of the creekbed. Follow the creek up and into an impressive valley and continue as far as the last trees.

93 MOSQUITO CREEK TO MOLAR MEADOWS

Ski touring

Grade Easy/intermediate
Distance 18 km return
Time This is a full day trip for most skiers
Height gain 450 m
Max elevation 2,270 m (at the meadows)
Map Hector Lake 82 N/9

This is a pleasant tour up a long and easy valley trail. Towards the end it climbs at a steady angle through the trees up to Molar Meadows. On a sunny day this is a beautiful place and you can spend the day making telemark turns on the slopes nearby.

Hazards Ski carefully in Molar Meadows and follows avalanche safety precautions.

Options For the well prepared and adventurous ski tourer it is possible to ski above Molar Meadows and up to North Molar Pass. Descent down the other side via Fish Lakes takes you into the Pipestone River which can be followed back to Lake Louise or you can ski via Skoki towards points south. These tours would take several days and require winter camping.

Photo Leon Kubbernus

Molar Meadows

Access Parking is at the plowed parking lot near the Mosquito Creek Hostel which is located on the left (west) side of the road, about 24 km north along the Icefields Parkway (Highway #93) from its junction with the Trans-Canada Highway (Highway #1). The parking lot is just before the highway crosses Mosquito Creek. Additional parking can be found across the bridge, on the west side of the road, in the Mosquito Creek Campground.

From the parking lot walk across the road and across the bridge. Put your skis on and locate the trail which starts very near to the bridge. To begin with, it climbs steeply through the trees up the hillside above. The trail eases off very quickly then climbs at a more gradual angle through the forest until it descends to the right down to the creek after about 3 km. The trail to this point is easy to follow.

Once the trail reaches the creek it follows the valley floor until after the valley curves to the right. At this point the trail crosses the creek and follows the right side of the creek bed for some distance, climbing more steadily until it eventually descends into the creek bed again. Finally the trail climbs up to the left to Molar Meadows. A moderately steep climb of about 120 vertical-m takes you to the edge of the trees and out into the meadows. The trail can be hard to follow during this last climb up to Molar Meadows but it is possible to switchback where necessary through the trees.

Dolomite Pass

Photo Alf Skrastins

94 DOLOMITE PEAK CIRCUIT
Ski touring/ski mountaineering

Grade Intermediate/advanced
Distance 19 km
Time This is a full day trip for most parties
Height gain 650 m
Max elevation 2,500 m
Map Hector Lake 82 N/9

The Dolomite Peak circuit is one of the finest ski tours in the Canadian Rockies. The route reaches above timberline, across high alpine snowfields, for much of the way, and the beauty of this trip is extraordinary. The early part of the trip up Helen Creek is straightforward, and the final run down Mosquito Creek is a fast and exhilarating way to end the day. The middle section of the trip high above timberline is beautiful, but in poor visibility can offer difficult route finding.

Hazards Route finding on this tour can be very tricky in poor visibility. It would be very easy to get lost in a whiteout.

There also is significant avalanche potential on this tour so caution and some knowledge are essential.

Much of the tour is above timberline so adequate protection against the elements and for emergency is a must.

Options Normally this is done as a one day tour. It could however be continued, over several days, up Mosquito Creek, over North Molar Pass and down the Pipestone River to Lake Louise (for the hardy and adventurous only).

Access Because this tour does not return to the same point on the highway as the departure point, two parking spots are described. It is customary to begin the trip at the Helen Creek trailhead, just north of the Helen Creek bridge, 29 km north on the Icefields Parkway (Highway #93). The trip finishes at the Mosquito Creek trailhead, just north of the Mosquito Creek bridge, 24 km north on the Icefields Parkway (Highway #93). Leave a car for your return as it is no fun to walk or hitch hike back up the road, at the end of the day. Normally there is a parking lot plowed at the Helen Creek trailhead and the parking lot for the Mosquito Creek Hostel is used at the Mosquito Creek trailhead. (There is also plenty of room for cars at the Mosquito Creek Campground, just across the road from the trailhead.)

The trail climbs steeply above the Helen Creek trailhead for about 100 m (vertical gain), until it reaches the crest of a ridge. The angle eases here and the trail continues north-west along the crest of the ridge for a short distance. Then it descends to the right to the creek bed. Cross the creek on a bridge and continue along the opposite bank. The trail along here crosses large avalanche paths and cuts through forests in between. After about 1.5 km the trail begins to climb, then crosses the creek again and works its way up through the trees to an elevation of about 2,150 m, where the trees begin to thin out. (As an alternative you can ascend an open trough at the base of a steep hillside just to the left of the trail — avalanche danger!).

From here there is no clearly defined trail and you simply work your way up and to the right over some steep rolls, and then over a rocky shoulder to gain a broad pass at about 2,400 m (avalanche hazard!). A gentle descent now takes you down to Katherine Lake.

Cross the lake, then continue on through Dolomite Pass itself (a huge boulder on the right makes a good wind break for a lunch stop). From here descend about 70 m (vertical loss) down the drainage to the north-east, until it is possible to begin turning back right (south-east) towards East Dolomite Pass which can now be seen about 2 km distant. It is not advised to cut this corner along a high line as some steep and potentially dangerous avalanche slopes will be encountered. The climb from this point to the pass, about 150 m (vertical gain), is straightforward.

From the pass descend the slope on the south-east side with some caution, then follow the drainage down to a large open area. Carry on descending the drainage until you reach a point where the right bank is threatened by slopes above. During periods of unstable snow it would be adviseable to continue, for a short distance, down the sparsely treed slopes on the left bank away from the danger. At an elevation of about 2,150 m cross the creek on a large bench to gain the right bank. Continue descending and traversing in a southerly direction (i.e. trending right). Some glades can be found through the trees, where you can get in a few turns. Do not descend directly down the creek bed because steep banks can pose a serious avalanche threat.

At the bottom, just before reaching Mosquito Creek, you will find the trail which is followed to the right back down to the Icefields Parkway.

Dolomite Pass circuit   Photo Alf Skrastins

On top of the headwall below Helen Lake looking over the Icefields Parkway to Crowfoot Pass

95 KATHERINE LAKE/HELEN LAKE CIRCUIT Ski touring

Grade Advanced
Distance 8 km return
Time 4-6 hrs
Height gain 650 m
Max elevation 2,470 m
Map Hector Lake 82 N/9

An outstanding trip which takes you high above timberline into the alpine area. The trip requires good weather and good visibility. There is some avalanche hazard so be prepared. This trip is really a variation of the Dolomite Peak circuit (see page 149).

Hazards You are in high alpine terrain far from shelter and should be prepared for emergencies. You are in potential avalanche terrain and should be knowledgeable of safety procedures.

Access Park at the cleared area on the north side of the Icefields Parkway (Highway #93), just across the bridge over Helen Creek, about 29 km north of the junction with the Trans-Canada Highway (Highway #1).

Follow the Dolomite Peak Circuit as far as Katherine Lake. From here ski easily to the west for about 1 km, up open slopes to gain the pass located immediately south of Cirque Peak. Descend the south-west slopes of the pass down to Helen Lake. At the top, the slopes are steep, and you should proceed with caution. Stay to the right on your descent as there are some small cliffs below on the left. Descend to the lake and cross it. From the south end contour at about the same level around to the left, through a notch and into a draw. Descend this draw or traverse a little further to your left and you will find your up-track. It is also possible to descend directly down Helen Creek from Helen Lake, but the creek can be a little awkward at the point where it reaches timberline, and there is also some avalanche danger.

151

96 CROWFOOT PASS

Ski touring

Grade Intermediate
Distance 10 km return
Time 5-6 hrs
Height gain 430 m
Max elevation 2,350 m
Map Hector Lake 82 N/9

The tour to Crowfoot Pass is one of the finest in the Rockies! It usually has lots of snow and there are excellent views down the Bow Valley to Mount Temple, Pilot Mountain and farther south to the tower of Mount Assiniboine. The sun lingers in the pass long into the afternoon

Hazards There is some avalanche danger skiing up the drainage towards the pass and a fatality has occurred here. Although the hillsides are small, slides are sufficiently large to be deadly.

Access Park at the Crowfoot Glacier viewpoint, located on the left (west) side of the Icefields Parkway (Highway #93) about 32 km north from the junction with the Trans-Canada Highway (Highway #1). This parking area is 3 km south of the turnoff into Num-ti-jah Lodge.

From the parking lot head straight over the snow bank and down a short steep hill to the trees below. This hill is about 20 m high and may require several kick turns. Once into the trees head out towards the valley bottom for a short distance, to reach the flats at the end of Bow Lake. Turn left and ski down the flats. After about 0.5 km there is a narrowing, then it opens up again. Follow the flats for another 1 km to where they jog to the right. Follow the jog, then turn left down the river again. The view of the surrounding peaks is outstanding.

Continue until the flats pinch off and the river begins, then ski up onto the right bank and proceed through the trees. The travelling is excellent along here and after about 1 km through the open forest you reach the drainage coming down from Crowfoot Pass. At this point it is a small canyon which is easily entered.

Put on your skins here and head straight up the creek. The travelling is easy and the angle is reasonable. Good snow cover is necessary so it is best to do this tour a little later in the season. The creek gains about 100 m (vertical) and approaches a cliff looming above through the trees. At this point the creek begins to curve to the left. Continue up the creek for some distance — it is usually quite distinct and easy to follow. At one point the creek levels out for a short distance but soon it begins to climb again through open trees, until it breaks out of the trees completely. Continue straight ahead up the drainage to the pass where there is a nice outcrop of quartzite to sit on.

Continuing down to Hector Lake is possible, but if you wish to make the traverse it is best to start at Hector Lake so as to ascend the steep, difficult section.

The Ramp Route

Many skiers take an alternative route to Crowfoot Pass which follows the obvious ramp high above the trees. To reach this ramp, follow the regular route along the river flats. Just before the end of the flats (GR 396222) ski up the drainage to the right to an open area below the Crowfoot Glacier. Ascend a narrow drainage to the southeast which climbs through the trees to the large ramp which is easily followed to Crowfoot Pass.

Following the Ramp Route to Crowfoot Pass

97 BOW SUMMIT
Ski touring/telemark skiing

Grade Easy/intermediate

Distance 1 km to the base of the ski slope

Time You can spend a few hours or the whole day skiing in this area

Height gain The most popular slope is about 100 m high

From the parking lot to the highest area normally skied is about 330 m.

Max elevation 2,250 m on the bench above the most popular slope 2,410 high in upper bowl

Maps Hector Lake 82 N/9
Blaeberry River 82 N/10

Bow Summit has long been a popular destination for ski touring and for making turns as well. On a sunny day in the spring it is a magical spot. There is lots of snow, the slopes are only a short distance from the car and the views are excellent. Note: the area may be closed to skiers until there is sufficient snow to prevent damage to the fragile alpine vegetation.

Hazards Bow summit has been the scene of avalanche fatalities in the past. Although the slopes are not large, they should be treated with caution.

Access Turn west off the Icefields Parkway at Bow Pass, 40 km north of the Trans-Canada Highway (Highway #1), and drive up the road towards the Peyto Lake viewpoint. In the winter the road is only plowed a short distance, to a parking lot.

From the parking lot, ski up the road several hundred metres, then angle out left to the base of a prominent hill. This hill is one of the most popular attractions at Bow Summit, and although it is not large, many hours can be spent climbing up and skiing back down. It is highly recommended.

There is also, a bowl higher up, where some good turns can be made. To reach this bowl, ski along the bench which runs on the top of the hill (there is an old road here). The trail (road) crosses a creek drainage after about 1 km and just beyond this turns up into a wild alpine cirque. Some of the slopes here are skiable but are potentially hazardous.

On rare occasions the snow is good high on the windswept shoulder above the Peyto Lake viewpoint. This is a forepeak of Mount Jimmy Simpson and it can at times offer a long and enjoyable run.

There are excellent opportunities for short tours at Bow Summit. Ski from the car park up the road for a few hundred metres, then angle out left below the prominent hill. Continue along the base of the hill until you reach the creek drainage, then work your way back, taking a lower line if you choose. This is a nice spot to introduce someone to the pleasures of ski touring.

From the parking lot you can ski up the road to the Peyto Lake viewpoint, then continue further up the hill on the old fire road. This road climbs in a southerly direction until it reaches the bench along the top of the prominent hill. Ski south along this bench for about 1 km to a point where the road crosses a creek drainage. You can ski a bit further along and have an outstanding view of the Bow Valley.

98 GLACIER LAKE

Grade Intermediate
Distance 14 km return
Time This is a moderate day tour
Height gain 250 m if following trail
50 m if following river
Max elevation 1,670 m following trail
1420 m following river
Map Mistaya Lake 82 N/15

This trail can offer a wonderful ski tour in a wilderness setting. However the valley is low in elevation and receives little snowfall. Consequently, the river flats are often blown bare of snow and when spring comes the snow disappears quickly.

Access Park at the plowed parking area on the southwest side of the Icefield Parkway about 1 km north of the David Thompson Highway turn-off.

The trail starts from the southwest corner of the parking lot and after heading south for a short distance, turns west and continues for about 1 km to a bridge over the North Sasketchewan River. Cross the bridge, then continue west until the trail descends to the flats of the Howse River.

From here follow the river flats for 5 km. At GR 125519, turn north up the creek which drains Glacier Lake. If the creek is open and it is not possible to ski up a short little canyon, climb up on the right bank and find the trail which is followed to Glacier Lake.

Instead of following the river flats it is also possible to follow the summer trail which works its way into the forest and climbs 250 vertical metres over a hill before descending steeply to the lake.

Spring ski touring at Glacier Lake

Photo Alf Skrastins

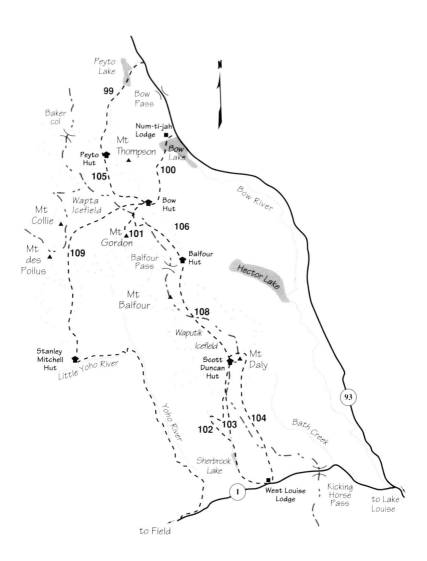

WAPTA ICEFIELDS

The Wapta Icefields has become, for good reason, the most popular area for ski mountaineering in Canada. The mountains are spectacular, the glaciers are extensive and relatively safe, access from the highways is easy and there is now an excellent system of huts operated by the Alpine Club of Canada.

The Wapta Icefields are really composed of two distinct icefields — the Wapta and the Waputik. They are normally both referred to simply as "The Wapta". This area comprises about 5-600 km² of which about 150 km² is actually covered by glaciers and icefields.

On a sunny day it is a joy to explore the icefields. You can make ski ascents of the surrounding peaks and there are enough different variations of the 'Wapta Traverse' to keep the ardent ski mountaineer busy for a number of years. There are also many fine slopes to satisfy the telemark skiers in the crowd.

The area is included in this book to help you in the transition from valley trail skiing to high alpine ski mountaineering.

The Wapta Icefields is normally the location where ski tourers make this exciting step to high mountain adventure.

Although the Wapta Icefields has come to be regarded as pretty tame adventure, one should not take lightly the dangers that are waiting for the unsuspecting. In the winter time, with extremely cold temperatures or violent storms, sheer survival can become an issue even for the most experienced ski mountaineer. With reduced visibility, navigation becomes a challenge for all of us and getting lost, with limited survival gear, is very serious indeed. Avalanche terrain and numerous crevasses require good route finding skills and experience in roped glacier travel. In the event of an emergency you should be prepared to locate and dig up the victim or extricate them from a crevasse. It is recommended that before venturing out onto these icefields you become trained in all the necessary skills, and for your first few trips travel in the company of an experienced ski mountaineer or even a guide.

A 13 photo panorama from the top of Mount Gordon.

Photo Gillean Daffern

There are four huts on the Wapta Icefields and a fifth hut in the Yoho Valley nearby (Stanley Mitchell Hut). It is worth remembering that in poor visibility it may be very difficult to locate some of these huts. You should be prepared to dig an emergency shelter and bivouac.

Bow Hut

Map 82 N/9 Hector Lake
Location NE of St. Nicholas Peak, on rocky ridge overlooking the main drainage leading down to Bow Lake GR 355203
Reservations Alpine Club of Canada
Capacity 30
Facilities Two buildings separated by vestibule. Foamies. Wood stove, Coleman stoves & lanterns and utensils in common room.
Water Snowmelt or drainage to south
Notes Common room locked when custodian not present. Combination required

Peyto Hut
(Peter & Catherine Whyte Hut)

Map 82 N/9 Hector Lake
82 N/10 Blaeberry River
Location On moraine below NW ridge of Mt. Thompson GR 314237
Reservations Alpine Club of Canada
Capacity 18
Facilities Foamies, Coleman stoves & lanterns, dishes
Water Snowmelt

Balfour Hut

Map 82 N/9 Hector Lake
Location West end of low, rocky hills which parallel the toe of the Vulture Glacier GR 375157
Reservations Alpine Club of Canada
Capacity 18
Facilities Foamies, Coleman stoves & lanterns, dishes
Water Snowmelt
Notes Difficult to find in a whiteout

The Wapta Icefields is covered by 4 topographical maps and this has been a nuisance in the past. However it is now possible to purchase one map which covers the entire region. It is printed on waterproof, tearproof and erasable paper, and on the back has aerial photographs showing the major routes. It is recommended that you purchase the map and use it as a companion to this guide book. It is referred to as "Touring the Wapta Icefields" and was prepared by Murray Toft.

Scott Duncan Hut

Map 82 N/9 Hector Lake
Location On a bench at the bottom end of the NW ridge of Mt. Daly
GR 417084
Reservations Alpine Club of Canada
Capacity 12
Facilities Foamies, Coleman stoves & lanterns, dishes
Water Snowmelt
Notes May be difficult to find in whiteout conditions

The Wapta Icefields are normally traversed in one of four ways, with some minor variations. These are:

- The Complete Traverse from Peyto Lake to Sherbrooke Lake (there are three possible exits).

- The Partial Traverse from Bow Lake to Sherbrooke Lake (three exits).

- The Mini Traverse from Bow Lake to Peyto Lake.

- The East to West Traverse from Bow Lake to the Little Yoho Valley.

All of the necessary components of these traverses are covered in this section.

99 PEYTO GLACIER APPROACH

Ski mountaineering

Grade Intermediate
Distance 10 km one way to the Peter &
Catherine Whyte Hut
Time 5-8 hrs
Height gain 550 m
Max elevation 2,480 m
Map Blaeberry River 82 N/10 or
Touring the Wapta Icefields (Murray Toft)

A very pleasant way to access the Wapta
Icefields. Depending on conditions, the
weight of your pack and your fitness and
skill level, it can be a either a half day trip
or a marathon march. The route is generally easy to follow.

Facilities The route passes by a glaciology research camp with a small wooden
cabin which has been known to provide
shelter in an emergency.

Hazards There are slopes on this tour that
could slide in certain conditions. Caution
should be exercised when circling around
the crevasses on the upper end of the
Peyto Glacier. The rope should be worn
when near these crevasses.

Options From the Peyto (Whyte) Hut the
traverse continues across to the Bow Hut
or to Balfour Hut. You can also ski to Baker/
Trapper col and descend to Mistaya
Lodge in Wildcat Basin

Access There is a plowed parking lot on
the west side of the Icefields Parkway
(Highway #93), about 2 kilometres down
the hill, north of Bow Pass.

From the parking lot find an old road
which is just a short distance away. It is
easiest to head north along the highway
for about 50 m then descend west down
the bank for another few metres to hit the
road. Descend the road for several hundred metres keeping your eyes open for

a trail which takes off through the woods to your left — usually there is a piece of flagging to mark the spot. Follow the trail as it rolls up and down through the woods for about 1 km to Peyto Lake. This section can be tricky and sometimes it is best to do it with your skins on!

Ski across the lake heading for the Peyto Creek drainage on the other side. Be certain that the lake is adequately frozen and snow covered.

Once you reach the gravel flats on the far side of the lake, head towards the gorge. At the first narrows, only a short distance from the lake, it is often necessary to climb up onto the left bank for a short distance, to avoid open water. Continue beyond this point along the gravel flats for about 0.5 km. When the stream begins to curve gradually to the left towards a narrowing gorge, climb up the slopes above on the right towards a large and prominent moraine that can be seen higher up.

Climb up into a protected little basin behind the moraine then continue up onto the moraine itself. Take off your skis and climb along the crest of the moraine until it butts up against the hillside. Climb the hillside (use caution — avalanche potential!) then continue on foot for another 75 m (vertical) until the angle lays back. Here you can usually put your skis back on and traverse to the Peyto Glacier passing by the Glaciology Research Camp.

Ascend the glacier in a south-west direction, aiming for the groove in the slope at the end. Ski up the groove staying well to the right of the crevasses. Continue until safely above them then circle back to the east. The Peyto Hut is directly to the east on a moraine knoll, below the slopes of Mount Thompson. The precise grid reference for the hut is 314237.

100 BOW HUT APPROACH

Ski mountaineering

Grade Intermediate
Distance 8 km one way to the Bow Hut
Time 4-6 hrs
Height gain 390 m
Max elevation 2,330 m
Maps Hector Lake 82 N/9
Blaeberry River 82 N/10 or
Touring the Wapta Icefields (Murray Toft)

The most popular and the easiest access onto the Wapta Icefields takes you to the Bow Hut which is the largest and most luxurious of the Wapta huts. The trail is usually broken and easy to follow, however, if there has been a heavy snowfall and you are unfamiliar with the route, it can be much more challenging.

Facilities There is a large lodge on the edge of Bow Lake (Num-ti-jah Lodge), but it is closed in the winter.

Hazards There is potential avalanche hazard on this route, particularly along the canyon, on the hillside above the canyon before entering the cirque, and then on the steep hillside below the Bow hut. Use caution!

Options This route ties in with all routes on the Wapta Icefields.

Access There is a large parking lot on the west side of the Icefields Parkway (Highway #93), about 6 km south of Bow Pass at the north end of Bow Lake at the turn off to Num-ti-jah Lodge.

From the parking lot ski gently down alongside the road, towards the lake. Just beyond Num-ti-jah Lodge head out across the lake (be certain that it is well frozen!). Cross the lake and ski across the gravel flats on the far side. Continue up the stream for about 0.5 km. until you

can see that a narrow gorge is coming up ahead. At this point, angle left and ski up through the trees on a trail which climbs gradually up the small side drainage until it bumps up against a steep mountainside complete with avalanche paths. Climb a short hill up to the right, traverse around the corner (west) then descend into the main drainage again. You have now circumvented the gorge.

Follow the creek, heading almost due south, up a narrow canyon. The walls above are steep and overhung with snow — you should not linger here. In the late spring the creek may be open in places and present difficulties. After about 1 km the way ahead becomes difficult and the route climbs up to the left, into the trees on the east bank. Continue through broken forest, climbing gradually, until the trees end and the route breaks out into a large open cirque.

Cross the cirque in a southerly direction, climbing gradually, and contour around to the base of the steep hillside, on your right. It is critical that you pick the right point to climb this hillside as there is the potential for avalanching. The route normally climbs a shallow groove up the left end of the hillside, with a series of traverses and kick turns, until it can break out over the right edge of the groove, onto the slopes above. Continue up these slopes to the hut which is about 100 vertical m higher up. The precise grid reference for the Bow hut is 355203. Please note that this is a new hut, built in 1989, and any information of an earlier date will give an incorrect hut location.

101 ASCENT OF MOUNT GORDON
Ski mountaineering

Grade Easy/intermediate
Distance 12 km return
Time An easy day trip
Height gain 850 m
Max elevation 3,200 m
Map Hector Lake 82 N/9
Blaeberry River 82 N/10 or
Touring the Wapta Icefields (Murray Toft)

One of the most scenic ski ascents on the Wapta. It is possible to see almost the whole icefields stretched out before you. The 13-page panorama above was taken from the summit of Mount Gordon. The ascent is straightforward in good weather, but can be tricky if visibility is poor.

Access The tour begins at the Bow Hut.

From the hut climb up the hill in a north-west direction. Climb the toe of the glacier in long switchbacks ascending west underneath the impressive north face of Mount Saint Nicholas. Continue angling south-west towards Mount Gordon. The route climbs easily to the right hand shoulder, passing a deep wind scoop below the outcropping rocks, then

works up and left to the ridge. Once on the ridge the angle eases and the summit is only a short distance away. Return by the same route — descending the ridge towards Vulture Col (although tempting) gets you into some very steep, avalanche-prone terrain.

102 THE SCHIESSER/LOMAS ROUTE

Ski mountaineering

Grade Intermediate in the upper section. Below Sherbrooke Lake where the trail descends through the trees to Wapta Lodge, the skiing is more difficult
Distance 12 km to Wapta Lodge
Time About half a day
Height loss 1,060 m
Max elevation 2,710 m
Maps Hector Lake 82 N/9
Lake Louise 82 N/8

The most pleasant and the safest descent from the Scott Duncan hut to the Trans Canada Highway (Highway #1) at Wapta Lodge. In reasonable visibility it is easy to follow. However, if you are unfamiliar with the terrain it can, in a whiteout, require navigational skills in the upper section.

From the Scott Duncan Hut descend to the glacier below. Traverse south towards the pass between Mount Niles and Mount Daly. Ski around the right side of the small peak in the centre of the pass and descend a slope which takes you out onto a broad bench high above the Niles Creek Valley. Descend along the bench for almost 2 km. Very near the end of the bench the route swings to the right and begins to curve back around the shoulder, towards the west. Be sure to swing right around to the west so that

you are clearly above the upper Sherbrooke Creek. Turn left, descend open slopes, then ski through the trees into upper Sherbrooke Creek. Continue directly down the creek bed to the flat, open meadows where it joins Niles Creek. There are a few short steep sections in this creek bed, but they are not too difficult to negotiate.

After you reach the junction of Niles Creek with Sherbrooke Creek, continue to the brow of a steep hill not far above Sherbrooke Lake. It is best to traverse

out to the right, through the trees, until you reach an open slope which descends to more gentle terrain. Ski down to the lake and cross it (be sure the lake is well frozen).

At the far end of the lake, continue above the left bank of Sherbrooke Creek for a short distance then search up to the left to find the trail. From here the trail turns east and heads down and around the shoulder of Paget Peak to Wapta Lodge. This section of the trail is steep and challenging —it is the most difficult part of the descent, particularly if you have a large pack and the trail is icy or rutted.

103 THE TRADITIONAL SHERBROOKE LAKE EXIT

The Scott Duncan hut was built to enable parties skiing the Wapta Traverse to get an early start and descend while conditions were still well frozen. There are several ways to descend to the Trans-Canada Highway (Highway #1) from the Scott Duncan Hut. The recommended route is the Schiesser/Lomas Route described on the previous page. The traditional exit down Niles Creek is dangerous and is not recommended unless the snowpack is very stable. The route goes through the pass between Mount Niles and Mount Daly, stays on the left side of the little peak in the pass then descends the Niles Creek drainage.

104 THE BATH GLACIER EXIT

The exit via the Bath Glacier offers an interesting variation and in good conditions can be a viable alternative to the Schiesser/Lomas Route. There is one very steep slope of about 300 m which you should feel very certain of before descending!

From the Scott Duncan hut head back to the north and curve around to the right (east). Ski through a gentle pass on the north-east side of Mount Daly and out onto the Bath Glacier. From here the route continues south across the Bath Glacier, high above the valley. The route is generally safe along here, but there are a few sections where the slope is steep

enough to be dangerous in certain conditions. After about 8 km the route climbs to a pass between Paget Peak and Mount Bosworth. The descent of the south side of this pass is extremely steep and should be undertaken only if you are absolutely certain of the safety of the slope. From the bottom of the hill continue south down the valley. After about 1 km swing right above the upper edge of the trees and work your way over to a large avalanche path which descends from Paget Peak. Ski down this slope then continue through the trees to Wapta Lodge, almost directly below.

105 PEYTO (WHYTE) HUT TO BOW HUT — Ski mountaineering

Grade Easy
Distance 6 km
Time 3-4 hrs
Height gain 150 m to Rhonda/
Thompson col
Height loss 300 m to Bow Hut
Max elevation 2,670 m
Map Hector Lake 82 N/9
Blaeberry River 82 N/10 or
Touring the Wapta Icefields (Murray Toft)

This connection is straightforward in good visibility, but can be a challenging route-finding problem in whiteout conditions.

From the Peyto hut ski south-east to the broad pass between Mount Thompson and Mount Rhonda. Continue south-east, traversing so as to maintain your height. The most common mistake here is to lose elevation too quickly, and be drawn down into the Bow Glacier drain-age. Stay high above the Bow Glacier and traverse through a little notch just above a small unnamed peak (GR 343209). From here descend south-east to the Bow Hut (GR 355203). Watch out for crevasses on this descent.

106 BOW HUT TO BALFOUR HUT — Ski Mountaineering

Grade Easy
Distance 7 km
Time 3-4 hrs
Height gain 580 m to Olive/St. Nicholas col
Height loss 430 m to Balfour Hut
Max elevation 2,930 m

Maps Hector Lake 82 N/9
Blaeberry River 82 N/10 or
Touring the Wapta Icefields (Murray Toft)

This connection is also very straightforward in good visibility but can be challenging in a whiteout.

From the Bow Hut climb up the hill in a north-west direction. Once you reach the glacier, the direction of travel becomes westerly. Climb up beneath the impressive north face of Mount Saint Nicholas and work your way around the west side of the peak, until you can ski up into the pass between Mount Olive and Mount Saint Nicholas.

From the pass, head east out onto the Vulture Glacier, then curve around to the right (there are a few crevasses to your right here, so be sure to take a wide enough arc). Continue descending in a south-east direction to the hut. There are numerous crevasses at the toe of the gla-

cier, directly in your path, so it is best to pick a line which takes you along the east side of the glacier, then curve around to the south at the very end.

In poor visibility the best tactic is to ski straight east from the Olive/St. Nicholas Col, until the escarpment which runs all along the east side of the Vulture glacier, can be seen. Then descend the glacier, using this escarpment as a handrail (it usually shows up through the mist as assorted cliffs and scree slopes). As you near the end of the glacier, the escarpment can actually be followed to the right (south) to the hut (GR 375157).

107 PEYTO HUT TO BALFOUR HUT — Ski mountaineering

Grade Intermediate
Distance 7 km
Time 5-6 hrs
Height gain 430 m to St. Nicholas/Olive col
Height loss 430 m to Balfour Hut
Max elevation 2,930 m
Map Hector Lake 82 N/9
Blaeberry River 82 N/10 or
Touring the Wapta Icefields (Murray Toft)

This tour offers the essence of icefields touring. It stays high and traverses across "endless" expanses of snow. In some conditions, the descent to the Balfour Hut can be fast and fun!

Many people ski directly from the Peyto (Whyte) Hut to the Balfour Hut. The trip is straightforward when there is good visibility. Refer to page 168 and 169 for the route. These two tours can be connected easily — instead of descending to the Bow Hut, when traversing from the Peyto (Whyte) Hut, simply continue across the top of the icefield to the Nicholas/Olive col and follow the usual route to the Balfour Hut.

Opposite: Daly Glacier and Mount Daly (right) from the south ridge of Mount Balfour. The Scott Duncan Hut is situated a little above the glacier on the rocky ridge of Mount Daly descending towards the camera

108 BALFOUR HUT TO SCOTT DUNCAN HUT Ski mountaineering

Grade Intermediate
Distance 10 km
Time 5-6 hrs
Height gain 520 m to Balfour High Col
Height loss 320 m to Scott Duncan Hut
Max elevation 3,020 m
Map Hector Lake 82 N/9
Touring the Wapta Icefields (Murray Toft)

This is one of the most challenging sections of ski mountaineering on the Wapta Icefields. It should only be undertaken in good visibility, as it is very hard to navigate by map and compass in the complicated terrain below Mount Balfour.

From the Balfour Hut, descend a short distance then ski across the flats in a southerly direction to reach the lower slopes of Mount Balfour. Ascend the slope and ski out onto the glacier, heading towards a rock cliff which sticks up prominently in the middle of the glacier. High above you on the right is another bench which is sometimes used as a route up the glacier. As you approach the rock cliff, the trail turns to the right and climbs steeply up a narrow ramp. The angle then eases off and it is possible to continue across for 1 km to the Balfour High Col. This route is subject to icefall from the north-east face of Mount Balfour and you should travel as quickly as possible, without rest stops!

From the high col the route descends in a south-east direction, almost directly for Mount Daly. There are a few crevasses across here, and one should still ski with caution. The hut is located at the base of the spur which descends in a north-west direction from Mount Daly (GR 417084)

Photo Rudi Setz Collection

171

109 THE YOHO TRAVERSE
Ski mountaineering

Grade Intermediate/advanced
Distance 20 km
Time This is a very full day tour
Height gain 820 m
Height loss 1,100 m
Max elevation 2,900 m
Map Hector Lake 82 N/9
Blaeberry River 82 N/10 or
Touring the Wapta Icefields (Murray Toft)

From the Bow Hut it is possible to traverse to the Stanley Mitchell Hut in the Little Yoho Valley. Most parties will find this a very long day — so be prepared to bivouac if necessary. There are several slopes which could provide serious avalanche potential in certain conditions, so it is best to wait for a period of high stability before attempting this trip. Routefinding in whiteout conditions on this tour is extremely challenging.

From the Bow Hut climb up the hill and head west out onto the icefields. Ski west to the broad open pass between Mount Rhonda and Mount Gordon. From the pass descend gently for several kilometres and ski across to the broken section of glacier descending south-east from Mount Collie. This is the first challenge of the trip — to find a way through these crevasses.

Once above them head south-west to the top of a very steep slope, above the des Poilus Glacier. This is the second challenge of the tour — to descend this slope safely. In certain conditions it may not be possible.

Cross the Des Poilus Glacier heading straight south. People often camp in this area on their night out, rather than stay at the Bow Hut. The third challenge is to ascend the steep ramp, which works its way from right to left under Isolated Peak, up to Isolated Col. Caution is required here as the slope is steeper than it appears.

The south side of Isolated Col (the notch in the centre of the picture) The steep portion of the slope directly below the col is prone to avalanche.

The descent of the south facing slope of Isolated Col is also steep and requires caution. Continue down the valley, then descend steeply through the trees to the Stanley Mitchell Hut which is located on the edge of a meadow, along the banks of the Little Yoho River. There is a trail through the forest which descends to the hut. To ski out to the highway refer to Little Yoho Valley on pages 135 & 136

Photo Leon Kubbernus

ICEFIELDS PARKWAY NORTH

The northern section of the Icefields Parkway (Highway #93) stretches from the David Thompson Highway at Saskatchewan River Crossing to Jasper. It is a remote highway and the section from the bottom of the "Big Bend" over Sunwapta Pass and past the foot of the Athabasca Glacier is subject to avalanches and whiteout conditions. There are no service stations, and few signs of civilization. Apart from a few hostels and campgrounds there is nowhere to stay. It is a bit of a backcountry experience to drive this road in winter. Be certain that you have enough gas to reach your destination and return to a service station, before you start.

The highway itself is an excellent road. It is well maintained and in good weather virtually any driver in any type of automobile can handle it. However during the big storms, when the snow comes, driving conditions can be very difficult. The highway is occasionally closed while avalanche slopes are bombed and snowplows do their work.

Be certain that you are prepared to deal with cold weather and snow. This includes a strong battery, good snow tires, jumper cables, survival gear and a shovel. Starting your car after a day or two of skiing in extremely cold weather can be a major problem. If you come from a warmer climate you may want to changer to a thinner oil and get a winter tune-up before you start.

Accommodation There are Hostels located at Ramparts Creek, Hilda Creek, and Athabasca Falls. Some of these have saunas which can be a real treat on a starlit winters night after a hard tour. In an emergency there are enclosed picnic shelters at the Columbia Icefields Campground, located just south of the Information Centre.

In emergency There are two warden stations, one at Saskatchewan River Crossing and the other at Poboktan Creek. There is a highway maintenance camp at Tangle Creek, just north of the exposed Athabasca Glacier area. There are pay telephones along the road at the tourist complex at Saskatchewan River Crossing, the tourist centre at the Columbia Icefields, at Poboktan Creek and at the Valley of the Five Lakes trailhead.

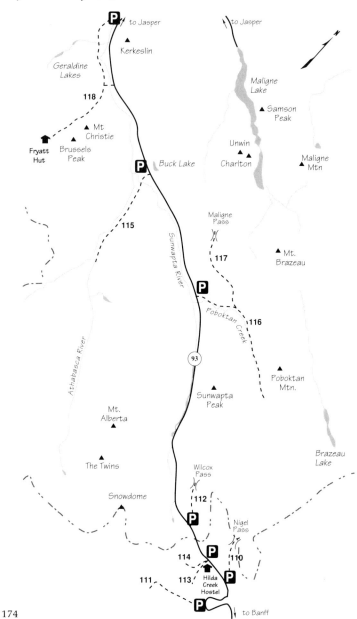

to Jasper

Kerkeslin

Geraldine Lakes

to Jasper

Maligne Lake

▲ Samson Peak

118

Fryatt Hut

▲ Mt Christie

Brussels Peak ▲

Unwin

Charlton ▲ ▲

▲ Maligne Mtn

Buck Lake

Maligne Pass

115

Sunwapta River

117

▲ Mt. Brazeau

Poboktan Creek

116

93

▲ Poboktan Mtn.

Athabasca River

Mt. Alberta ▲

▲ Sunwapta Peak

The Twins ▲

Brazeau Lake

Wilcox Pass

Snowdome

112

Nigel Pass

114

110

113

Hilda Creek Hostel

111

to Banff

110 NIGEL PASS

Ski touring

Grade Intermediate
Distance 16 km return
Time 4-6 hrs
Height gain 280 m
Max elevation 2,120 m
Map Columbia Icefield 83 C/3

A very pleasant tour through spectacular mountain terrain. It is varied and interesting, but not too difficult. The valley gets a lot of sun as it is oriented north/south. The trip offers an easy day tour with lots of time for lunch breaks and exploring around.

Hazards Approach the pass with caution as cornices can overhang the cliffs above the Brazeau River.

Options To continue over the pass and down the Brazeau River it is necessary to climb up to your right (east), about 1 km before the pass. Gain about 100 m elevation and cross into the Brazeau drainage which is followed back down to your left (west).

Access Park in the cleared parking area at the Nigel Pass trailhead on the east side of the Icefields Parkway (Highway #93) about 7 km south of Sunwapta Pass.

From the parking lot ski straight ahead, climbing gently up the old road. (Do not follow the trail which is off to the right, across the stream.) After about 1.5 km, where a large avalanche path descends from the left, cut right into the trees for a short distance, to the old Camp Parker Warden Cabin. Ski past the cabin on the left side, and angle down through open timber to Nigel Creek (a steep but short descent). Follow the creek bed for another kilometre until the sides begin to pinch in. It is possible to continue up the creek if there is lots of snow, but it is better to climb up onto the right bank and gain a bench about 50 m higher up. There is a trail in the woods. Follow the trail along this bench for 1 km until the terrain starts to open up and the canyon

disappears. Continue easily, just above the creek, for another kilometre until it is necessary to climb up the right bank again to pass a rocky canyon below. Soon the trail descends to the creek and the way ahead is clear. Follow the drainage straight ahead, climbing gradually through meadows and clumps of trees, up to Nigel Pass. If you stay to the left and ski to the lowest point in the pass, you will end up looking down a very steep cliff into the headwaters of the Brazeau River.

Of interest Joe Weiss was a Swiss adventurer who lived in Jasper. Between 1929 and 1933 he undertook five major ski adventures in the Rockies. On two occasions he and his group skied from Jasper to Lake Louise. They crossed Nigel Pass en route and spent a few days resting at the Camp Parker Warden Cabin. Joe is 96 years old and lives in Edmonton.

Looking down onto the Saskatchewan Glacier from the Castleguard Meadows   Photo Alf Skrastins

111 CASTLEGUARD MEADOWS

Ski mountaineering

Grade Easy
Distance 28 km return
Time Most parties would do this tour in two days, camping overnight at Castleguard Meadows.
Height gain 580 m
Max elevation 2,240 m
Map Columbia Icefield 83 C/3

An ideal trip for an introduction to glacier travel and overnight mountain camping. The scenery is magnificent, the climb is gentle and the glacier is reasonably safe.

Hazards This is a high mountain, glacier tour and you should be prepared to deal with extremely inclement weather, glacier travel, crevasse rescue, avalanche hazard and whiteout navigation.

Options The Saskatchewan Glacier can be used as an approach route to the Columbia Icefields.

From the Castleguard Meadows you can continue over into the Castleguard River then on to the Alexandra River, which is followed back to the highway.

Access There is a large, plowed parking area at the "big bend" on the Icefields Parkway (Highway #93), located at the bottom of the big hill, 12 km south of Sunwapta Pass.

From the parking lot, angle south a short distance, crossing the creek and crossing the open flats to the trees (note that the highway is no longer as marked on edition 1 of the topo map). Here you will find an old road heading up the hill through the forest (marked on the map). Do not attempt to follow the creek through the canyon — it is impassable. Climb up the road, gaining about 75 m of elevation, then pass through a bit of a notch and follow the road down the other side. The descent is exposed to avalanches from the slopes on the left above and you should proceed as quickly as possible to the safety of the valley flats below.

Cross the open gravel flats for several kilometres, then climb easily onto the toe of the glacier. Continue up the Saskatchewan Glacier for about 5-6 km keeping to the right-hand (true left) side of the glacier until you are almost opposite the Castleguard Meadows. There is a lateral moraine running up this side of the glacier which provides a landmark in poor visibility. Angle left (south) and climb steeply up the moraine into the meadows, which are located between Castleguard Mountain and Mount Saskatchewan.

If you are considering skiing farther up the Saskatchewan Glacier and onto the Columbia Icefields, be aware that you will be undertaking some serious ski mountaineering. Be sure to give the corner where you swing right around Mount Andromeda a very wide berth — there are some enormous crevasses.

112 WILCOX PASS

Ski touring

Grade Intermediate/advanced
Distance 8 km return
Time 4 hrs
Height gain 360 m
Max elevation 2,360 m
Map Columbia Icefield 83 C/3

An exciting tour that gets you up high very quickly. The view towards the great peaks of the Columbia Icefields is excellent.

Hazards The steep initial section of this tour may be tricky to descend.

Access Park at the plowed turnoff into the Wilcox Creek Campground, on the north side of the Icefields Parkway (Highway #93), 2.5 km south of the Columbia Icefields Chalet.

The trail climbs up the hillside almost immediately above the parking area. It is advisable to put your skins on for the initial part of this tour. The trail can be found in the trees straight ahead of the parking area. At first the trail climbs at a reasonable, although steep, angle. After a short distance, the trail enters a gully,

and it becomes necessary to make about three switchbacks, rather than climb straight up. After gaining about 50 m elevation, cut out left to the brow of the hill. The angle eases off here and the way ahead follows a gentle bench which climbs gradually through the trees. After a short distance you can climb up to your right through some trees for about 75 m (vertical), from this lower bench onto a higher bench. Follow the higher bench easily to the north-west for about 3 km to Wilcox Pass.

Photo Leon Kubbernus

113 PARKERS RIDGE

Ski touring/telemarking

Grade Intermediate
Distance 2 km
Time 2 hrs
Height gain 410 m
Max elevation 2,440 m
Map Columbia Icefield 83 C/3

Parkers Ridge is the classic telemark location in the Rockies. The slope is excellent, the views are outstanding and the snow is deep. The hillside starts within a stones throw of the car and if you choose to stay overnight, there is even a hostel right at the bottom of the run. Because the snow comes early and stays late, it is a favorite autumn and springtime ski hill. Note: The area may be closed to skiers until there is sufficient snow to prevent damage to the fragile alpine vegetation.

Facilities Hilda Creek Hostel is located at the bottom of Parkers Ridge.

Hazards Parkers Ridge is avalanche country. There have been several fatalities here over the years. Ski with caution and use all avalanche safety procedures.

Access Parking is available in a lot on the north side of the Icefields Parkway (Highway #93) overlooking Hilda Creek, about 3 km south of Sunwapta Pass.

From your car, walk across the highway and continue a short distance east along the highway until it is possible to put your skis on and ski up to the hostel which is located just south of the road. From the hostel make your way up through the trees for several hundred metres, then angle off to the right about the point where you begin to break out of the trees. Above you on your left the slope steepens. Ski a short distance to the right, to where the angle of the hillside lays back, and there is a poorly defined drainage.

Climb the hillside at the lowest and safest point to reach the bench above. Now begin to work your way to the south-east, climbing very gradually towards Parkers Ridge. Once you reach the ridge you can continue climbing along the crest for another 150 m (vertical). Most people stop about this point, where the ridge becomes narrower, and admire the incredible view.

The safest descent is to return along the route you climbed. There are however, many alternatives lines of descent, if conditions are adequately stable.

Of interest Parkers Ridge was the scene for many years of the Sunwapta Giant Slalom. This ski race, organized by the Calgary Mountain Club, was held on the Victoria Day long weekend during the early and mid 60's. It was a great spring time event and attracted up to 2000 spectators, skiing and partying in the sun and snow. A young skier by the name of Nancy Greene was a winner one year.

179

114 HILDA RIDGE

Ski touring/telemarking

Grade Intermediate
Distance 2.5 km
Time 2 hrs
Height gain 410 m
Max elevation 2,440 m
Map Columbia Icefields 83 C/3

An enjoyable alternative to Parkers Ridge which will often be in shape when Parkers Ridge is either skied out or windblown.

Facilities Hilda Creek hostel offers rustic accommodation.

Hazards Some of these slopes are steep enough to avalanche in certain conditions. Ski with caution and use all avalanche safety procedures.

Access Park your car and make your way to the Hilda Creek Hostel (see Parkers Ridge).

Ski west beyond the hostel, through the trees, over to Hilda Creek and up the creek bed for a short distance until it appears reasonable to begin climbing the hillside on your right (north). Work your way up through the trees for about 180 m (vertical) until you break out of the forest, onto the crest of a ridge. Continue working your way up the ridge for another 100 m. You can descend to Hilda Creek a number of different ways. The 200 m descent straight down to Hilda Creek is the obvious line. Use caution!

115 SUNWAPTA FALLS/ATHABASCA RIVER

Ski touring

Grade Intermediate
Distance 26 km return to the ford of the Athabasca River
Time You can ski along this trail for a few hours or all day if you like
Height gain 100 m
Max elevation 1,390 m
Map Athabasca Falls 83 C/12
Fortress Lake 83 C/5

This is a pleasant and popular trail which offers some enjoyable skiing. The trail is wide and the views along the river are good. The trail is unique in that it descends on the way out and climbs coming back to the cars.

Access Park at the Sunwapta Falls access road, 55 km south of Jasper along the Icefields parkway (Highway #93)

Ski down the access road for 0.5 km to the falls then cross the footbridge over the Sunwapta River. Ski south down the trail as it descends gradually. After 5 km the trail joins the flats along the Athabasca River. For the next 8 km the trail follows the valley bottom, in the forest most of the way. If you like you can ski all the way to the confluence of the Chaba and the Athabasca Rivers.

116 POBOKTAN CREEK

Grade Easy
Distance 26 km return
Time A full day tour for most skiers.
Height gain 400 m
Max elevation 1,940 m
Map Sunwapta Peak 83 C/6

Facilities Toilets at the parking area.

Hazards Do not attempt to ski the creek bed of Poboktan Creek. There is a narrow canyon about 4 km below the Waterfall Warden Cabin which is impassable.

The ski up Poboktan Creek is a pleasant valley trip. The trail through the trees is usually hard-packed by snowmobiles used by the wardens to transport hay to their back country outposts.

Options The tour up Poboktan Creek can be continued farther on to Poboktan Pass or to Jonas Pass and Nigel Pass to make a loop back to the Icefields Parkway.

Access There is a large parking lot on the east side of the Icefields Parkway (Highway #93), on the south side of Poboktan Creek (just across the creek from the Warden Station).

From the parking area, descend almost directly down to Poboktan Creek. Cross the creek on a bridge, then ski for about 0.5 km along the north side of the creek. At this point the trail begins to climb steeply, and soon gains about 100 m (vertical). It now continues high on the north slope, working its way back into the valley. After about 3 km the trail drops down to the creek again and follows it along for a short distance. Then once again, it climbs up onto the north bank and for several kilometres works its way through the trees, until it reaches Poligne Creek.

Cross this creek and follow the trail as it winds its way through the woods for about 1 km, until it reaches another creek. The trail crosses this creek and continues up the valley, climbing steadily. After several kilometres of traversing along the north-east side of the valley, the trail descends to Poboktan Creek. Follow the creekbed for about 1 km to a major fork. The way up the left fork looks clear but it is actually a dead end. Follow the right fork for a very short distance then climb the open slope up onto the left bank. In the angle between the two forks you will find the trail again (and the Waterfall Camping Area as well). Follow the trail through the trees for about 1 km until it descends to the open meadows along Poboktan Creek. Ski across the meadows to the far end (1.5 km) where the Waterfall Warden Cabin is located at the edge of the trees, on the north-east side of the meadow.

Photo Alf Skrastins   *Maligne Pass*

117 MALIGNE PASS   Ski touring

Grade Advanced
Distance 28 km return
Time This is a full day ski tour
Height gain 700 m
Max elevation 2,240 m
Map Sunwapta Peak 83 C/6

A challenging ski tour. The way up the narrow valley of Poligne Creek is difficult and the route does not get any easier until very near Maligne Pass. The tour should only be undertaken by experienced skiers who can handle very tricky downhill skiing on narrow trails. The descent to Poboktan

Creek is an exciting ride to say the least. However Maligne Pass itself is well worth the trip and is a beautiful high alpine pass.

Facilities Toilets at the parking area.

Hazards This tour should only be undertaken when the avalanche hazard is low as the upper part is very exposed.

Options It is possible to continue across Maligne Pass and on to Maligne Lake. This would require several days.

Access There is a large parking lot on the east side of the Icefields Parkway (Highway #93), on the south side of Poboktan Creek (just across the creek from the warden station).

From the parking lot follow the Poboktan Creek trail for 7 km, to its junction with Poligne Creek (see page 181). From the junction ski north, up the hill, for a few hundred metres, then cross a bridge to the east bank of Poligne Creek. The trail climbs very steeply now and skins are recommended. It does one very long switchback to the right then comes back to the left and begins to head back into the valley at a more reasonable angle. The trail continues along horizontally for some way then descends to the creek.

Cross a bridge, then continue along the trail as it climbs into the trees on the west bank. The trail descends to the creek again after about 1 km. Cross the creek on a bridge located at the edge of a large avalanche path. Follow the trail through the trees, climbing steadily, high above the east bank of the creek. After another kilometre the trail again descends to the creek. Cross a bridge to the west bank. You are now in the V angle formed by the junction of two creeks, about 2.5 km up the trail, north of Poboktan Creek. Continue through the trees, following a trail, to reach the most westerly of the two creeks, the one which descends from Maligne Pass. Follow this creek, staying on the east bank, for about 0.5 km until you cross it on a small bridge. You are now on the west bank of the most westerly creek. Continue angling up the treed hillside above and soon the trail peters out. Traverse right into the creek bed itself.

Follow the creek bed for a short distance until you come out into the open at a giant avalanche path. Cross the avalanche path and ski up a draw to your right to regain safer ground in the trees. Now work your way up towards the pass, through the trees, staying well back from the avalanche slopes on your right. After a while the trees thin out, then disappear. Continue skiing for several kilometres, climbing gently to the pass. The last 4 km, beyond the giant avalanche path is very beautiful, and the pass itself is outstanding.

118 FRYATT CREEK

Ski touring

Grade Advanced
Distance 13 km one way from the
Athabasca River crossing
Time A full day tour to reach the hut and
a bit faster on the way out.
Height gain 780 m
Max elevation 1,980 m
Map Athabasca Falls 83 C/12

An adventurous ski tour with a pleasant
cabin as your reward. The scenery is
excellent and the snow deep. The head-

wall up to the cabin can be a killer — try to
leave plenty of time to deal with this ob-
stacle in daylight.

Facilities The Sydney Vallance Hut is
located just above the headwall at the end
of Fryatt Valley. Note that it is incorrectly
marked on the map. The correct location is
GR 403174.

Hazards Use care when crossing the
Athabasca River. Be sure it is well frozen.

Access Park along the highway 7.5 km
south of Athabasca Falls where the river
is near to the road.

Ski across the river at the old aerial
cableway (marked incorrectly on the
map) and continue a short distance up
the opposite bank to the main trail.

If it is not possible to cross the river
you can follow the summer trail from
Athabasca Falls. Ski along the road for a
short distance from the Athabasca Falls
parking lot, crossing the bridge over the
Athabasca River and rounding the
curve. Turn left up the Geraldine Fire
Road and follow this for 2 km to the
junction with the Fryatt trail. Turn left
again and follow the trail along the valley bottom for 6 km to reach the river
crossing point.

From the river crossing point follow
the trail for 3.5 km to where it crosses
Fryatt Creek. From here the trail climbs
steeply through forest along the south
side of the valley for the next 4 km. The
creek is reached again and the way becomes easier. Follow the drainage back

up the valley, cross the lake, then continue up the drainage to the headwall.
The summer trail is hard to follow up the
steep headwall and the skiing is very
difficult. It is often a good idea to just
take off your skis and climb the hill on
foot. Start to the right of the waterfall and
ascend the hill on a diagonal from right
to left. The cabin is just above the north-
west side of the creek not far beyond the
rim of the headwall.

Sydney Vallance Hut

Map 83 C/12 Athabasca Falls
Location Above headwall at head of
Fryatt Creek. GR 403174
Reservations Alpine Clubs of Canada
Capacity 16
Facilities Coleman stove and lamp,
wood stove, tick mattresses for 6, pots
and utensils
Water Creek few metres east of hut
Notes Locked when hut custodian not
present. Combination required

JASPER AREA

Jasper Park is the largest of the mountain parks covering 10,878 km². It offers extensive opportunities for cross country skiing. Compared to Banff Park this region is very quiet and it still has a special wilderness feel to it. The town itself is much less commercialized than Banff or Lake Louise and is still a place where people actually live and raise families.

Access Jasper is most easily reached after a 362 km drive by car or bus from Edmonton via Highway #16. One can also reach Jasper after a 230 km drive along the Icefields Parkway (Highway #93) from Lake Louise. Another option is to take the train from points east (Edmonton) or west (Vancouver). Mount Robson Park which is a British Columbia Provincial Park is located 88 km west of Jasper, along the Yellowhead Highway (#16). Many of the ski trails in this book are found along the Maligne Lake Road which branches off Highway #16, 5 km east of town.

Facilities The town of Jasper has a population of about 2500, and offers most of the amenities a ski adventurer could want. There are any number of gas stations, grocery stores, book stores, restaurants and hotels. The most prestigious hotel is The Jasper Park Lodge, which is attempting to promote itself as a cross country ski destination. The best bargain in town is the Whistlers Youth Hostel, located 7 km from town along the road to the Sky Tram. There is a government liquor store and a post office. However the town has no real back country mountain equipment shop. The best you can do here is Totem Men's Wear & Ski Shop.

Information There is a Park Information Centre located across from the VIA Rail Train Station in the centre of downtown. The Warden Office is located a short distance along the Maligne Lake Road just east of town. Fork left not long after crossing the bridge over the Athabasca River.

In Emergency The Warden Office can be reached at 852-6156 or the RCMP at 852-4848.

History Jasper has a rich skiing history. As far back as the late 1920's major ski trips were undertaken in the area. The first of note was a solitary ascent of Mount Resplendent, near Robson, by an adventurer by the name Parsons. Soon after, ski explorer Joe Weiss made a solo trip to the Columbia Icefields. Over the next four years he was to undertake four major ski expeditions, including two all the way from Jasper to Lake Louise. Weiss's companions on many of these trips were Vern & Doug Jeffery, Pete Withers and Frank Burstrom.

Through the 1930's and 40's the Alpine Club of Canada Hut in the Tonquin Valley was the scene of much ski activity. Rex Gibson, who was to become president of the ACC was a leader at the time. He was killed in 1957, climbing in the Coast Mountains, and the hut was named in his honour (and that of Cyril Wates).

Several ski cabins were built in the area near Maligne Lake. Most famous of these is the Shangri-la Cabin which was built at the head of Jefferys Creek. The skiing above the cabin in Snow Bowl is perhaps the finest in the Canadian Rockies. The Watchtower Cabin, in the next valley north, unfortunately burned down in the 1970's.

During the war a number of British troops trained in the Jasper area. The Lovat Scouts, as they were called, were instructed by some of Canada's most prominent ski guides — Joe Weiss, Ken Jones and Bruno Engler. The Lovat Scouts were led by noted mountaineer, Frank Smythe and the Canadian officer in charge was none other than Major Rex Gibson. Unfortunately, many of the soldiers were to lose their lives in the Italian campaign.

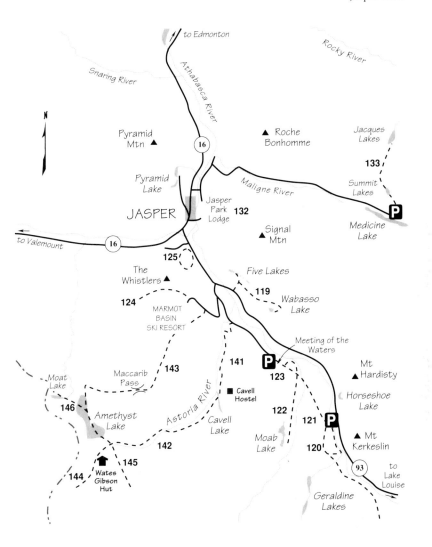

119 VALLEY OF THE FIVE LAKES/WABASSO LAKE   Ski touring

Grade Easy/Intermediate
Distance 2 km one way to the Valley of the Five Lakes
6 km to Wabasso Lake one way.
Time 1 hr one way Valley of the Five Lakes. 2 hrs to Wabasso Lake one way
Height gain 75 m
Max elevation 1,130 m
Map Jasper 83 D/16
Medicine Lake 83 C/13

A short and pleasant ski tour, which can be lengthened quite substantially by skiing to Wabasso Lake. The terrain is rolling and on an overcast day it would be quite easy to get turned around. It is recommended you carry a map and compass.

Facilities There are telephones, picnic tables and an outhouse at the trail head.

Hazards Note that the trails are incorrectly drawn on the topographical map. Also the Fifth Lake is incorrectly labelled Wabasso Lake. Wabasso Lake is about 4 km farther south-east (GR 352482).

Options Although there are trails which lead from the Valley of the Five Lakes back to Jasper they are very difficult to follow. You should not attempt to ski them unless you are skilled at route finding in complicated terrain.

Access There is a parking lot located on the north-east side of the road, 9 km south of Jasper, along the Icefields Parkway (Highway #93).

From the parking lot, ski straight back into the woods. Follow a clear trail, in a north-east direction, through the lodgepole pine forest. After 800 m the trail drops down to a creek bed. From here you have two choices — Wabasso Lake is along the creek to the right and the Valley of the Five Lakes is straight ahead.

Wabasso Lake turn right and ski along the creek bed. The terrain is gentle and makes easy travelling. The summer trail is actually on your left in the forest most of the time, but it is best to simply follow the creek. After about 5 km the woods close in around the creek and it is best to find the trail which curls around to the right, turning almost 180 degrees around the end of a ridge. It then travels west a few hundred metres to Wabasso Lake.

Valley of the Five Lakes from the junction at the creek, climb the hill above in a north-east direction (be careful of snow stability). At the top of the hill you have two choices. You can angle off to the left, climbing at a gradual angle for about 200 m, to a crest. Then descend the other side for 0.5 km to the First and Second Lakes. To reach the Third, Fourth and Fifth Lakes angle to the right from the top of the hill and climb through the woods for several hundred metres to the top of a crest. Descend sharply down the other side, ski along a small open space then climb to another crest. Descend sharply again and continue down for about 200 m to the lakes.

120 ATHABASCA FALLS LOOP
Nordic skiing

Grade Easy
Distance 7 km loop
Time 2 hrs
Height gain 40 m
Max elevation 1,220 m
Map Athabasca Falls 83 C/12

A very pleasant trail over varied terrain.

Options You can continue up the Geraldine Fire Road for another 7 km and gain over 500 m in elevation. The view from the top is excellent but the road is extremely steep and relentless.

Access Drive south for 31 km along the Icefields Parkway, then follow Highway 93A a short distance to the Athabasca Falls parking lot.

Ski along Highway #93A (not plowed) and cross the bridge over the Athabasca River. The impressive frozen falls will be seen on your left. Continue along the road for about 0.5 km as it curves north, to the turn off for the Geraldine Fire Road. Turn left and ski up the fire road for about 2 km through the forest, gently gaining elevation, to the Fryatt Creek trailhead. Turn left and follow the trail for about 1 km until it veers left along a marsh. Follow the trail east, for one more kilometre, to the Athabasca River then turn left again and ski along the shore, back to the road and the parking lot.

121 ATHABASCA FALLS/MEETING OF THE WATERS
Nordic skiing

Grade Easy
Distance 10.5 km one way
Time 3-4 hrs
Height gain 60 m
Height loss 120 m
Max elevation 1,240 m
Map Athabasca Falls 83 C/12

A gentle trail which follows the unplowed Highway 93A. There are some good views of the valley and surrounding peaks.

Options Can be skied in either direction or you can leave a car at one end and begin your tour from the other end. It can be extended by skiing the Moab Lake Trail and/or the Whirlpool Campground Loop.

Access This trail is most often skied from south to north. One car should be left at the Meeting of the Waters picnic site on Highway #93A. The road is only plowed as far south as this point. Then drive around via Highway #93 to the Athabasca Falls parking lot (31 km south of Jasper) and begin your tour here.

From the parking lot the trail simply follows Highway #93A. It begins by crossing the bridge over the Athabasca River, passing the frozen power of the falls on the left. It continues around a long curve, past the intersection with the Geraldine Fire Road and then climbs very gradually for about 4 km. Just beyond Leach Lake, which is on your left, the trail begins a gradual descent for about 2 km, then levels off towards the bridge over the Whirlpool River. The trail then continues level for another 2.5 km as far as your car at the Meeting of the Waters.

189

122 MOAB LAKE
Nordic Skiing

Grade Easy
Distance 18 km return
Time 5-6 hours return
Height gain 110 m
Max elevation 1,230 m
Map Athabasca Falls 83 C/12

Another long, easy trip much of which is along a forested road. Some portions of the trail runs parallel to the Whirlpool River, offering expansive views.

Options Can be extended up the Whirlpool River along the fire road for another 8.5 km to the Tie Camp Warden Cabin.

Access Drive south along Highway #93A and park at the Meeting of the Waters picnic site. This is as far south as the road is plowed.

From the parking lot ski south along the road. After 2 km turn right onto the Whirlpool River Fire Road and follow it for another 6.5 km to what is the summer parking lot and trailhead. Continue about 0.5 km beyond this point and you will see the trail for Moab Lake leaving the road, to the right (large

sign). The lake itself is just a short distance down the hill.

Of interest The Meeting of the Waters and the trail up the Whirlpool River to Athabasca Pass is indeed historic. This is the route of the early fur traders and was discovered by David Thompson in the winter of 1810-11. Be sure to read the fascinating historical signpost at the Meeting of the Waters, then think of the early explorers and fur traders as you slide peacefully along the snowy trail.

123 WHIRLPOOL CAMPGROUND LOOP
Nordic Skiing

Grade Easy
Distance 4.5 km return
Time 1-2 hrs
Height gain Nil
Max elevation 1,130 m
Map Athabasca Falls 83 C/12

A short and pleasant trip with some fine views.

Access Drive south for 7 km along the Icefields Parkway, then follow Highway 93A to the Meeting of the Waters parking lot. This is as far south as the road is plowed.

From the parking lot ski 2.2 km south along the unplowed road, as far as the Whirlpool River Bridge. Turn left and circle back through the campsite along the Whirlpool River to return to the parking lot

124 WHISTLERS CREEK

Ski touring

Grade Easy as far as creek, then intermediate/advanced beyond this
Distance 10 km to upper creek return
Time 4-5 hrs return
Height gain 300 m
Max elevation 2,100 m
Map Jasper 83 D/16

This tour is popular with locals, particularly when there is little snow in the valley near Jasper. It is a pleasant and easy ski for the first 2 km, as far as the intersection with Whistlers Creek but beyond this it is more difficult.

Facilities The tour starts from the Marmot Basin Ski Resort where all amenities are available.

Hazards The steep slopes at the head of the valley offer avalanche potential and only experienced skiers, taking all the appropriate precautions, should venture beyond this point.

Options There is good potential for ski mountaineering and telemark skiing in the upper basin.

Access Drive south of Jasper along the Icefields Parkway (Highway #93) for 7 km then turn right onto Highway #93A. After 2.5 km turn right again on the Marmot Basin access road and follow it for about 11 km to the ski area. If possible park in parking lot #3.

The trail begins across the road from parking lot #3 and a few metres down the hill. Climb over the bank and head north into the trees. Climb gradually for about 400 m along a good trail until it reaches a small lake. Round the lake on the right, along a trail through the trees, then continue north along the brow of the hill. A diversion of a few metres out to the right here will give you a view across to Jasper and the Athabasca Valley. The trail gains elevation very gently and curves around to the left for about 1 km then just after crossing the bottom of an avalanche path it descends down to the right to reach the creek bed. To this point the trail is fairly level and wide.

From here the trail follows the stream bed and climbs more steeply. It is a tricky trail to descend so it is only recommended for more experienced skiers. After several kilometres the trees open up and views improve. Beyond this point is ski mountaineering terrain for experienced skiers only.

125 WHISTLERS CAMPGROUND LOOP
Nordic Skiing

Grade Easy
Distance 4.5 km
Time You can spend a few hours here or the whole day if you choose.
Height Gain Nil
Max elevation 1,060 m
Map Jasper 83 D/16

The track set trails of the Whistlers Campground provide excellent skiing for skiers of all ages and abilities.

Facilities There are tables and fire pits for picnics. The campground lights are turned on seven days a week for night skiing.

Access Drive south from Jasper along Highway #93 and turn right after 3 km at the Whistlers Mountain Road. Immediately turn left again along the campground road and follow this to the plowed parking lot.

From the parking lot ski a short distance along the access road to join the campground perimeter road. This road forms a loop around the campground and offers enjoyable easy skiing.

126 MARJORIE AND CALEDONIA LAKE
Ski touring

Grade Easy
Distance 4 km to Marjorie Lake return 8 km to Caledonia Lake return
Time 1.5 hrs to Marjorie Lake return 3 hrs to Caledonia Lake return
Height gain 70 m
Max elevation 1,170 m
Map Jasper 83 D/16

This tour starts right at the edge of town. It is an easy way to get out and spend a few hours in the woods.

Options Adventurous skiers can carry on around the Saturday Night Circle, an additional 20 km of skiing and, most likely, trail breaking

Access The trail starts at the south-west edge of town, along Cabin Creek Road, where the access road to the water supply begins.

The trail immediately crosses a creek, travels behind some houses for a short distance, then turns up to the right. Ski up the hill for about 100 m, turn back sharply to the left and climb to a crest overlooking the houses of Jasper and the Athabasca Valley. The trail continues gaining elevation through the forest for 0.5 km then descends and breaks out into a clearing. Cross the clearing, descending slightly and enter the forest on the far side. The trail now climbs gradu-

ally for another kilometre along the south facing slope, then levels off and continues for 0.5 km to Marjorie Lake.

Follow the trail along the right shore of the lake to an intersection at the far end. Stay to the left at the intersection and carry on ahead through the forest. Follow along the edge of the delta at the end of the lake, then ski up a draw for about 1.0 km. The trail then traverses along a south facing hillside, through aspen and pine, for a kilometre to another intersection. Climb a few metres up to the right then break out left and continue for about 1.0 km to Caledonia Lake.

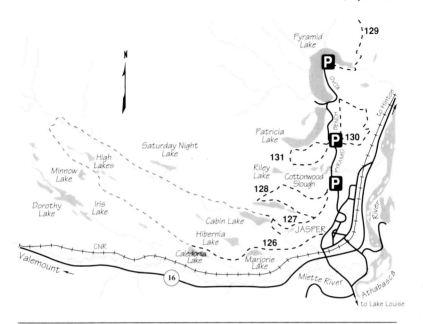

127 CABIN LAKE FIRE ROAD
Nordic Skiing/ski touring

Grade Easy
Distance 6 km return
Time 2 hrs
Height gain 80 m
Max elevation 1,200 m
Map Jasper 83 D/16

A pleasant tour along an easy trail.

Options The adventurous can attempt to ski the Saturday Night Lake Circle. This 27.5 km tour is not often skied and the route finding can be tricky.

Access There is a parking lot on the left, about 2 km up the Pyramid Lake Road, next to Cottonwood Slough.

From the parking lot ski south-east along a trail parallel to the road. After about 200 m turn right onto the Cabin Lake Fire Road. Head up the hill and in a few metres the road opens up into a large swath through the trees (this is the Town of Jasper fire break). The tour continues along this fire break all the way to the lake. The trail passes under some power lines in about 0.5 km, jogs left then climbs to the brow of a hill. It descends a short distance, passing some large Douglas Firs, climbs over another hill then descends to Cabin Lake.

For an outstanding view, ski south along the dike at the east end of the lake, then descend to the left for about 0.5 km to the brow of the hill which is an excellent viewpoint, looking south over the Athabasca Valley.

193

128 MINA LAKE LOOP
Nordic Skiing

Grade Easy/Intermediate
Distance 6.7 km
Time 2 hrs
Height gain 110 m
Max elevation 1,230 m
Map Jasper 83 D/16

An excellent trail which is varied but never too difficult.

Options This trail can be combined with a trip to Cabin Lake for a longer day. A side excursion to Riley Lake is also possible.

Access As for Cabin Lake Fire Road.

From the parking lot head south, parallel to the road for about 200 m to reach the Cabin Lake Fire Road. Turn right and follow the road up the hill. Within a few metres the road becomes a wide swath cut through the trees (it is actually the towns fire break). Follow the open path up the hill, under some power lines and continue up the clearing. The trail ascends for about 1 km and crosses over a hill and descends gently down the other side. You will see a trail on the right entering the forest, marked (#8). Turn here and ski up a wide trail through the forest for about 0.5 km to the first lake. Ski along the right bank of the lake, then cross 100 m to the second lake. Ski along the right side of this lake through an open forest of mature Douglas Fir trees. From the end of the second lake the trail curves around to the right and descends quite steeply to a junction with the Riley Lake trail. If you choose to make a side trip to this lake it is off to your left about 0.5 km. The way descends steeply at one point, and can be hard to follow.

To continue along the Mina Lake Loop turn right at the junction and climb easily for about 0.5 km until the trail begins to descend. The last part of this tour is a fun down hill run for about 1 km through the woods to rejoin the Cabin Lake Fire Road. Turn left for some more downhill fun back to your car.

129 PALISADE LOOKOUT
Ski touring

Grade Intermediate
Distance 22 km return
Time 6-8 hrs return
Height gain 890 m
Max elevation 2,070 m
Map Jasper 83 D/16

A ski trip up a fire road which gives great views if you reach the top.

Access Park your car at the end of the Pyramid Lake Road, 6 km from Jasper.

This tour follows the road through forest all the way to the lookout. The grade is moderate along the early part of the tour. After 7.5 km the road forks and you should follow the right-hand branch. The view from the top is worth the effort. Bundle up for the run back down.

130 PYRAMID BENCH TRAIL

Nordic skiing

Grade Easy
Distance 4.5 km
Time 1 hr
Height gain Nil
Max elevation 1,200 m
Map Jasper 83 D/16

The view across the valley towards the Colin Range is outstanding and there is an excellent chance of seeing wildlife, particularly sheep, along the bench. This trail should be avoided when there is little snow cover.

Access Same as for Patricia Lake Loop.

The trail starts from the end of the parking lot and undulates through aspen forest in a north-east direction to a junction. Turn right here and ski up the trail through Douglas Fir forests. Soon you arrive at the top of the bench overlooking the Athabasca Valley. If it is not too windy this is a lovely spot to take a break. Turn right and ski along the bench through the Douglas Firs. Eventually the trail turns back to the right, away from the bench, and the depth of snow immediately increases. Along this section there is a downhill which may be a challenge for novice skiers. The trail winds its way back to the parking lot.

Photo Gillean Daffern

Photo Gillean Daffern

131 PATRICIA LAKE LOOP

Nordic skiing

Grade Intermediate
Distance 6 km
Time 2 hrs
Height gain 100 m
Max elevation 1,210 m
Map Jasper 83 D/16

One of the most interesting trails in this area. The terrain is varied, the scenery is excellent and the trail holds the snow better than some of its neighbours. It is best skied in a clockwise direction.

Options The trailhead for this loop and the Pyramid Bench Loop are the same. You can ski both trails easily in a day.

Access Follow the Pyramid Lake Road from town for 3 km, then turn right into the Pyramid Riding Stables parking lot.

Ski back to the Pyramid Lake Road along a narrow trail paralleling the access road. Cross the road and the trail proper begins on the other side. In a very short distance the trail divides and you are urged to turn left. Work your way through the trees to the top of a bench overlooking Cottonwood Slough. Descend to the creek then follow it west to the beaver pond. At this point the trail

begins to climb quite steeply to the outlet creek from Patricia Lake. It crosses and re-crosses the creek before reaching the south shore of Patricia Lake. There is a long flat section along the lake with views of Pyramid Mountain and other peaks in the Victoria Cross Ranges. Make a sharp turn to the right near a building on the lake, then climb steeply up and over a ridge crossing two powerlines en route. A long pleasant downhill is your payoff and this takes you back to the intersection with the start of the trail.

132 JASPER PARK LODGE TRAILS

Nordic Skiing

Grade Easy and intermediate
Distance 29 km of trails
Time A few hours or all day if you choose
Height gain Minimal
Max elevation 1,060 m
Map Jasper 83 D/16

A fun place to get some exercise if there is adequate snow in the valley. The Lodge is attempting to establish itself as a nordic ski centre.

Facilities A ski centre which offers rentals and lessons. The world-famous Jasper Park Lodge is nearby.

Access From Jasper, drive east from town and turn right. Cross the Athabasca River and turn right again. Follow the road to the Lodge.

There are almost 30 km of trackset trails with loops of up to 10 km.

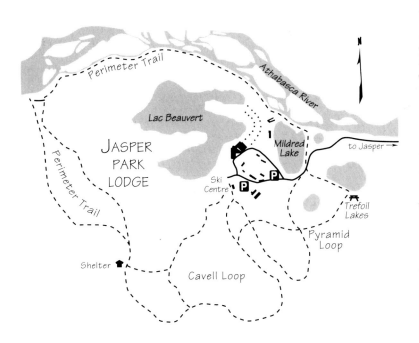

Photo Gillean Daffern

133 SUMMIT LAKES/JACQUES LAKE
Nordic skiing

Grade Easy to First Summit Lake
Intermediate to Jacques Lake
Distance 5 km one way to Summit Lake
12 km one way to Jacques Lake
Time 1.5 hrs to first Summit Lake
It is a full day trip to ski to Jacques Lake.
Height gain 80 m to First Summit Lake
Max elevation 1,530 m at Summit Lake
1,490 m at Jacques Lake
Map Medicine Lake 83 C/13

An excellent novice trail as far as Summit Lake. The trail follows a valley along Bea-

ver Creek between the Colin Range and the Queen Elizabeth Range and is very scenic. To carry on to Jacques Lake is more challenging and it may be necessary to break trail along this narrow path.

Facilities There is a picnic shelter just before reaching Beaver Lake.

Hazards Do not linger in the obvious avalanche path which crosses the valley just before Summit Lake.

Access Drive 27 km up the Maligne Lake Road to the Beaver Creek picnic area which is on your left at the south-east end of Medicine Lake.

Because this trail is an old road it is wide and gentle as far as Beaver Lake. The trail continues along the west shore of Beaver Lake, offering superb views of the immense slabby wall of the Queen Eliza-

beth Range. Beyond the lake the trail crosses to the east side of the valley briefly, then returns to the west side. Shortly after crossing an avalanche path the road ends at the first Summit Lake. To carry on to Jacques Lake follow the right-hand (north-east) lakeshore of both lakes before finding the summer trail again. Follow this trail through dense forests to Jacques Lake.

MALIGNE LAKE TRAILS

The maintained trails at Maligne Lake offer superb nordic skiing. The snow is usually excellent, the scenery is beautiful and there are a variety of trails to choose from. The touring into the alpine terrain high above tree line is amongst the finest in the world and there is great scope for telemark skiing, and overnight camping.

The Maligne Lake trails are located at the end of the Maligne Lake Road, 45 km from Jasper. There are two parking lots. The first one that you reach, on the north-east shore of the lake, serves Lake Loop only. All the other trails in the area are accessed from the parking lot on the west side of Maligne Lake, across the bridge.

The trails are normally snowmobile track set and offer a mix from short and easy, to fairly long and advanced

Many of the trails begin along the Bald Hills Fire Road which starts where the access road turns left into the second parking lot.

The Maligne Lake Chalet has not been open in the past but it is rumoured that it may be in the winter of 1992-93. This would indeed help to establish this area as a premier nordic ski location

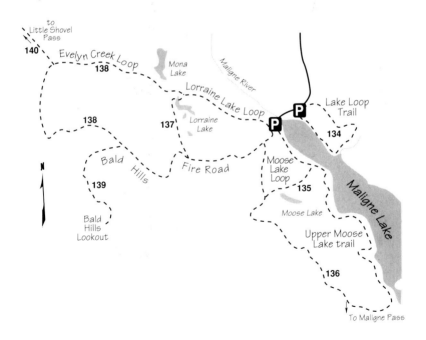

Lake Loop

Photo Gillean Daffern

134 LAKE LOOP TRAIL Nordic skiing

Grade Easy/intermediate
Distance 3.5 km
Time 1 hr
Height gain 80 m
Max elevation 1,720 m
Map Athabasca Falls 83 C/12

This is supposedly the beginners trail but the steepish hill over the ridge belies the grading. Although the section along the

lakeshore is very easy and the views are excellent, the trail through the dense forest over the ridge can be awkward for beginners.

Facilities There are picnic tables along the lakeshore.

Hazards Watch out for open water on the lake

Access See introduction.

The trail starts from the end of the parking lot and immediately passes by a kettle (deep hole in the ground made by melting ice) on the left. Continue southeast, past a large meadow on the left and gradually turn to the right before climbing over a forested ridge. The descent on

the far side can be difficult for beginners as it is narrow and winding. The trail continues down more easily to an indent on Maligne Lake. It follows the right shoreline out of the indent and back to the north-west along the lake. The trail passes the boathouse, built by Curly Phillips. Just beyond the boathouse climb back up the bank to the parking lot.

135 MOOSE LAKE LOOP Nordic skiing

Grade Easy/intermediate
Distance 4.5 km
Time 1 hr
Height gain 60 m
Max elevation 1,740 m
Map Athabasca Falls 83 C/12

This would be an easy trail if it were not for the hill down to the lake. The trail should probably be skied in an anti-clockwise direction. Moose Lake is a lovely spot for a break.

Hazards Watch out for open water on the lake

Options This trail can be linked with upper Moose Lake Loop

Access See introduction.

Start along the Bald Hills Fire Road. In about 100 metres, turn left at the Maligne Pass trail sign. There is some very nice undulating skiing to the junction with the Upper Moose Lake Loop. Turn left

here and ski a fast downhill to Moose Lake. From here the trail continues more easily to the shore of Maligne Lake. Turn left again and ski past the warden cabin to the lower level of the parking lot.

136 UPPER MOOSE LAKE LOOP

Nordic skiing

Grade Intermediate
Distance 7.6 km
Time 2 hrs
Height gain 90 m
Max elevation 1,780
Map Athabasca Falls 83 C/12

This is a fun trail. It is always interesting and the views along the lakeshore are beautiful. It should be skied in the anti-clockwise direction.

Hazards Watch out for open water on the lake.

Options You can carry on up the Maligne Pass Trail and, if you are really adventurous, cross the pass and descend Pobok-tan Creek to the Icefields Parkway (2 days or more)

Access See introduction.

The first part of this trail is as described above for the Moose Lake Loop but at the junction continue ahead up the steep hill. After this it is a winding and narrow trail to the Maligne Pass trail junction. After this the fun begins. Turn left and

descend a draw, curving easily back and forth, to the lake. Turn left again and follow the trail along the lakeshore, winding in and out at every indentation, rounding immense boulders to eventually join up with the last part of the Moose Lake Loop.

Skiing past one of the immense boulders along the lakeshore

Photo Gillean Daffern

137 LORRAINE LAKE LOOP
Nordic skiing

Grade Intermediate
Distance 7.3 km
Time 2 hrs
Height gain 120 m
Max elevation 1,820
Map Athabasca Falls 83 C/12

An entertaining trail which is a little more challenging than the Moose Lake Loops.

Hazards Watch out for the blind corners

Options This loop ties in with the Evelyn Creek Loop

Access See introduction

Begin along the Bald Hills Fire Road. Ski easily up the fire road for about 1.5 km then turn right at the sign, onto a much narrower trail. The trail rolls along, finishing with a downhill and a sharp left corner to Lorraine Lake. Ski around the north-west shoreline to join the Evelyn Creek Loop. Turn right at this junction and ski along a narrow twisting trail. It is mostly down hill with blind corners, and emerges on the access road just to the north of the trailhead. Be careful of other skiers ascending this trail. There is another impressive kettle formation on your right just before you reach the access road.

138 EVELYN CREEK LOOP
Nordic skiing

Grade Intermediate/advanced
Distance 12 km
Time 3 hrs
Height gain 280 m
Max elevation 1,960 m
Map Athabasca Falls 83 C/12

A longer trail with a challenging downhill section. Apart from this, the trail is reasonable. It is best skied in a clockwise direction to get the thrill of the long downhill run (140 m elevation loss).

Access See introduction

Head up the Bald Hills Fire Road for about 3.5 km and at the end of a long straight section leave the fire road and continue straight ahead on the narrow Evelyn Creek Trail. Make a long traverse across the hillside then, just past the Evelyn Pass hiking trail turnoff, turn right and descend to Evelyn Creek (at this point you will see, on your left, the bridge over Evelyn Creek). This is a long and exciting downhill run and it keeps the snow very well. Turn right again and continue along a very pleasant rolling section to join the Lorraine Lake loop just past Mona Lake.

Looking east over Maligne Lake from the Bald Hills Lookout   Photo Gillean Daffern

139 BALD HILLS LOOKOUT   Ski touring

Grade Intermediate
Distance 10.5 km return
Time A most enjoyable day trip
Height gain 480 m
Max elevation 2,170 m
Map Athabasca Falls 83 C/12

This trail takes you high above treeline.
where the terrain and the scenery are
beautiful. It is worth spending a few hours
up here exploring the area.

Hazards If you wander off into the meadows be careful of avalanche terrain. Be
prepared up here for the cold and the
wind. Be careful on the descent. If you
attempt the short cut down the steep
east facing slopes, there is real potential
for avalanches.

Options This is the start of the Six Pass
and Eight Pass routes.

Access See introduction

The trail begins along the Bald Hills Fire
Road and follows this to the site of the
old fire lookout. After the Evelyn Creek
Loop turnoff the fire road steepens con-
siderably and climbs to the open ridge at
tree line. The trail continues along the
ridge in a southerly direction, over
meadows and rises, to gain the lookout

site, which is on the left (east) side of the
ridge. All along here there are wonderful
views, to the right and behind you, of
Mount Tekarra and the ridges of the
skyline trail. However when you reach
the lookout site you are treated to the
celebrated view of Maligne Lake and the
major surrounding peaks. It is very
tempting, if you have time, to explore
across the meadows to the south.

140 LITTLE SHOVEL PASS

Ski touring

Grade Intermediate/advanced
Distance 20 km to Little Shovel Pass return
Time A full day trip to the pass. Usually combined with some telemark skiing.
Height gain 650 m
Max elevation 2,320 m
Map Athabasca Falls 83 C/12
Medicine Lake 83 C/13 (Snow Bowl and Jefferys Creek)

One of the finest tours in the Jasper area. You climb very quickly into open alpine terrain, where the scenery is beautiful and there is limitless opportunity for telemark skiing. Snow Bowl, on the north side of Little Shovel Pass offers some of the finest ski touring in North America. Be sure to bring your sun cream and your camera.

Facilities The Shangri-la Ski Cabin is located at the head of Jefferys Creek, below Snow Bowl (GR 479447).

Hazards This tour takes you high above timberline. Be prepared to deal with avalanche terrain, extreme weather and limited visibility.

Options From Little Shovel Pass you can continue north out into Snow Bowl and find endless potential for touring or making turns. It is also very popular for parties to descend Jefferys Creek (which drains Snow Bowl) back to the Maligne Lake Road. If you intend to do this, leave a second car in the plowed parking area beside the bridge over the Maligne River (GR 535468).

The trail down Jefferys Creek follows the creek itself for the first 3 km, then climbs out of the creek and into the trees on the right flank. The trail crosses over the shoulder, then descends steeply into the Maligne valley well to the south of Jefferys Creek. Eventually, the trail works its way south above the Maligne River to reach the road at a bridge over the river.

Access The tour begins at Maligne Lake. Drive past the Chalet, cross the bridge over the Maligne River and continue a short distance to the parking lot.

From the parking lot head back along the access road a few metres then turn left up the Skyline Trail (this is also the exit from the Lorraine Lake and Evelyn Creek Loops). The trail climbs steeply with blind corners, past Lorraine Lake and Mona Lake, then after 5 km reaches the bridge over Evelyn Creek. Keep a sharp eye out for skiers coming down the hill. From this point the trail begins to climb in earnest. If there is enough

snow, it is best to follow the creek bed to the pass. Ski up the creek and after a very short distance take the right branch which may appear less distinct. Normally this trail is packed by the wardens on snowmobiles and provides easy travelling. Towards the head of the valley turn to the right and follow another side drainage up to the pass which is unnamed on the map but is located at grid reference 485430. The summer trail which switchbacks up the right hillside, above the creek, is not recommended as it traverses several open slopes higher up.

141 MOUNT EDITH CAVELL ROAD

Ski touring

Grade Easy
Distance 11 km one way to hostel
Time 4-5 hrs one way to Hostel
2-3 hrs one way back to vehicle
Height gain 500 m
Max elevation 1,730 m
Maps Jasper 83 D/16
Amethyst Lakes 83 D/9

The trail follows a road which is not plowed in the winter. It is a steady uphill plod but it takes you to the Mount Edith Cavell Hostel where you can spend a pleasant

night. Nearby the views of the north face of Mount Edith Cavell are impressive.

Facilities The Mount Edith Cavell Hostel is the destination for this trip. There is a telephone at the parking lot.

Options This trail is the start of the tour into the Tonquin Valley and Amethyst Lakes. It is advisable to ski to the hostel the first day, spend the night, then continue the next day up the Astoria River to the Tonquin Valley.

Access From Jasper, drive south on the Icefields Parkway (Highway #93). Turn off onto Highway #93A after 7 km and follow this for another 5 km, past the turn-off to Marmot Basin, to a large parking lot for the Mount Edith Cavell Road, located just across the bridge over the Astoria River, on the left (east) side.

The trail (road) begins directly across the highway from the parking lot. It climbs for several kilometres, in long

switchbacks, and then it rounds a shoulder into the drainage of the Astoria River. The rest of the way it climbs more gently and is very easy to follow. The hostel is on your left. After getting settled in and drinking a hot cup of tea it's nice to round the day off with a short ski up the remainder of the road to Cavell Lake, and admire the impressive north face of Mount Edith Cavell.

Location of and route to Wates-Gibson Hut

Photo Vance Hanna

TONQUIN VALLEY/ROBSON

The Tonquin Valley offers some excellent touring and has long been the scene of Alpine Club ski camps. The scenery is outstanding, the snow is deep and there is a good variety of terrain to explore. The Wates-Gibson Hut makes a perfect base for many of these trips. One can ski into the hut in one long day and exit in another equally long day. However, it is best to allow several days or even a week to get to know the valley. Although there are only three tours described here, there is potential for many more.

The Tonquin Valley was pioneered as a ski touring area by the Edmonton Section of the Alpine Club of Canada. Cyril Wates and Rex Gibson, who were both prominent members of the club spent a great deal of time in the area. The cabin at Outpost Lake, which bears their names, is the third incarnation in this valley and it is in excellent condition thanks to major renovations performed by the Edmonton Section of the ACC.

Facilities The Wates-Gibson Hut, owned by the Alpine Club of Canada, is located on the banks of Outpost Lake (GR 152353). There is a commercial lodge (open in the winter) located at the north end of Amethyst Lakes (Dixon's Lodge). There is a locked warden cabin along the east side of Amethyst Lakes and another commercial lodge (closed in winter), near the isthmus on Amethyst Lakes.

Dixon's Lodge

This rustic lodge offers winter accommodation for 14 skiers. Meals are served in a central dining building and guests sleep in cabins. Wood burning heaters and outdoor plumbing are part of the experience. The lodge is located at the north end of Amethyst Lakes in the Tonquin Valley, a 23 km ski from the Marmot Basin access road.
The season is from Christmas until springtime. Accommodation is $80 per person and all meals are included. Phone (403) 852-3909 for information and reservations.

Wates-Gibson Memorial Hut

Map 83 D/9 Amethyst Lakes
Location NW corner of Outpost Lake GR 152353
Reservations Alpine Club of Canada
Capacity 40
Facilities Fully equipped
Water Outpost Lake
Notes Locked when custodian is not present. Combination required

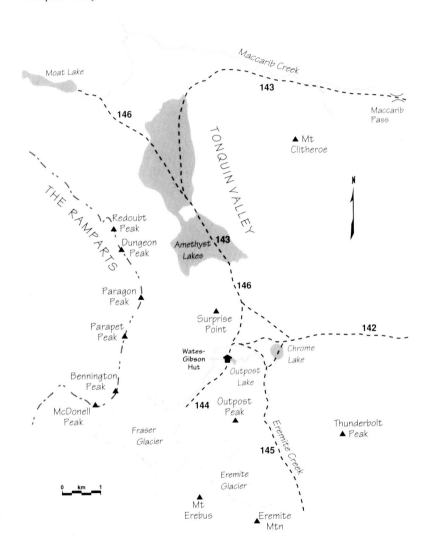

142 TONQUIN VALLEY VIA THE ASTORIA RIVER   Ski touring

Grade Intermediate
Distance 14 km to Wates-Gibson Hut
16 km to Amethyst Lakes
Time 6 hrs one way
Height gain 150 m to Wates-Gibson Hut
240 m to Amethyst Lakes
Max elevation 1,970 m Amethyst Lakes
Map Amethyst Lakes 83 D/9

A classic tour which takes you into the heart of one of the most beautiful regions in the world. It is really worth while to spend a few days here, at the Wates-Gibson Hut, exploring the area.

Hazards Many parties arrive late in the day and have trouble locating the Wates-Gibson Hut. Plan your schedule so that you arrive in daylight, and have a few hours to hunt around if need be.

Options It is common for parties to ski into the Tonquin via the Astoria River, then to return to the road via Maccarib Pass and Portal Creek.

Access This trail begins at the Mount Edith Cavell Hostel (see page 206).

From the Edith Cavell Hostel ski up the road for about 75 m then turn down a trail to your right. This trail crosses a bridge over Cavell Creek and after a few metres passes some outfitters shacks and corrals. The trail proper starts here, and for the first 5 km stays high on the north-west flank of Mount Edith Cavell, above the Astoria River. The trail traverses horizontally at first, then actually climbs for a short distance. Eventually it works its way down the hillside and reaches the Astoria River, shortly after crossing Verdant Creek.

The trail crosses to the right (north) bank of the Astoria River and for most of the next 9 km, as far as Chrome Lake, it continues along the north bank. Sometimes the trail follows the river bed itself but usually it is up on the north side of the river. The travelling along this trail is almost always easy due to the snowmobile traffic into the Tonquin Valley.

Just before reaching Chrome Lake a branch of the trail begins to climb up to the right, following the drainage which descends from Amethyst Lakes. This trail is packed because it is the snowmobile route. On the map this drainage divides into two streams — follow the left (west) branch up to the lake. Here you will be treated to one of the most beautiful views in the world, the Ramparts above Amethyst Lakes.

To reach the Wates Gibson Hut on Outpost Lake you should however continue along the Astoria River to Chrome Lake. The trail will normally become more difficult to follow, because the snowmobiles have turned off and the trail will, at the most, be ski packed. As well, the Astoria River is not as clearly defined along here.

From Chrome Lake to Outpost Lake the route finding is a little tricky. Starting from the outlet of Chrome Lake, there are two ways to go.

You can ski across the lake, angling left (south) to the inflow stream. Climb up a few metres to your right (west), through a notch and into the meadows above. Now turn right (north west) and ski back up the meadows for a few hundred metres, to the north end. This route has simply followed the drainage.

The Ramparts from Maccarib Pass

Photo Alf Skrastins

Alternatively, you can take a short cut from Chrome Lake to the meadows just beyond. From the outlet of Chrome Lake, angle up to the right (west) and follow clearings through the trees for about 0,5 km, over to the meadow previously mentioned.

From this meadow the trail climbs up Penstock Creek for about 50 m of elevation gain before it flattens out into a meadow below Surprise Point. On your right (north) you will see a huge pile of jumbled rocks. Ski along the left (south) side of the meadow for about 300 m. The trail then curves around a bit of a corner to your left, and you will see on the hillside, about 50 m in front of you, a V-shaped open slope. Climb the hillside through the trees, just before reaching this open slope. After gaining about 75 vertical metres, climbing back and forth through the trees, you will come up behind the cabin and pop over the hillside to the shores of Outpost Lake. The cabin is nestled in the trees, a few metres above the north-west corner of the lake.

210

143 TONQUIN VALLEY VIA MACCARIB PASS   Ski touring

Grade Intermediate
Distance 12 km to Maccarib Pass
28 km to the Wates-Gibson Hut
Time An easy afternoon ski to the
junction of Portal and Circus Creeks.
A full day ski to Maccarib Pass & return.
To ski to Outpost Lake, in one push, is a
long, hard day indeed.
Height gain 300 m to the junction of
Portal and Circus Creeks
740 m to Maccarib Pass
Max elevation
2,200 m at Maccarib Pass
Maps Jasper 83 D/16
Amethyst Lakes 83 D/9

The ski up to the junction of Portal and
Circus Creeks is pleasant, however the
really nice terrain starts at this point and
the next 8 km up to Maccarib Pass is
beautiful touring country. The tour to the
pass is highly recommended. For those
contemplating the trip into the Tonquin
Valley it is really best to ski in via the
Astoria River then ski out over Maccarib
Pass (when your packs are light and the
skiing is mainly downhill)

Options This route can be combined
with the Astoria River trail for a circuit.

Access There is a cleared parking area on the left (west) side of the Marmot Basin Ski Area access road, at the point where the road crosses Portal Creek. Drive south from Jasper along the Icefields Parkway (Highway #93) for 7 km then turn right onto highway #93A. Follow the road for another 2.5 km then turn right again onto the road to Marmot Basin. Drive up this road another 6 km to Portal Creek.

From the parking lot walk across the bridge to the north side of Portal Creek. Put on your skis and start up the trail. The trail is straightforward to follow and provides easy going. It runs through the trees just above the right bank of the creek. In heavy snow years or later in the season, it is easy to follow the creek bed itself. After about 4 km the trail drops into the creek bed of Portal Creek, just beyond its junction with Circus Creek. The point where you break out of the trees is a nice spot to stop for a drink and a bite to eat.

Beyond here the travel becomes much more pleasant and the skiing is lovely. For 5 km follow the creek up the valley through open, rolling terrain until you begin to approach the end of the valley. Just before the end start climbing up to the right towards Maccarib Pass. It is an easy and simple climb. The route follows open alpine terrain and the slopes are of mostly of a lower angle. Be sure not to turn up to the right too soon. The pass you are looking for is tucked up close to the north side of Mount Maccarib (there is another pass which turns up a little earlier and looks inviting). The last part of the climb to the pass and then through the pass is easy, however in whiteout conditions could provide tricky route finding!

From the pass descend gently down the other side for 5 km, losing 180 m. At the point where the valley is about to close in and the creek bed begins to narrow and descend steeply (you can see evidence of a campground across the creek), angle to the left through the trees. A gently descending traverse, around the corner through open woods, for about 1 km, brings you down to the valley bottom, at the north end of Amethyst Lakes.

Ski due south along the north arm of Amethyst Lakes, cut across a narrow spit of land which sticks out into the lake, then continue south again to the far shore. From this point the going gets tricky. You want to traverse high around the head of the Astoria River, just below Surprise Point, to gain the upper valley of Penstock Creek. This 2 km stretch can prove difficult, or it can be not too bad if done correctly.

From the end of the lake follow the right-hand drainage, which exits the lake on the west flank, near to Surprise Point for about 1 km until it begins to descend more steeply towards the valley. At this point begin angling around through the forest to the right. It is not necessary to climb up at all and a traverse through the trees should bring you into the upper reaches of Penstock Creek. There is no well defined trail through here in the winter, and you will be forced to do a bit of bushwhacking.

You should aim to reach upper Penstock Creek in the open meadow, below Surprise Point. Above you to the north, on Surprise Point, you will see a slope strewn with large boulders. Cross the meadow over to the south side where there is an obvious open slope on the treed hillside above. Climb back and forth through the trees, up the hillside, to the left of this slope, for about 75 vertical metres, to reach the Wates Gibson hut on the shores of Outpost Lake.

144 FRASER GLACIER

Ski touring/ski mountaineering

Grade Intermediate
Distance 2 km one way to the edge of the glacier
4 km one way to the shoulder of McDonnell Peak
Time 2 hrs one way to toe of glacier
4-5 hrs one way to shoulder of McDonnell Peak
Height gain 400 m to toe of glacier
1,060 m to shoulder of McDonnell Peak
Max elevation 2,940 m shoulder of McDonnell Peak
Map Amethyst Lakes 83 D/9

An exciting tour which is included because many people explore up this way when they visit the Wates-Gibson Hut. To go all the way to the shoulder of McDonnell Peak is a ski mountaineering trip, on a glacier, and should not be attempted unless you are familiar with glacier travel in the high mountains.

However it is a nice afternoon tour to explore up to the edge of the glacier. Some telemark turns can be made in this region.

Access This tour begins at the Wates-Gibson hut on the edge of Outpost Lake.

From the hut work your way up the hillside, through the trees in a westerly direction. After about 50 m of vertical gain the terrain lays back and you can continue west over rolling hills, through sparse trees. Make your way out into the open drainage of Penstock Creek. Be certain not to cut the corner on your left too tight across the steep open slope! The trail up to the edge of the glacier follows the drainage and is open and straightforward. Stay well back from any steep slopes or hanging glaciers. At about 2,200 m the angle lays back again just before the glacier begins. For the ski mountaineers the tour continues westerly, climbing up onto the Fraser Glacier. You can continue under the face of Bennington Peak and higher up to the shoulder of McDonnell Peak. There are crevasses and avalanche hazards in this area.

Skiing towards the Fraser Glacier
Photo Vance Hanna

213

145 THE EREMITE VALLEY
Ski touring/ski mountaineering

Grade Easy/intermediate
Distance 5 km one way to toe of glacier. 7 km one way to the Alcove/Angle Pass
Time 2-3 hrs one way to toe of glacier
4-5 hrs one way to Alcove/Angle Pass
Height gain 400 m to toe of glacier
700 m to the Alcove/Angle Pass
Max elevation 2,510 m to Alcove/Angle Pass
Map Amethyst Lakes 83 D/9

A beautiful day trip from the Wates-Gibson Hut. You can explore around, make a few turns high in the Eremite Valley and generally pass a lovely day here. If you are equipped and prepared for glacier travel, you can continue up to the Alcove/Angle Pass. The descent from this pass is excellent. You can also explore an unnamed pass on the east side of the valley.

Hazards Do not linger beneath the avalanche slopes off Outpost Mountain.

Options If you are really adventurous you could cross the unnamed pass described here into the Whirlpool River, and follow this drainage back to the road!

Access This tour begins at the Wates Gibson Hut on the edge of Outpost Lake.

From the hut ski north, down the hill through the trees, to the open meadow below Surprise Point. Continue down Penstock Creek, losing about 75 m elevation, to reach the meadows just above Chrome Lake. Continue south along the meadows bordering Eremite Creek. Generally the route follows the creek bed up the valley, eventually breaking out into open alpine terrain after about 2.5 km, at Arrowhead Lake. The slopes on your right on Outpost Peak contain some obvious giant avalanche paths, so you should travel quickly across any area which is threatened.

If you choose to travel beyond this point you can ski without difficulty up to an unnamed pass on the east side of the valley, which looks down into the head of the Whirlpool River. Ski mountaineers, with the proper equipment, can ski without difficulty to the pass between Alcove Mountain and Angle Peak. The descent back down the glacier offers excellent skiing.

TELEMARK AREAS

The most popular telemark area near the Wates Gibson Hut is the north facing lower slope of Outpost Mountain. Looking out of the front door of the hut, you can see the slope across the lake. This slope is sufficiently steep to be a real avalanche hazard, so treat it with caution. There is room for many hours of happy skiing here and the runs are about 150 m high.

Photo Alf Skrastins

146 AMETHYST LAKES/MOAT LAKE

Ski touring

Grade Easy/intermediate
Distance 20 km return to Moat Lake
Time Allow a full day for this round trip
Height gain 120 m
Max elevation 1,940 m
Map Amethyst Lakes 83 D/9

This tour is a little tricky to start. It is not completely straightforward to work your way around from Penstock Creek to Amethyst Lakes. Once you are there, the tour across the lake, underneath the wall of The Ramparts, is outstanding.

Access This tour begins at the Wates-Gibson Hut on the edge of Outpost Lake.

From the hut, ski north down the hill to the meadows along upper Penstock Creek. From here you must work your way north-east, around the slopes of Surprise Point towards Amethyst Lakes. There is no well defined trail in the winter and you may have to do a little bushwhacking and route finding. You should gradually climb as you work your way around the hillside, gaining about 100 m over 1 km. If you are unsure of this route you can also descend Penstock Creek to Chrome Lake, then descend the Astoria River for a short distance to reach the drainage coming down from Amethyst Lakes. It is then a simple matter of climbing back up this drainage, perhaps along a well packed snowmobile trail, to reach the lakes. This route, however, will add at least an hour extra to the tour (each way).

Once you reach Amethyst Lakes the imposing mountain wall of the Ramparts appears. The rest of the tour across the lakes and around the corner to Moat Lake is straightforward and one of the most spectacular tours in the world. Be sure to take your camera.

215

147 BERG LAKE VIA KINNEY LAKE

Ski touring

Grade Advanced

Distance 17 km one way

Time Depending on the depth of the trail breaking, the strength of the party and the weight of the packs, this may be a one or two day trip to get to the lake.

Height gain 780 m

Max elevation 1,640 m

Map Mount Robson 83 E/3

A real adventure tour that takes you well into the backcountry. You feel like you have truly "got away from it all" at Berg Lake. The scenery is outstanding.

Facilities There is a camp shelter along the north-east shore of Kinney Lake and another at the Whitehorn campground, located on the east side of the Robson River, just after the suspension bridge, near the start of the Valley of a Thousand Falls. There is a cabin/shelter at Berg Lake itself along the north-west shore towards the north end of the lake. This cabin is completely enclosed and has heating stoves.

Hazards The climb at the north end of the Valley of a Thousand Falls alongside White Falls and Emperor Falls is steep and potentially dangerous.

Access Mount Robson Provincial Park is located 88 km west of Jasper along Highway #16. Turn right at the information booth and follow a short access road to the trailhead.

The trail initially is wide and easy. It follows alongside the Robson River gaining elevation gradually. Just before Kinney Lake cross a bridge to the east shore. Continue around the lake along the right shore (camp shelter) then head easily across the gravel flats at the end of the lake. The valley narrows and you must climb up on the left flank of the valley to gain the higher Valley of a Thousand Falls. This can be a tricky route finding problem. After the trail levels off, cross a suspension bridge over the Robson River

to the east bank. Near here you will see the Whitehorn shelter. Carry on up the east bank of the river for a little more than a kilometre then cross another suspension bridge. Above the bridge the trail climbs steeply, switchbacking up the hillside. You must use caution here. Beyond Emperor Falls the angle lays back and the skiing becomes more reasonable. Follow the trail until it breaks out into the open gravel flats and ski cross these to the lake. Ski along the north shore of the lake most of the way to the far end to the Berg Lake Shelter.

MULTI-DAY ADVENTURES

One of the nice things about ski touring is that you can pursue it at any level which suits you. You can ski for an hour or two along an easy trail, tour for 10 or 15 km into the backcountry or if you are really adventurous try one of these multi-day adventures which require a very high level of experience and skill. When you head off on these trips no one is expecting you back for weeks, so if something goes wrong you may have a long wait for assistance. You must be prepared to deal with all eventualities yourself.

The history of this type of trip goes back 60 years. In 1929 a Swiss adventurer by the name of Joe Weiss, who lived in Jasper, made a solo ski trip to the Columbia Icefields and back. Over the next 4 years he and his companions were to make 4 more mammoth ski tours including 2 tours from Jasper to Lake Louise (in those days there was no Icefields Parkway).

The 4 multi-day adventures included here are just a sample of what you can do if you are so inclined. In the Rocky Mountains in winter, you can point your skis up almost any valley and just go where the spirit takes you. In this world of overcrowded ski resorts and contrived adventure it is nice just to let your spirit roam. The finest ski adventure of all, the Jasper to Lake Louise High Level Traverse, which crosses the icefields of the Great Divide for 300 km is not included, as it is a ski mountaineering trip.

The North and South Boundary Trails are infrequently done. Unless you have some "in" with Jasper National Park and can get a key to the warden cabins, be prepared to camp. The Jasper to Banff Traverse has only been done twice to my knowledge, by Don Gardner and Larry Mason in 1976 and by Bob Saunders and Mel Hines in 1979. Both times the trip was done in 14 days — and these fellows are strong skiers. It is a long way. The Southern Rockies Hut to Hut traverse has never been done as described although almost all of the components of the tour have been done many times. However it looks to me like a natural and I personally intend to ski the trip the winter of 1993. Perhaps with this bit of information others may be inspired to leave the tyranny of the rat race behind for a short while and discover something that is still whispered on the wind, out there along the wilderness trail.

Before heading out on one of these trips it is a good idea to have a chat with the wardens and let them know your plans. They will probably have some good advice to offer and always like to know of folks undertaking major adventures in their parks.

148 SOUTH BOUNDARY TRAIL

Grade Advanced
Distance About 200 km
Time 7-10 days
Height gain 1,500 m
Max elevation 2,200 m
Maps Medecine Lake 83 C/13
Mountain Park 83 C/14
Southesk Lake 83 C/11
George Creek 83 C/10

Job Creek 83 C/7
Sunwapta Peak 83 C/6
Columbia Icefields 83 C/3
Jasper National Park MCR 221

A wilderness adventure. You will be camping and breaking your own trail the whole way. The trail follows the valley bottoms so route finding is reasonably simple.

Access Park as for Summit/Jaques Lakes along the Maligne Lake Road (page 198. Leave a second car at the Nigel Pass trail head (page 175).

The tour roughly follows the east and south boundaries of Jasper National Park. It normally begins by skiing to Summit Lakes and Jacques Lake, then continues north-east to the Rocky River. Turn south-east and ski for several days along the Rocky River and the Medecine-Tent River to Southesk Pass. Descend the Cairn River to the Southesk River, then turn east and follow the Southesk River to its confluence with the Brazeau River. Turn sharply to the south-west and follow the Brazeau River for about 60 km to Nigel Pass. Descend Nigel Creek back to the Icefields Parkway.

149 NORTH BOUNDARY TRAIL

Grade Advanced
Distance About 200 km
Time 7-10 days
Height gain 1,200 m
Max elevation 2,000 m
Map Jasper National Park MCR 221
Mount Robson 83 E/3
Twin Tree Lake 83 E/6
Blue Creek 83 E/7

Another wilderness adventure. The trail follows the valley bottoms so route finding is relatively simple.

Options There are several variations to this trip. Blue Creek offers an alternative to the upper Snake Indian River.. Moose Pass and the Moose River offer an alternative finish to the trip.

Access The trip begins from Highway #16 at the east end of Jasper Lake. Leave a second car at the Berg Lake trailhead (see page 216).

This tour roughly follows the north and west boundaries of Jasper National Park. It begins by ascending north up the Snake Indian River for almost 100 km to Snake Indian Pass. It then descends Twintree Creek to the Smoky River. The route then turns south and follows the Smoky River to Robson Pass. It finishes along the Berg Lake trail via Kinney Lake to the Yellowhead Highway (Highway #16).

Grade Advanced
Distance About 350 km
Time 14-21 days
Height gain About 7,500 m
Max elevation 2,500 m
Maps Jasper National Park MCR 221 &
Banff Kootenay & Yoho MCR 220
Medecine Lake 83 C/13
Athabasca Falls 83 C/12
Southesk Lake 83 C/11
Sunwapta Peak 83 C/6
Job Creek 83 C/7
Cline River 83 C/2
Pentland Lake 82 N/16
Hector Lake 82 N/9
Lake Louise 82 N/8
Castle Mountain 82 O/5
Banff 82 O/4

About as challenging a ski adventure as possible. It has only been done twice and then only by very strong skiers. Plan this one well, train all winter then give it everything. March is a nice time of year, when the days are longer and warmer and the snow is deep. It is possible to bail out from this expedition at a number of points along the way (Poboktan Creek, Nigel Creek, Pipestone Creek and several more). More food can be picked up when you cross the David Thompson Highway, about half way along the tour, and food caches could be placed in advance from the Icefields Parkway (Highway #93).

Hazards This trip is big time adventure and you must be prepared and strong. Good planning is absolutely essential.

Access If you do this trip in its entirety you can start almost from the town of Jasper and ski all the way to the town of Banff.

The trip begins by skiing up the Signal Mountain Fire Road just outside of Jasper. It then continues across the Skyline Trail to Little Shovel Pass and down to Maligne Lake (see page 205). From here climb back up to the Bald Hills Lookout (see page 204) and continue south across the rolling alpine terrain of the Eight Pass Route to Maligne Pass. Descend Poligne Creek to Poboktan Creek (see page 181, 182) and continue up to Jonas Shoulder and Jonas Pass. Descend to the Brazeau River then ascend to Cline Pass. Descend the Cline River all the way to

the David Thompson Highway (you can pick up a food cache here and maybe a change of clothes).

It is necessary to walk along the highway for about 5 km to reach the Siffleur River which is followed all the way to Pipestone Pass. Descend the Pipestone River then climb back up Little Pipestone Creek and Skoki Creek (see page 123) to Skoki Lodge (it might be nice to spend a night in luxury here!). Ski over Deception Pass (see page 113) then down Baker Creek. Follow Wildflower Creek up to Pulsatilla Pass then descend Johnston Creek. Cross Mystic Pass (see page 54) and follow Forty Mile Creek (see page 52) back to the Mount Norquay Ski Resort.

151 SOUTHERN ROCKIES HUT-TO-HUT TRAVERSE — Ski touring

Grade Intermediate/advanced
Distance 125 km
Time 7-10 days
Height gain 4,000 m
Max elevation 2,600 m
Maps Spray Lakes Reservoir 82 J/14
Mount Assiniboine 82 J/13
Banff 82 O/4
Castle Mountain 82 O/5
Lake Louise 82 N/8

This multi-day tour takes you through some of the most beautiful and dramatic mountain terrain in the world. There are huts along the way so you can travel with a light pack.

Facilities The huts along the way are: the Bryant Creek Shelter, Assiniboine Lodge or the Naiset Cabins, the Policeman Meadow Cabin, Sunshine Village Ski Resort, Egypt Lake Shelter, Shadow Lake Lodge, Baker Creek Chalets, the Moraine Lake Picnic Shelters and the Elizabeth Parker Hut. Most of these shelters are described elsewhere in this book. They vary from first class back country lodges with four star meals, to wilderness cabins and even camp shelters. Reservations are required at most huts so be sure to take care of this before you start.

Hazards Avalanches are always a real threat.

Options This trip can be skied in part if desired. The road is reached at Sunshine Village and at Castle Junction. It is also possible to cut the end of the trip short by skiing out the road from Moraine Lake.

Access The tour begins at the Mount Shark trailhead (page 28) and ends at the Lake O'Hara Fire Road (page 131)

Most of the individual sections of this trip are described in detail in the text. This tour is simply a matter of stringing them all together.

The first section of the tour follows Bryant Creek, crossing Assiniboine Pass to the Assiniboine Meadows. This can be done in two days if you choose to overnight at the Bryant Creek Shelter. At Assiniboine you can stay at the Naiset Huts or at Assiniboine Lodge.

The next section continues via Citadel Pass to the Sunshine Village Ski Resort. There are old cabins at Policeman Meadows which can be used to overnight if necessary.

From Sunshine Village the tour continues via Simpson Pass and Healy Pass to Egypt Lake then down Pharoah Creek to the Brewster Lodge at Shadow Lake. From Shadow Lake the route crosses Gibbon Pass and descends from Twin Lakes to the highway. A pleasant night can be spent at the Baker Creek Chalets or you can end the trip here if you like.

The last part of the trip is a bit more demanding. The trail climbs to Taylor Lake then traverses around the corner to Moraine Lake. The Moraine Lake Lodge is not open in the winter but there are picnic shelters which could provide protection. From here the route crosses Wenkchemna and Opabin Passes, the highest points on the route, and the last night is spent at the Elizabeth Parker Hut at Lake O'Hara. The last morning ski to your waiting vehicle at the end of the access road.

This is a new tour in the Rockies but is destined to become a great classic. Eventually people from around the world may travel here for this adventure.

USEFUL PHONE NUMBERS

Park Administrative Offices

Kananaskis Country Office, Canmore	(403) 678-5508
Parks Canada Regional Office	(403) 292-4401
B.C. Parks, East Kootenay Office	(604) 422-3212

Information Centres

Waterton	(403) 859-2352
Banff	(403) 762-4256
Banff (French language information)	(403) 762-4834
Lake Louise	(403) 522-3833
Yoho	(604) 343-6324
Jasper	(403) 852-6176

Travel Alberta

Field	(604) 343-6446

Weather Reports

Banff	(403) 762-2088
Jasper	(403) 852-3185

Reservations

Alpine Club of Canada Huts	(403) 678-3200
Banff National Park Huts	(403) 762-4256
Canadian Alpine Centre Lake Louise	(403) 522-2200
Southern Alberta Hostelling Assoc.	(403) 283-5551
Alberta Hostelling Association	(403) 439-3139

Helicopter Companies

Canmore Helicopters	Tel (403) 678-4802
PO Box 2069, Canmore, AB T0L 0M0	Fax 678-2176
Canadian Helicopters Canmore	Tel (403) 678-2207
PO Box 2309, Canmore, AB T0L 0M0	Fax 678-5600

INDEX

IN AN EMERGENCY

In an emergency, contact the Royal Canadian Mounted Police (RCMP)
or the nearest Ranger or Warden Office

RCMP Offices
Waterton (Nov - Apr)	653-4932
Kananaskis	591-7707
Canmore	678-5516
Banff	762-2226
Lake Louise	522-3811
Field	343-6316
Radium	347-9393
Jasper	852-4848

Park Ranger or Warden Offices
Waterton	859-2477
Kananaskis Country Emergency	591-7767
Banff	762-4506
Kootenay	347-9361
Lake Louise	522-3866
Field	343-6324
Saskatchewan Crossing	761-7077
Poboktan Creek	852-5383
Jasper	852-6156

AVALANCHE HAZARD & SNOW STABILITY

Public Avalanche Information Bulletin
(Canadian Avalanche Association)

1-800-667-1105

Banff Park Avalanche Information   762-1460 (recording)